C000004585

EASTERN EUROPE
1939-1989

EASTERN EUROPE
1939-1989

THE FIFTY YEARS WAR

PATRICK BROGAN

BLOOMSBURY

All rights reserved; no part of this publication may be reproduced, stored in a retrieval system, or transmitted by any means, electronic, mechanical, photocopying or otherwise, without the prior permission of the Publisher.

First published 1990 by Bloomsbury Publishing Limited,
2 Soho Square, London W1V 5DE

Copyright © 1990 by Patrick Brogan

The moral right of the author has been asserted.

Acknowledgements
'The Solution' on p. 30 from *Poems 1913–56* by Bertolt Brecht, translated by Derek Bowman, Methuen, London.

British Library Cataloguing in Publication Data
A CIP record for this book is available from the British Library

ISBN 0 7475 0754 6

Designed by Geoff Green
Typeset by Hewer Text Composition Services, Edinburgh
Printed by Richard Clay Ltd, Bungay, Suffolk

Contents

Introduction   1

1   East Germany   13
2   Poland   45
3   Czechoslovakia   77
4   Hungary   115
5   Yugoslavia   145
6   Albania   171
7   Bulgaria   185
8   Romania   209
9   The Baltic Republics   241

Postscript   253
The Collapse of Communism: a Chronology   259
Bibliography   265
Index   271

Introduction

Communism collapsed in Europe on the night of 9 November 1989, when the Berlin Wall opened and a million East Berliners poured through the gates to freedom. It was, at last, the symbolic end of World War II, the final restoration of democracy and freedom to the city that had once been Hitler's capital. The East German regime had disintegrated, to be followed within six weeks by those of Bulgaria, Czechoslovakia and Romania, and the revolution then swept eastwards into the Soviet Union itself. Marxism and the Cold War died together that one night in Germany, where both had been born. The great enterprise begun by Lenin in 1917 and carried forward by Stalin and his successors had failed irredeemably, and the empire they had inherited from the tsars was on the brink of ruin.

The most evocative sights of that extraordinary year were the rejoicing crowds dancing on the Berlin Wall, and the body of Nicolae Ceauşescu, shot on Christmas Day, sprawled in a barracks yard. The one symbolized peaceful change; the other was a reminder of Europe's violent and repressive past. The first was a picture to pair with images of the liberation of Paris in 1944, the second with those of Mussolini and his mistress strung up by their feet at a filling station in Milan.

The event transcended Eastern Europe. The Berlin Wall fell, and the East Germans became free again, but so did the West Germans and all other Europeans. They had been prisoners of the Cold War for two generations, their economies and politics distorted by the unceasing enmity between East and West. That hostility had extended across the globe, leading Americans to fight Communism in Korea and Vietnam, and Soviets to fight counter-revolution in

Afghanistan – and both to impose their conflict on Africans, Asians and Latin Americans.

The European revolution began in the Soviet Union when the regime was at last forced to confront the failure of its most fundamental economic principles. In 1979, it was still sufficiently self-confident to invade Afghanistan. Two years later, Brezhnev, in his dotage, could still insist that General Jaruzelski in Poland must suppress Solidarity. These were the dying gestures of Russian imperialism and Communist messianism. By the time Brezhnev died in 1982, it was already obvious that the Afghan intervention had failed. Then came the worldwide collapse of oil prices. Its effects on the Soviet Union, the world's major oil producer, were particularly severe: oil was, except for armaments, its only major export; it was the currency that paid for all its foreign adventures – in Africa, Latin America and Asia – and for imports from the West that were essential for the entire Eastern bloc's economic survival.

These were the immediate causes of the crisis. The underlying problem was that Stalin's economic system was based on force, waste and bureaucracy. The miserably low Soviet standard of living was deteriorating, and this deterioration accelerated throughout the 1980s. The Soviet social and economic system could not save itself.

The secret – that Communism had failed – was known to everyone in the Soviet Union, though no one dared say it aloud. It was several years before Mikhail Gorbachev, who became general secretary of the Communist party in 1985, could admit publicly the failure of the system he now directed, but from the start, he discussed, and allowed everyone else to discuss, particular failures. Openness (*glasnost*) preceded restructuring (*perestroika*). People were permitted to complain in public about the shortages of everything from housing to shoelaces; they were allowed to reveal the crimes of Stalin. Within two years, everyone had discovered not only that the economic disaster was far worse than even the greatest pessimists had imagined, but also the essential secret: that everyone else in the Soviet Union also knew that Communism had failed. The emperor himself was the first to declare that he had no clothes, and once that crucial admission was made, it was impossible ever to restore the old official hypocrisy.

Glasnost, while spreading rapidly in the Soviet Union, was repressed in most of Eastern Europe because the regimes there saw clearly that such an admission of failure would destroy them. It did not occur to Gorbachev until later that he had perhaps released a genie that would consume him, but Honecker, Husák and Ceauşescu were under no such illusions. They stood firm against the tide until it overwhelmed them.

The Poles were the first to respond to the news from Moscow. They had resisted Soviet Communism more consistently and more successfully than the other Eastern Europeans, and were ready to respond to the first signs of weakness. In May 1988, there was a rash of strikes, which the government defeated – with much difficulty – with a mixture of concession and suppression. Lech Wałęsa returned to the Lenin shipyard at Gdańsk and the strikes ended, but the underlying dissatisfactions were as acute as ever, and the strikes resumed in August. That was the moment when the revolution began. Jaruzelski's government was forced to retreat step by step as Solidarity was reborn from its ashes. One day the archives will be opened and we will discover what advice Jaruzelski sought and was offered in Moscow. Perhaps Gorbachev told him from the start that he must resolve his own problems, that whatever happened there would be no help from the Red Army. Perhaps the new Soviet policy of non-interference evolved as the need and the difficulty of intervention became more pressing. In any event, Jaruzelski surrendered at every point, and in August and September 1989, a non-Communist government was formed in Warsaw.

By that time, the government of Hungary also was in full retreat. The Hungarian Communist Party, following in the footsteps of János Kádár, believed that it could stay ahead of the opposition reformers and remain master of a changing situation. That was also Gorbachev's position in the USSR. Indeed, the Hungarian party boasted that it had invented *glasnost* 20 years before Gorbachev. Then *glasnost* swept the party into oblivion, a result that may have given Gorbachev a moment of disquiet.

In Poland and Hungary, the regimes gave way to political pressures from the opposition and from below. In East Germany and Czechoslovakia, in October and November 1989, the regimes were repudiated in mass demonstrations of 'people's power', as Marcos in the Philippines had been in 1988. Still the Red Army did not intervene. Honecker ordered his troops to fire on the demonstrators in Leipzig, and he was not obeyed. A first demonstration in Prague on 17 November, the protestors emboldened by the news from Berlin, was broken up violently, but after that, the police, the army and the militia abandoned the government. Even the secret police in East Germany and Czechoslovakia did not defend their masters.

In Bulgaria, the Communist party abruptly reformed itself. It was the only successful case of a revolution from above: Todor Zhivkov was removed from office on 10 November, the day after the Berlin Wall was opened, and in the succeeding months, reformers took over every level of the party, which they renamed the Bulgarian Socialist Party. In June 1990, they won Bulgaria's first free elections.

The revolutions spread from country to country by emulation and by television. At the end of 1989, Ceauşescu in turn fell victim to people's power. His secret police, the *Securitate*, tried to resist, and up to 1000 people were killed in the fighting. Romania then fell into the hands of a group of opposition Communists who had been disgraced under the Ceauşescu regime. They repudiated the dictator's odious and corrupt social and economic policies, but were not true democrats and relied on the old Balkan techniques of intimidation, manipulation and demagoguery to remain in power. Communism, as it had been practised for 45 years, was overthrown in Romania, but it was not replaced by the hopeful democracy achieved in Poland, Hungary and East Germany.

As for the rest of the Balkans, Yugoslavia moved inexorably nearer to abandoning Communism. Two of its six republics elected non-Communist governments in April 1990, and by then, the federation was on the verge of dissolution. Albania's leaders, like East Germany's and Romania's before them, tried to resist the changes sweeping Europe. There was scant hope they could succeed, and the first crack in the monolith occurred in July 1990, when thousands of Albanians took refuge in foreign embassies in Tirana, and demanded the right to emigrate. No one believed the regime could survive very long as a last relic of Stalinism.

The whole world marvelled at the speed of the transformation. On 7 June 1990, the annual summit of the seven members of the Warsaw Pact assembled in Moscow. Only Presidents Gorbachev of the USSR and Jaruzelski of Poland had attended the 1989 summit, and Jaruzelski was now accompanied by the non-Communist ministers who had stripped him of all his powers. President Václav Havel of Czechoslovakia, chosen co-chairman of the Pact, had been in jail at the time of the previous meeting. Two of the missing men had been jailed, two others were in disgrace and Nicolae Ceauşescu had been put against a wall by his own soldiers and shot.

The end of empires is not usually peaceful. The dissolution of the Soviet external empire in Eastern Europe was not violent, except in Romania, but now the Soviet Union itself – the internal empire – has begun to break up in blood and hatred. The assembled presidents of the Warsaw Pact, gathered to give their alliance a decent burial, were faced with a reversal of all precedent in their dealings. Once the Soviet leader gave orders to his European vassals, who ruled by his grace and protection. Now all was changed: the Europeans, except for the Romanians, could be confident in their countries' future, and a new period in their histories was opening – but the future of the Soviet Union was quite unpredictable. Gorbachev himself might not survive to attend the next Warsaw Pact summit – if, that is, there is such a thing in 1991.

The explosions in Eastern Europe were not, in themselves, surprising. Many people had predicted them, and had even predicted that more than one country would rise in revolt at the same time. The real surprises were that it had happened peacefully (again, except for Romania), and that the Soviet Union had permitted its entire external empire to collapse so rapidly. Evidently the USSR itself was in a far worse condition than its harshest critics had imagined, and its sense of mission had completely dissipated. George Orwell's image of Stalinism as a boot endlessly grinding in its victim's face proved mistaken. The old tyrant's successors eventually lost the taste for tyranny, and Communism itself proved a long, miserable parenthesis, a false turning, for the Soviet Union as well as for Eastern Europe.

The party in the USSR claimed its legitimacy from its victories in 1917, in the civil war and in World War II. In Eastern Europe, with the exceptions of Yugoslavia and Albania, the Communist regimes were all the creations of the Red Army. They were installed and sustained by force, and when that force was relaxed, they all fell together.

In 1944, Stalin told Milovan Djilas, a Yugoslav Communist, 'This war is not as in the past: whoever occupies a territory also imposes on it his own social system. Everyone imposes his own system as far as his army can reach.' Stalin applied this doctrine ruthlessly. In the autumn of that year his armies reconquered the Baltic republics and immediately restored the Soviet order. As soon as the Red Army crossed the 1940 frontiers into Poland, Czechoslovakia, Romania, Hungary and Bulgaria, 'national fronts' were set up that were soon to be developed into the new governments of the liberated countries. In every case, the Communists were dominant. The spectrum ranged from Czechoslovakia, where the pre-war president, Eduard Beneš, gave his authority to the new regime, to Bulgaria where the old Bolshevik Dimitrov sent his agents to suppress all opposition immediately. But the result was always the same. The conqueror imposed his own social system upon his conquests. In Yugoslavia, meanwhile, the indigenous Communists achieved the same result, and set up a client state in Albania, and in Germany, the first steps towards partition were taken in April 1945.

In most of Eastern Europe, the Communists continued to rule through coalitions for several years after the war, and the full rigours of Stalinism were not imposed until 1948. To begin with, many people rallied to the new regimes which swept away the old governing classes and gave real advantages to workers and landless peasants – for instance, the Communists were the largest party in Czechoslovakia's elections in 1946. Some 45 years later, in 1990, the new government in Romania showed once again how a ruthless and demogogic government can call upon social resentments to maintain itself. However, the technique does not work for long unless the country is prosperous enough to guarantee the favoured proletariat a better standard of living than the 'class enemy' – and a rising standard, too. In Central Europe after World War II, those relatively favourable conditions and sentiments did not last long, as the East German regime discovered in 1953 and the Polish and Hungarian governments in 1956.

Those popular revolts comprised the second crisis to confront the parties after the war. The first consisted of a series of purges and show trials between 1948 and 1954, in which Stalin and his satraps expelled, tried and often executed party leaders who were deemed insufficiently loyal to the USSR. Gomułka in Poland, Rajk in Hungary, Kostov in Bulgaria, Xoxe in Albania, Slanský in Czechoslovakia and Patrascanu in Romania were all purged and, except for Gomułka, murdered. Stalin had intended the chief victim to be Tito himself, the only real hero to emerge from the Communist resistance in Eastern Europe and the only man with the authority to defy Stalin. From 1948 until Stalin died in 1953, party leaders only survived by servile submission to him, and lived in constant terror of his disfavour.

In the last months of his life, the old, mad, evil dictator conceived a new plot to destroy his enemies, and by 'enemies' he meant his closest collaborators. The Slanský trial in Prague was to be followed by a wholesale purge of the Soviet party: Beria, Molotov, Mikoyan, Malenkov and the rest were to go the way of Trotsky, Bukharin, Kamenev and Zinoviev – the Bolshevik leaders whom Stalin had purged and killed in the 1930s.

Just as those purges had been heralded by the murder, on Stalin's order, of the Leningrad party leader Sergei Kirov in 1934, so the new purge was heralded, in January 1953, by the arrest of nine professors of medicine, who all served as house physicians in the Kremlin, and most of whom were Jews. They were accused of murdering two members of the government who had died earlier, and of plotting against Soviet military leaders. They were not accused of plotting against Molotov (whose wife had been deported to the *gulag*), or Mikoyan (whose sons had been arrested), or any other Kremlin leader: evidently the leaders themselves were to be accused of directing the 'doctors' plot'. Their lives – and the doctors' – were saved when Stalin died of a stroke on 5 March 1953.

The tyrant's death was followed by a great outpouring of public mourning, and by riots in the labour camps and the uprising in East Germany three months later. In February 1956, Nikita Khrushchev, who had won the fight for the succession, convened a party conference and revealed some of the details of Stalin's crimes in a speech to a closed session of delegates. Stalin had ruled by terror and now, in the 'secret speech', Khrushchev denounced state terrorism. Soviet authority was badly shaken in Eastern Europe: the crisis in Poland and the Budapest uprising in October 1956 were direct consequences of the 'thaw' that Khrushchev introduced.

In the crisis of 1956, the USSR decided that Communism must be maintained in Eastern Europe at all costs, and the shadow of Budapest was to hang over the bloc until 1989. The Hungarians' lesson was repeated in Czechoslovakia in 1968, and the threat of Soviet intervention allowed Jaruzelski to impose martial law on Poland in 1981. From 1944 to 1989, therefore, the history of Eastern Europe was one of repression by the Soviet Union.

Revisionist historians in the West have argued that the Cold War was as much the fault of Truman, Churchill and their colleagues as it was Stalin's. Certainly the latter's chief concern was for the Soviet Union's own security: he was determined that never again would German armies march on Moscow and Stalingrad, and he thought the best defence was to establish a glacis of client states to protect his western borders. Perhaps if the West had recognized and welcomed the Iron Curtain from the start as a legitimate Soviet fortification, if it had pacified and appeased the USSR instead of confronting it with Nato, Soviet paranoia might have subsided earlier and the captive nations might therefore have recovered their freedom sooner. After all, strict Stalinist Communism was not imposed on most of Eastern Europe until after the onset of the Cold War in 1948. However, none of this proves that Truman, Attlee and Adenauer were wrong to take drastic measures to protect their countries. Stalin's attitude towards the West was always one of relentless hostility, and it was not unreasonable for Western nations to take him at his word and to protect themselves against the fate of East Germany and Czechoslovakia.

The events of 1989 were a further answer to the revisionists. All those cold warriors who had insisted that the division of Europe was entirely imposed by the Soviet Union were proved right. Containment worked – though it took far longer than the US State Department's George Kennan had expected when he had proposed the policy in the early 1950s. He had suggested that the way to deal with an aggressive and paranoid USSR was to 'contain' it – not to attack it, not to try to 'roll back' the Iron Curtain (that was Dulles's later, demagoguic formulation), but to wait for the Soviets to discover, through the passage of time, that they had taken the wrong road. When at last *glasnost* broke through the carapace of official mendacity and self-deception, showing Soviet citizens that the Communist party did not have the scientific answer to all social and economic problems, Eastern Europe was allowed to escape without regret. Then the Soviets turned to their own concerns.

The history of Communist rule in Eastern Europe ended in 1989, except in Yugoslavia, Albania and the three Baltic republics. It may be that the history of the Soviet Union is also coming to an end, but it would be most foolish to write its obituary so soon. It is never wise to predict the course of an avalanche, except to say that it will probably sweep away all superficial features from the landscape, leaving only the underlying structures exposed to the sun, and a vast mass of debris for the survivors to clear up.

This book is a history of Eastern Europe from 1945 to 1990, not a history of Communism, of the Cold War or of the Soviet Union. I have described some of the earlier history of the eight Communist states of the bloc, and of the three Baltic republics, because it is impossible to understand contemporary politics there without remembering the past. Take, for example, the parliamentary elections in Czechoslovakia in 1990: the leader of a Slovak nationalist party campaigned on the proposition that 'centuries of slavery under the Hungarians was preferable to 70 years of oppression by the Czechs.' The country's underlying landscape thus re-emerged a mere six months after the overthrow of Communism.

It will be many years before Europe, east and west, recovers from Communism, and it is already clear that there cannot be an easy transformation of eleven very different nations from totalitarianism to democracy. They will all go their separate ways; their individual histories have resumed, after a long interval. The history of Eastern Europe – of the 'captive nations', as the Americans used to call them – is over.

EUROPE 1938

North Sea
SWEDEN
ESTONIA
LATVIA
LITHU-ANIA
Moscow
U S S R
DENMARK
Baltic Sea
Danzig
UNITED KINGDOM
NETHERLANDS
London
Berlin
Warsaw
BELGIUM
GERMANY
POLAND
Paris
Prague
CZECHOSLOVAKIA
Munich
FRANCE
SWITZ.
AUSTRIA
Budapest
HUNGARY
ITALY
Belgrade
YUGOSLAVIA
Bucharest
ROMANIA
Black Sea
Rome
ALBANIA
BULGARIA
Sofia
GREECE

EUROPE 1990

Helsinki
SWEDEN
ESTONIA
LATVIA
LITHU-ANIA
Moscow
U S S R
DENMARK
UNITED KINGDOM
NETHERLANDS
London
Berlin
Warsaw
BELGIUM
GERMANY
POLAND
Bonn
Paris
Prague
CZECHOSLOVAKIA
FRANCE
SWITZ.
AUSTRIA
Budapest
HUNGARY
ITALY
RUMANIA
Belgrade
Bucharest
YUGOSLAVIA
Rome
BULGARIA
Sofia
ALBANIA
GREECE
TURKEY

Areas under Communist control

NORWAY
Oslo
SWEDEN
DENMARK
Copenhagen

MECKLENBURG
Szczecin
BRANDENBURG
Hamburg
Wandlitz
Berlin
Potsdam
Oder

WEST GERMANY
EAST GERMANY
SAXONY-ANHALT
Leipzig
THURINGIA
Dresden

NETHERLANDS
The Hague
UNITED KINGDOM
London
Brussels
BELGIUM
Bonn
Rhine
Frankfurt
SUDETENLAND
Lidice
Pra
Plzeň (Pilsen)
BOH
C
Budweis

English Channel
Seine
Paris
LUXEMBOURG
Nuremberg
Danube
Strasbourg
Munich

F R A N C E
Berne
SWITZERLAND
A U S T R I A
(Allied occupation 1945-5

Po
SLOV
Trieste
Fium (Rijek
Istrian Peninsula
I T A L Y
Adriatic
Rome

EUROPE IN 1945

0   100   200   300 km
0   50   100   150 miles

▪▪▪▪ Boundary between the Soviet
and Western Allies' occupation zones,
(the Iron Curtain since 1948)

Stockholm

Helsinki
Leningrad

Tallinn

ESTONIA

Baltic Sea

Riga

LATVIA

Klaipeda
(Memel)

Kaliningrad
(Königsberg)

LITHUANIA
Kaunas   Vilnius

1945 to
Russian SSR

Gdynia
Gdánsk

incorporated into
Poland 1945

...NIA

Bydgoszcz

Poznań

Vistula

Warsaw

U   S   S   R

to USSR

1945

Moscow

N

Kiev

OLAND

Wrocław
ŁESIA

Łodz

Radom

Lublin

Kraków

UKRAINE

Ostrava
RAVIA
Tĕšin (Teschen)

Zlin (Gottwaldov)

Brno

nna

HOS
SLOVAKIA

SLOVAKIA

Bratislava

RUTHENIA
to USSR
1945

MOLDAVIA to USSR 1944

Budapest

MOLDAVIA

Prut

MOLDAVIA

HUNGARY

Cluj

Tîrgu Mureş

TRANSYLVANIA

ROMANIA

VOJVODINA

Timisoara

Braşov

IA
BANAT

WALLACHIA

Tîrgovişte

Belgrade

S
E
R
B
I
A

Bucharest

Danube

DOBRUJA

Black
Sea

SNIA-
RCEGOVINA

YUGOSLAVIA

BULGARIA

MATIA

MONTENEGRO

Prištína

KOSOVO

Sofia

Sea

Shköder
(Scutari)

MACEDONIA

Tiranë (Tirana)

ALBANIA

Istanbul

Strait of Otranto

GREECE

Aegean Sea

TURKEY

Corfu

1 East Germany

The first act in the revolutions of 1989 occurred in Hungary, in May, when television cameras were invited to the borders to record soldiers rolling up barbed wire and demolishing watch towers. No one thought it was very important: Hungarians had been free to cross their borders for years. The government wanted to improve relations with the West and to encourage Western investment, so it ostentatiously dismantled the Iron Curtain. A Hungarian statesman visiting Washington presented a strand of barbed wire to President Bush as a momento. The whole affair was simply a small, symbolic gesture – like the fall of a few stones high in the mountains which starts an avalanche.

Some East Germans, watching on West German television, booked themselves holidays in Hungary. Perhaps, if the borders were really open, they thought, they could cross to freedom. In the course of the summer, there were dramatic political developments in Hungary and Poland, but the German Democratic Republic – *Deutsche Demokratische Republik* (DDR) – remained locked in the Stalinist embrace of its ruling gerontocracy. Soviet publications, writing of *glasnost*, were banned in the DDR, and people became desperate to escape.

A steady trickle of them slipped across the Hungarian border with Austria, which police made no excessive effort to patrol. In August, thousands presented themselves to the West German embassy in Budapest, asking for help. Others camped out in a nearby church-yard, and all vowed they would never return to the DDR. Far larger numbers, scores of thousands, stayed in camp grounds all over Hungary, waiting on events. West German television, followed by West German politicians, visited the refugees. The Hungarians were caught between their obligations to their Warsaw Pact ally and their hopes for better relations with the West. Moscow offered no guidance, and Hungary opted for hope. On 10 September, it lifted all restrictions.

This time there was no mistaking the event's significance. Tens of thousands of East Germans poured through the breach in the wall that had blocked them for a generation, and hundreds of thousands more prepared to follow them. Others took to the streets in East Berlin, Leipzig and Dresden to demand, first, the right to emigrate. Then they demanded democracy, and the crowds swelled to enormous proportions. They demanded the government's resignation; they proclaimed, 'We Are the People,' and, finally, 'We Are One People.' The avalanche was rushing down the mountain and nothing could stop it.

The German Democratic Republic was a creation of the Cold War. It was born in 1949, when tensions between East and West were at their height – and when those tensions ended and the Cold War with them, the DDR died. It lasted 40 years, one month and two days, from 7 October 1949 to 9 November 1989, and its overthrow was the most uplifting and dramatic moment of 1989, that year of revolutions. The Berlin Wall had become the symbol of the division of Europe and the failure of Communism. On the night the barriers were lifted, one million East Berliners poured through the Wall, free citizens again. Forty years of socialism had failed. They were Germans, not 'East Germans', and the 'Democratic Republic' had never been democratic or a real state. Outsiders and East German intellectuals had often speculated – and the Communists had endlessly proclaimed – that 40 years of indoctrination had created a real East German patriotism, a pride in the DDR's achievements, a desire to retain a distinctive nationality and to remain free of the crass materialism of the West. But it was all illusion.

There had been a growing separatism in the German Federal Republic – *Bundesrepublik Deutschland* (BRD) – in the sense that people there no longer much regretted the country's division, or put reunification very high on their list of priorities. West Germans had peered over the Wall, disliked what they saw and turned their backs on the separated brethren. The national holiday on 17 June, commemorating the East German uprising in 1953, no longer meant anything special at all.

Then the Wall fell, and a generation of self-delusion, on both sides, evaporated like the morning mist. There was only one Germany. It had been divided by force, and the division had been maintained by force, Soviet force – and once the Soviets abandoned the effort, the two halves of Germany flowed together again, irresistibly. The only questions that remained were matters of book keeping: the exchange rate of the East German *Mark* as it was swallowed by the *Deutschmark*, or pensions for former Communist bureaucrats. The government ministries and foreign embassies in Bonn prepared to move back to the capital Berlin.

Post-war Germany

When General Lucius Clay, the American commander in Berlin, first saw it in June 1945, he found a 'city of the dead'. It was a wilderness of rubble, with the sickly smell of death permeating everything. Survivors crouched in cellars, grubbed through the ruins looking for food, or lined up in their hundreds at water stand-pipes. There were thousands of defeated soldiers dressed in the rags of the *Wehrmacht*, but the great majority of those who had endured were women, and they were all starving together. The Soviet soldiers who had captured the city were the élite of their army, disciplined, well-behaved. They were followed by a rabble who looted everything they could find and raped every woman.

Twenty per cent of Berlin's buildings were totally destroyed; another 50 per cent were virtually uninhabitable. For months on end, the US Air Force had bombed by day and the RAF by night. During the worst of the firestorms, people fled the shelters and cellars of burning buildings and took refuge in the wide boulevards, lying head to toe down the centres of roads while the flames from the blazing city met over their heads. For the last two months of the war, as the Germans put up a last savage defence of the city, Berlin was bombarded by Soviet artillery. That final battle cost 300,000 Soviet casualties, an even greater number of German soldiers and 100,000 civilian dead. Hitler killed himself on 30 April, a Red Army soldier hung the Red Flag from the roof of the *Reichstag* that evening, and the last German forces surrendered on 2 May. The Soviets had taken Berlin, and they were to exercise all the political advantages their victory gave them.

The Americans and British had advanced well into the future Soviet occupation zone by the end of the war, and could have taken Berlin themselves if Eisenhower had given the order. However, he thought the city had no military significance, ignored its political significance and preferred to allow the Red Army to fight for a city that was to be in their own occupation zone, as established at Yalta in February 1945. Therefore, immediately after the German surrender on 8 May, American and British troops were pulled back to the borders of the occupation zones, and it was three months before they could get to their own sectors of Berlin.

The Soviets showed an unrelenting obstructionism from the start, beginning with a series of obstacles to delay their allies' arrival in the capital. Then the two Western allies (soon to be joined by the French) were told that they must supply their own sectors: nothing would be available from the Soviet zone, neither food nor fuel.

Furthermore, the Soviets imposed strict restrictions on western access routes into Berlin by road, rail and canal. The only unrestricted access they permitted were by air, along three recognized corridors. This was not then thought a significant concession. The Western military men and politicians – and President Truman when he came to the Potsdam summit in July – took a conciliatory approach to Soviet intransigence, believing that satisfactory arrangements could be worked out later, for the rest of Eastern Europe as well as for Germany. This period of American naïveté did not last long, and many Americans (including George Kennan, in Moscow) protested at the time, but while it lasted, Truman, Eisenhower and the others made mistakes that were later to cost them dear.

The Soviets, meanwhile, had set up an 'anti-Fascist' administration for Berlin, and they established local governments in each of the five *Länder* (states) in their zone: Saxony–Anhalt, Brandenburg, Mecklenburg, Saxony and Thuringia. These were all, from the start, dominated by the German Communist Party (KPD), although the most conspicuous positions were occupied by compliant non-Communists.

In 1933, when Hitler came to power, the KPD had been the most powerful Communist party in Europe outside the Soviet Union, but then it had been ruthlessly suppressed by the Nazis, and those of its leaders who had not escaped abroad were shot or incarcerated (its chief, Ernst Thälmann, was shot in prison in the last days of the war). Stalin probably killed more prominent German Communists than Hitler ever did: those German comrades who were in Moscow during the purges of 1936–38 were mostly shot. Late in the war, the survivors were instructed to prepare themselves for the tasks to come, and on 30 April 1945, Walter Ulbricht, Wilhelm Pieck and the others returned to Germany, accompanied by some trustworthy socialists, led by Otto Grotewohl. They immediately set about creating local committees to take charge of feeding the population, restoring public services, clearing the rubble, preserving public order – and directing the affairs of the 'anti-Fascist' local administrations. It was a first step towards that greatest of 19th-century Communist ambitions, a socialist Germany.

At any rate, that was Ulbricht's ambition. Stalin had other priorities. It has been observed that when the Red Flag was hoisted over Berlin, it symbolized the victory of the Russian Revolution over its greatest enemy, not the victory of a German Communist revolution. Stalin's objects were to obtain reparations from Germany and to ensure that it could never again rise up and endanger the Soviet Union. These two policies were contradictory: Germany could only pay for the restoration of the Soviet Union if it were itself restored to economic health, and that meant a centralized and powerful German government. The history of the next four years, and the start of the Cold War, was dominated by Soviet attempts to resolve this contradiction. In the event, Stalin chose to dismember Germany, by creating a separate German state in the Soviet zone, and to extract what reparations he could from that fragment.

The Potsdam conference ran from 17 July to 2 August 1945. It was the first foreign venture for President Truman and for Clement Attlee, who became British prime minister halfway through the conference. These diplomatic novices were confronted by Stalin, who knew exactly what he wanted, who was surrounded by his victorious armies, and who set the scene for the future by announcing to his allies that Poland had already taken possession of the parts of Germany that lay east of the Oder–Neisse line. This had been discussed at Yalta, when the Western allies had agreed that Poland's eastern frontier should be the line of the Soviet occupation in 1939 – the 'Curzon line'. Poland was to be compensated at Germany's expense, but the final status of the territories and the exact frontier were to be established at the peace conference. Now Stalin had taken matters into his own hands. Silesia and Pomerania and the ancient German cities Breslau, Danzig and Stettin were to become Polish and their German citizens expelled – and Stalin arbitrarily decreed that the frontier would be on the western or Lusatian Neisse, and not on the eastern Neisse as had been discussed at Yalta. Truman and the others, while protesting against this abrupt geographical rearrangement (especially the new British foreign secretary, Ernest Bevin) let it pass. They also conceded that East Prussia should be divided between Poland and the Soviet Union, with the USSR taking the capital, Königsberg (and renaming it Kaliningrad).

These lost territories amounted to about a quarter of Germany as it had been in 1937. Their entire population, about 10 million people, together with another 3 million Sudeten Germans in Czechoslovakia, were now to be driven from their homes. They headed west with whatever possessions they could carry, and flooded into the devastated heartlands where millions of other Germans were already homeless and the whole population was on the verge of starvation.

An equally important decision taken at Potsdam, one that made the partition of Germany inevitable, was that final authority in each of the zones was to be entrusted to military governors, whose only superior was the Allied Control Commission – the decisions of which had to be unanimous. This meant that the Western allies renounced all control or even influence over the way the Soviets administered their zone, and thus renounced any unified German government. This was not what they said; on the contrary, the 'Big Three' proclaimed that Germany would not be partitioned, merely de-Nazified, demilitarized, and decentralized. But these pious hopes did not long survive the bleak reality.

The conference also agreed that each of the four allies would be entitled to take reparations from its own zone and that the USSR would be entitled to a further 10 per cent of the reparations taken by the Western allies. The Soviets had already begun to strip their zone: factories were shipped east, together with rolling stock, vehicles, even railway track. East Germany, having suffered the extremes of the air war and the ground war, was now comprehensively looted. As for the territories to the east formerly occupied by Germany, the Soviets stripped them completely of their industrial plant. The Poles, who hoped to inherit working mines and factories, found a devastated and empty country.

The Soviets extended their control in their zone. Two hundred of the companies that were not dismantled were taken under Soviet ownership and worked exclusively for the USSR until 1954. German technicians were deported to the Soviet Union to work in factories there, and German prisoners of war were also held to labour for the Soviets. Opposition was crushed in the approved manner. Between 1945 and 1950, 200,000 Germans were sent to the concentration camps that had recently been liberated: Buchenwald and Sachsenhausen were now filled with German democrats and other dissidents, teachers, landowners, factory owners and former Nazis. The Soviet secret police, like the *Gestapo* before it, did not limit itself to imprisonment and deportation: in 1990, after the overthrow of Communism, many mass graves were discovered, containing the bodies of thousands of people who had been summarily executed by the Soviets.

In the Soviet zone, the KPD co-opted the SPD – the Socialists – as well as the two other democratic parties that had revived from the embers: the Christian Democrats and the Liberals. They were all forced into the 'Anti-Fascist Alliance', led by the KPD employing the usual methods of intimidation and corruption. Berlin was different, however; here, from the beginning, the Soviets and their German clients had to cope with the baleful influence of the West. The SPD in Berlin, which had resolutely opposed Hitler, was now sustained by its national leaders in the West. Their detestation of Communism, nurtured in the street wars of the 1920s and early 1930s, had survived the Third Reich undimmed. In March 1946, the Berlin SPD staged a party referendum on the question whether it should merge with the KPD. The vote was sabotaged in East Berlin, but in a free vote in the West, the proposed merger was defeated four to one. The Communists in the Soviet sector responded by staging a series of rallies, culminating in April with a ceremony in the *Admiralspalast*, a public assembly hall in East Berlin, at which the KPD and a rump of the SPD, led by Grotewohl, were merged. Ulbricht and Grotewohl solemnly marched on to the stage, from either side, and shook hands in the middle to wild applause from the audience. Thus was formed the Socialist Unity Party of Germany – the SED – which remained in existence, as the governing party of East Germany, until it was swept away in the cataclysm of 1989.

The new SED and the old SPD then did battle in the first post-war election in Berlin in October 1946, to choose a new government for the city. It was the first free election there since 1932, and the last in the east until 1990. Other German cities and *Länder* in the Soviet zone had already voted in municipal elections. The Communist success in these latter elections had depended upon the thoroughness with which party militants had intimidated the opposition. In Berlin, despite the party thugs' best efforts in the Soviet sector, the Socialists won 48 per cent over all, the Christian Democrats 22 per cent, the Liberals 9 per cent – and the Communist SED just under 20 per cent of the vote. It was a dramatic defeat for the new party, and demonstrated to its leaders, and to Stalin, that they could never win elections fairly in Germany, and would have to attain their ends by other means.

The post-war German economy

In the first year after the war, Germany's economic situation deteriorated sharply – and, with it, the rest of Europe's. The Soviets and the French insisted on reparations and on reducing German industry to a fraction of its pre-war level, and to compound the problem the Soviets refused all cooperation between the four zones. For a century, western Germany had been fed by the farms of the east, mainly in the areas now annexed by Poland, and that supply was now abruptly cut off. Soon, the three Western powers were keeping alive the millions of Germans under their care with food imports, which they paid for themselves. There was barely enough to feed the population, and then only at a starvation level. Meetings of the four foreign ministers grew increasingly rancorous. The British and American governments began to face the fact that no cooperation was possible with the Soviet Union except on Soviet terms – and those terms were quite unacceptable. One result of this realization was Winston

Churchill's 'Iron Curtain' speech, given at Fulton, Missouri on 5 March 1946.

In the summer of that year, with the prospect of disaster in the coming winter, the Americans proposed merging their zone with the British zone, for economic purposes, arguing that the only way to feed the Germans was to allow them to work and produce, and for this they needed a united country, not a series of starving fragments. The British agreed at once. The US secretary of state, James Byrne, announced that the administration of this new 'Bizone' would be handed over to the Germans themselves as soon as possible. He also reversed American policy with the promise that the United States army would stay in Europe as long as it was needed. The subsequent history of Western Europe followed from these two essential decisions.

The second winter after the war was a hard one, and the Germans were starving in Berlin and in the rest of the country. A further foreign ministers' conference in Moscow was utterly fruitless, and convinced the new US secretary of state, General George Marshall, that the Soviet Union was perfectly content to allow Germany to collapse altogether, in the hope of driving out the allies and precipitating a Communist revolution. Furthermore, it became obvious that Europe as a whole could not recover on its own. Britain, on the verge of bankruptcy, was forced to end its assistance to the Greek and Turkish governments*. The United States stepped into the breach when President Truman announced the 'Truman Doctrine' under which the United States would 'support free peoples who are resisting attempted subjugation by armed minorities or by outside pressures'. The Germans were allowed to set up an economic council in the Bizone to direct economic policy, its members being drawn from the elected representatives of the *Länder*.

Finally, in June 1947, Marshall announced the American proposal to restore Europe: the Marshall Plan. The United States would provide the capital Europe needed, on condition that Europeans worked together to restore their economies. Ernest Bevin immediately persuaded the French to join him in convening a conference

---

* Greece was in the throes of a civil war between the government and Communist insurgents, and Turkey was faced with immense pressure from the USSR over territorial questions in Anatolia and Soviet access from the Black Sea.

in Paris to discuss European recovery and the Marshall Plan. It met in July, and marked the formal division of the continent: the Soviet Union and the rest of Eastern Europe, on Stalin's instructions, refused to attend. Two months later, they formed the Cominform, the latest reincarnation of the old Comintern, the Third International.

The third winter was again hard. Most Germans had to survive on 1000 calories a day or less. Inflation was rising steadily, and farmers had nothing to buy with what they earned, and anyway, the currency was worthless – so they made no effort to supply the cities. The Americans and British expanded the German-run Economic Council and turned over to it most economic policy decisions. Then, in February 1948, the Communists in Czechoslovakia staged a *coup d'état* and seized power. By a coincidence, the American, British, French and Benelux foreign ministers were then meeting in London to consider the future of Germany. After the Czech coup, the Europeans responded by signing the Treaty of Brussels setting up the West European Union, a military alliance that was the nucleus of NATO. For his part, President Truman proposed peacetime conscription for the first time in American history.

The Soviets reacted to this military alliance by walking out of the Allied Control Commission in Berlin on 20 March. Then on 1 April, they interrupted all military rail traffic between Berlin and the western zones of Germany. Four days later, a Soviet fighter that was buzzing a British civilian plane (a Vickers Viking) flying into Berlin flew too close and crashed into it. The crew and seven passengers (two of them Americans) in the British plane and the Soviet pilot were all killed. This proved to be a warning of dangers to come, not the opening shot of a major offensive.

The next two months passed quietly, until a further meeting of Western ministers in London decided, on 1 June, to call a constituent assembly in the three western zones to set up a German federation. On the same day, the three allies also decided that the time had come to institute currency reform; the Germany economy could not recover without it.

The political consequences of the reform would be immense. It would mark the final division of Germany, since the Soviets would not accept the new currency in their zone. As for Berlin, that city, too, would be divided if the Western powers introduced their new currency there – and if they did not, West Berlin would be absorbed into the eastern zone. On 18 June 1948, the new currency – the *Deutschmark* – was introduced in the three western zones. The Soviets were told that its introduction in West Berlin would be held up, in the hope of a four-power agreement on the issue. Germans were allowed to trade in 60 *Reichmarks* for 60 *Deutschmarks*, other arrangements were made for commercial enterprises – and the rest of the nation's pre-war currency became completely worthless.

A second reform took place at the same time, directed by Professor Ludwig Erhard on behalf of the new German economic authorities in the west. Choosing a weekend, when the occupying powers were distracted, he abolished all price controls, rationing (except basic foodstuffs) and other restrictions that had come into force during the previous 15 years – during the Depression, under Hitler and under the occupation. It was the classic 'big bang' in economics, and it was a dramatic success. The German 'economic miracle' began immediately.

The Soviets produced their own new currency – the *Ostmark* – and tried to impose it on all of Berlin, the Berlin Assembly having been instructed to approve it. The Western powers then allowed *Deutschmarks* to be used in West Berlin and asked the Assembly to approve the move.

On 24 June, the Soviets cut off all land and water communications between Berlin and the West. The Berlin blockade had begun.

The Berlin blockade

The Cold War settled upon Europe and the world in 1948. Stalin ordered that all residual opposition parties in Eastern Europe be suppressed, and purged the Communist parties themselves, to ensure slavish obedience to the Soviet Union. In February, Czechoslovakia fell into the Communist camp (*see* Chapter 3). In June, Yugoslavia was expelled from the Cominform (*see* Chapter 5), just as the Berlin blockade was beginning. Evidently Stalin had concluded that he had reached the limits of diplomacy, and that future victories must come through a show of force. His choices *vis à vis* Germany were clear: he could either abandon East Germany, leaving the Western allies to set up a new, united and capitalist Germany to replace Hitler's *Reich*; or else he could dismember the country and set up a permanent Communist government in the Soviet zone. He did not hesitate.

It was then necessary for the Soviets, if possible, to drive the Western powers out of Berlin. The currency reform was a pretext, not a cause, of the crisis. The western sector was a large, indigestible foreign body in the heart of the future Democratic Republic, what Khrushchev later called 'a bone stuck in [his] throat'. By annexing it, Stalin would greatly strengthen Communist Germany – and it was always possible that such a major defeat for the West would drive the Americans back across the Atlantic and permit the Communist parties in France, Italy and West Germany to seize power.

The Western allies, seeing the danger as clearly as Stalin, resolved to hold Berlin. Their determination, and eventual success, was made possible by the courage and steadfastness of the Berliners themselves, led by Walter Reuter (who had been elected mayor but had been prevented from taking office by a Soviet veto) and his deputy Willy Brandt. They were both socialists, who had spent the Hitler years in exile.

The belligerent American commander, Lucius Clay, wanted to send a heavily armoured convoy up the *autobahn* to blast its way through to Berlin, but wiser councils prevailed: Berlin was to be supplied by air. The two sides prepared for a long siege. The Soviets walked out of the *Kommandatura*, the four-power military administration of Berlin (they did not return until 1990). The Americans held their ultimate weapon in reserve: several squadrons of B-29s, which could carry nuclear weapons, were moved to Britain, to remind the Soviet Union of the dangers of pushing their tactical advantage too far.

The airlift began in improvisation. Every plane that the Americans and British could find was pressed into service, together with air and ground crews. The city's essential needs in food and medical supplies were met, at the minimal level the Germans had become accustomed to. The daily average of the airlift in June was 1404 tons*. In July, the figure was 2225 tons, 3838 in August and 4641 in September. These amounts were impressive, but not enough. They totalled only 40 per cent of the city's imports

* All figures are in American tons, i.e. 2000 lbs.

before the blockade had begun (which, even then, gave Berliners a miserable standard of living), and the minimum figure needed during the winter months was 5500 tons, including 2500 tons of coal. It was fortunate that the blockade began in summer, although the weather in 1948 was particularly bad.

The airlift was steadily and rapidly expanded, and by the time winter set in, there were enough daily flights to carry sufficient coal for the power plants as well as food for the Berliners. The airports were all enlarged and a new one built, and hundreds of cargo planes were brought in from the United States. The airlift involved immense logistical problems in the western zones, which were still devastated by war damage. For instance, thousands of tons of coal a day had to be delivered, in regular quantities and packed in standard coal bags, to former *Luftwaffe* bases. Air traffic control, too, was an endless difficulty: the Americans had to set up a special school, in Montana, which turned out 100 controllers a month. By the end of the year, the application of formidable American technical competence and seemingly limitless resources had demonstrated that Berlin could be supplied indefinitely.

Some diplomatic efforts to resolve the crisis were tried in the autumn. They failed: the Soviet Union insisted that the *Ostmark* must be the only currency in Berlin, and that the London agreement to set up a federal government in the western zones must be abandoned. In September, the Berlin city government was broken up by Communist mobs storming the *Stadthaus*; the Assembly's members took refuge in the western sector, and set up a separate administration. Berlin was now officially divided.

In September 1948, representatives of the western *Länder* gathered to discuss the 'Basic Law' (a rather coy phrase used to conceal the fact that they were drawing up a new constitution). They met in Bonn, which happened to be the residence of the Christian Democratic leader, Konrad Adenauer. Elections for a new Berlin Assembly were called for 5 December, and the Communists prepared for their defeat by staging a rally of their supporters at the city opera house on 30 November, voting the old city government out of existence and replacing it with a new one wholly dominated by the Communist party. The December elections were restricted to the western section, and the SPD won easily. Walter Reuter was at last able to take office as mayor, but in a divided city.

As for the airlift, Berlin was saved by the weather: the winter of 1948/49 was the mildest on record, with clear skies and very little frost. Because of this, the airlift could continue uninterrupted, and it reached 5546 tons a day in January and 5436 in February. Berliners not only survived, but because food supplies had by then been extremely well organised, they were actually better fed than at any time since the war. Loads continued to increase, reaching 7845 tons a day in April.

Meanwhile, plans for establishing NATO were moving briskly forward, as were discussions on the West German 'Basic Law'. The North Atlantic Treaty was signed in Washington on 4 April 1949, and in May, the Basic Law was approved by the German parties and ratified by the *Länder*.

By then, Stalin had concluded that the Berlin blockade had failed and that its continuance was against Soviet interests. He agreed to lift all travel restrictions in exchange for the promise of a new foreign ministers' conference to discuss the future of Germany. On 11 May, electricity from power plants in the east was restored to West Berlin, and the first convoy set out down the *autobahn* just after midnight; rail and canal traffic resumed at the same time. The airlift was kept in place for several months more, to build up stocks and supplement ground traffic, and by July, 8184 tons a day were being flown in. During the course of the airlift, a total of 2,325,808 tons of supplies were flown into Berlin.

The German Democratic Republic

After the Berlin blockade ended, the four allied foreign ministers assembled for a last, fruitless meeting in Paris in May 1949. The West was determined to set up a democratic German government and to protect West Berlin. The Soviets once again demanded that Germany be kept under the control of the four powers, each of whom would have a veto over every decision. No agreement was possible. The Federal Republic (BRD) was set up in August, and the German Democratic Republic (DDR) was formally established on 7 October 1949, with Wilhelm Pieck as president and Otto Grotewohl as prime minister. Walter Ulbricht retained the key position of secretary general of the SED.

The new DDR was a thoroughly Stalinist state right from the

beginning. Ulbricht set about purging the party of all opponents, real and imagined, concentrating on those old Communists who had served the cause in Spain and elsewhere in the West and whose loyalty was therefore suspect. As in other Soviet satellites, Stalin wanted only loyal 'Muscovites' in command. The same ruse was used in the DDR that had worked so well elsewhere: an unfortunate American Communist, Noël Field, had been arrested in Hungary and accused of being a CIA agent; then everyone he had ever met in Eastern Europe was charged with spying, and the net spread across the whole bloc. The most senior German victim of this absurdity was Paul Merker, a member of the Politburo since 1926. The big difference between the DDR and other satellites was that Merker was not executed.

Economic conditions continued to be grim and depressing. By 1947, 65 per cent of the zone's industrial capacity had been shipped to the USSR, and more than one third of the remaining companies were owned directly by the Soviet Union and sent their entire production east, without payment. All East German industries were turned from their normal paths of trade with the rest of the country and made over to Soviet specifications. The Berlin blockade had disrupted the economy of East Berlin almost as much as it had that of the Western sector. The DDR was deprived of aid from the Marshall Plan as well as of the beneficial effects of the Erhard reforms; thousands of technicians and professionals were conscripted into the Soviet economy; the country suffered from agricultural policies which broke up existing farms and big estates; its industry was progressively nationalized; and it continued to carry the full cost of the Soviet occupation. Hundreds of thousands of East Germans emigrated to the west: 165,000 in 1951, 182,000 in 1952 and 331,000 in 1953. While West Germany was beginning to enjoy its 'miracle', East Germany remained locked in misery.

The June revolt

Stalin died on 5 March 1953. The struggle for the succession began at once, and the East European regimes were pawns in the battle. Some powerful men in Moscow, including Beria and Malenkov, considered settling their differences with the West in one sweeping gesture, by abandoning the DDR. Their advocacy of a 'new course' in East Germany was one of the events that provoked the 17 June revolt.

The possibility that a general settlement might have been achieved in 1953 has tantalized historians ever since. Churchill, then in his last term as British prime minister, went to see Eisenhower, who had taken office as president in January, and proposed a joint approach to Moscow. He thought the opportunities brought about by the Soviet disarray should be seized. Eisenhower spurned the idea, and in any event, the man who eventually came out on top in Moscow, Nikita Khrushchev, showed himself a firm believer in maintaining Soviet hegemony in Eastern Europe. Later, the proposal for 'abandoning' the DDR was one of the charges made against Malenkov.

Unlike most of the other satellite leaders, Walter Ulbricht refused to follow Khrushchev's example (or orders) and de-Stalinize after the dictator's death. Ulbricht knew that he was the most vulnerable of all: if the USSR chose to abandon the DDR, it would simply cease to exist. Ulbricht therefore had nothing to lose: until such time as the fate of his Democratic Republic was decided over his head, he would govern it himself, to the bitter end. Collectivization, five-year plans, concentration on heavy industry and still more purges continued to be his policy.

In the middle of May 1953, the SED Politburo broadcast an astonishing, wide-ranging resolution. It denounced saboteurs, Trotskyites, Zionists, Freemasons, 'morally depraved individuals' and enemies of the state. It said that the DDR had much to learn from the Slanský trial in Czechoslovakia the previous year (*see* Chapter 3), and announced the purging of the most prominent German survivor of the International Brigade in Spain, Franz Dahlem, who was probably the only member of the party with the authority to challenge Ulbricht. The resolution also announced a 10 per cent increase in the workers' 'norms': every worker must now increase his productivity by 10 per cent without any increase in wages. The announcement provoked furious protests. The party countered by launching a new cult of Ulbricht's personality, proposing lavish celebrations to mark his 60th birthday.

The Soviet Communist Party, or at least the Malenkov–Beria wing of the Politburo, took these suggestions ill and sent a new Soviet high commissioner to Berlin. He recommended that Ulbricht's birthday be marked in the same way that Lenin had marked his own 50th birthday: 'He invited a few friends to drop in for dinner.' The Commissioner continued by proposing a 'new course' for the Germany party, and this programme was duly published on 11 June. In it, the government admitted some of its past mistakes. Investment would be shifted from heavy industry to consumer industries. The party confessed that it had unjustly discriminated against farmers, artisans, intellectuals and their children: former 'bourgeois' citizens were to get their ration cards back; and on 14 June, 4000 political prisoners were released, joined later by a further 1500. Some price increases were withdrawn. However, the most remarkable part of this programme was the proposal that the party should seek a rapprochement between the two German states and 'reunify all German people into a national German state'. This was the first sign of 'the thaw' that later swept the Eastern block.

The workers noted, however, that the new norms had not been rescinded, and on 16 June, an article in a party newspaper stated that they would be maintained. Building workers at a site in East Berlin on the *Stalinallee* spontaneously downed tools, marched on SED headquarters and demanded to see Pieck and Grotewohl. Lesser officials were sent out to talk to the crowd, and were shouted down. The workers kept up their demonstration until evening and then went home – but not before calling for a general strike the next day and a mass demonstration in the centre of the city. News of the dispute spread like wildfire. That evening, the radio station in the American sector of Berlin broadcast the workers' call for a general strike, and the following day, there were strikes and demonstrations throughout the country. Mass meetings of workers denounced the government, the regime and Communism itself, to the utter dismay of party functionaries who had devoted their lives to the workers' cause and now saw themselves repudiated.

That day, 17 June, about 350,000 workers came out on strike, and a large crowd marched through the centre of East Berlin and demonstrated outside party headquarters, demanding free elections as well as reduced norms. It was entirely spontaneous – there were not even any strike committees. Nor was it violent, to begin with. Then some young demonstrators began throwing stones at the police, and soon there was rioting throughout the city.

Whatever their internal debates about a general settlement, the Soviet Politburo had no intention of allowing the Germans to reassert their independence. As the demonstrations got out of hand, the Soviet commandant declared martial law; Soviet troops were deployed in large numbers in the major cities, notably Berlin, and helped the DDR police put down the disturbances. The Soviet role was limited, for the most part, to sending tanks rumbling through the streets to intimidate the population, and when they fired, it was usually over the heads of the demonstrators. None the less, the enduring image – for the citizens of West Berlin watching helplessly through the Brandenburg gate – was one of Soviet tanks and armoured cars shooting down the last remnants of the worker and student demonstrations. By official count, 21 people were killed; unofficial estimates put the number at several hundred.

The party and state did not collapse, as their counterparts in Hungary did in 1956. There was no time for popular fury to overturn the government – the Soviets acted too quickly. However, there is no doubt that, without Soviet intervention, the DDR would never have survived.

The June revolt was not nearly as serious as the periodic Polish uprisings, let alone Budapest in 1956, but the memory haunted the regime for the rest of its existence. In October 1989, when news of the mass demonstrations in Leipzig reached him, Erich Honecker asked, 'Is it another 17 June?'

Bertolt Brecht wrote a poem about the revolt:

The Solution
After the rising of the 17th June
The Secretary of the Writers' Union
Had leaflets distributed in the Stalinallee
stating that the people
Had forfeited the confidence of the government
And could win it back only
By redoubled efforts. Would it not be easier
In that case for the government
To dissolve the people
And elect another?

Ulbricht's Germany

The regime was badly shaken by the revolt. After a brief period of hesitation, during which the SED admitted the possibility of its own errors, Ulbricht imposed a hard line. The revolt was blamed on Western provocateurs; strikers and demonstrators were arrested, 1300 were jailed and six were sentenced to death. Although there was a wholesale purge inside the SED, to get rid of those whose doubts or criticism of the leadership might have contributed to the confusion that led to the revolt, the party dispute between the Stalinists and those who supported the 'new course' continued. The West Germans exploited their propaganda advantage to the hilt, proclaiming 17 June a day of national mourning for the oppression suffered by the East Germans, and using each anniversary for fiery speeches denouncing the 'Zone'.

Ulbricht's position had been strengthened by the abrupt removal of Beria from the Soviet government three weeks after the revolt (he was shot the following December), and by Khrushchev's ascendancy. However, after Khrushchev's 'secret speech' denouncing Stalin in February 1956, even Ulbricht had to allow some loosening of the reins. Many of the victims of earlier purges were rehabilitated and the DDR went through a brief liberal phase. It did not last, and in any event, it was confined to party intellectuals who were loyal to the principles of Communism. The explosions in Poland and Hungary in October and November 1956 showed the dangers of liberalism, and Ulbricht reinstated the purges and restored the full rigours of German Stalinism. The leading theoretical revisionist, Wolfgang Harich, was sentenced to ten years' imprisonment in March 1957 for illegal contacts with West Germany.

When Adenauer visited Moscow in 1955, the Soviet Union agreed to recognize the Federal Republic, without demanding that West Germany in turn recognize the separate existence of the DDR. On the contrary, the West Germans, as they recovered their economic and diplomatic strength, insisted that no state anywhere in the world could have diplomatic relations with both East and West Germany at the same time – with the sole exception of the USSR. This came to be called the Hallstein doctrine*, and it effectively ensured that East Germany remained isolated until Bonn relented. In 1967, the West Germans recognized Romania, and in 1968, Yugoslavia, but still refused to recognize the DDR.

Whatever the external difficulties, Ulbricht's position in the DDR and in the Eastern bloc was stronger than ever. Khrushchev had full confidence in him: the DDR remained quiet throughout 1956, and supported the Soviet Union vociferously in the invasion of Hungary. In 1954, the USSR had relinquished the German industries and firms it had controlled (it made the same concession to Romania and the other satellites at the same time), the last reparations were paid in 1956; by then, the remaining German prisoners of war had also been released. As a result, the DDR's economy advanced rapidly, and in 1958, Ulbricht announced to a party conference that East Germany would catch up with the Federal Republic within three years. It was a year of illusions: Khrushchev also promised to overtake the United States by 1972, and in China, Mao proclaimed his 'Great Leap Forward'.

The improvements of the late 1950s, which had at last brought some semblance of normality to people's lives, soon began to unravel. There was an upsurge of inflation as the government poured investment into consumption, instead of into services, infrastructure and business. The worst danger was emigration: there were strict border controls along the frontier between East and West Germany, but the border in Berlin was open. Anyone who wanted to cross had merely to take the *S-Bahn* (the elevated railway), and every year hundreds of thousands of East Germans did: 261,622 in 1957 alone. In 1959, the figure fell to 143,917, the lowest since 1950, but still an intolerable drain on the country. Between 1949 and 1961, 3.5 million East Germans (including about a million who were also refugees from the lost eastern territories) went to the West. Instead of catching up with the West, the DDR fell further behind.

In November 1958, Khrushchev sparked off a new crisis when he proclaimed that West Berlin should be united with the rest of the city, proposing that it should become a demilitarized 'free city' within six months. The Soviet Union would sign a separate peace treaty with the East Germans, giving them control of all access

* Named after Walter Hallstein, the head of the West German foreign ministry and, later, first president of the European Commission.

routes to West Berlin – in other words, the city would become a Soviet satellite. The West defied the challenge, Khrushchev backed down and nothing happened. All the same, East Berliners feared that the borders were going to be closed. Coincidentally, the collectivization of agriculture was completed, and the push to increase industrial production reached a new level of frenzy. The exodus accelerated.

In 1960, 199,000 people fled the country; in the first seven and a half months of 1961, 207,000 people left; and in the last weeks of that period, they were going at a rate of 10,000 a week. In June, Khrushchev renewed his threat to sign a separate peace treaty with the DDR.

The wall

On 13 August 1961, at one o'clock in the morning, Soviet and German troops and police began to close off the crossing points in Berlin.

Troops gathered at each one, with machine-guns, armoured cars and tanks. The entire 28-mile border, running through the heart of the city, was sealed. Then came squads of workers. It was all meticulously planned, under the direction of Erich Honecker, Ulbricht's ultimate successor. Trucks delivered rolls of barbed wire and concrete posts and slabs, and soon the human barrier of armed troops and police was reinforced by an impenetrable physical barrier. Concrete slabs were erected across open spaces between east and west, blocking off streets and intersections. The *Potsdamer Platz* was cut in two, and the Wall was built in front of the Brandenburg Gate. The *S-Bahn* stations were closed off. Workers heading for their jobs across the border, in either direction, were told they could do so no longer.

Desperate East Berliners still tried to escape – jumping out of windows on the border, rushing across the barbed wire, smashing through the barriers in homemade tanks. The opportunities were few and soon eliminated. Honecker rapidly and efficiently closed off every exit, bricked up every window, and built his monstrous Wall right around West Berlin. Within a week, West Berlin was completely shut in – and the East Germans were locked into the world's largest concentration camp.

There was one moment of extreme tension on 28 October, when American and Soviet tanks faced each other at Checkpoint Charlie. However, it was soon clear that the West was not about to go to war to rescue East Germany and it also transpired that, despite all his bluster, Khrushchev's intention had been merely to protect the DDR, not to annex West Berlin. He withdrew his threat to sign a treaty with the DDR ten days before the Checkpoint Charlie episode. American politicians began a regular pilgrimage to Berlin, the most memorable being John F. Kennedy's visit in June 1963, during which he proclaimed in Boston German, '*Ich bin ein Berliner*.' Berliners noted that all these Americans merely repeated their long-standing promise to sustain West Berlin. They did nothing to remove the Wall.

Over the next 28 years, a steady trickle of East Germans did manage to defeat the odds and escape across the Wall. Some dug tunnels; some flew across in private planes or balloons. A few were rescued by an American freelance helicopter pilot. Others tried crashing through the checkpoints in armoured cars or buses. One family, dressed in homemade Russian uniforms, simply drove across. Still others tried to smuggle themselves across in an astonishing variety of hiding places, and the bravest or most foolhardy tried to scramble across the Wall itself. Many of them were killed in the attempt. In August 1962, after being shot trying to cross it, Peter Fechter bled to death in the shadow of the Wall.

On its eastern side, the Wall was progressively strengthened as the years went by. Its western face was covered with graffiti, and dotted with little shrines, decorated with small bunches of flowers, at the points where people had been killed. There was now a dead zone, on both sides, running through the heart of a great city, with the implacable Wall offering a grim image of tyranny.

Behind the wall

Walter Ulbricht's Germany prospered, after a fashion, behind the Wall, and it remained at all times totally loyal to the USSR: in 1968, Ulbricht took the lead in denouncing the 'Prague spring', and that August, German troops once again invaded Czechoslovakia, some of them taking the same roads that their fathers had taken 30 years earlier. Ulbricht himself was forced to resign as first secretary of the SED in 1971, although he remained head of state (he died in 1973). He was succeeded by Honecker, who pursued the same policies with the same drab, methodical thoroughness. In 1981, Honecker insistently urged the USSR to use every means to suppress Solidarity in Poland.

East Germany remained quiet for a generation. Westerners who had speculated that the Wall would so enrage the East Germans that they would rise in revolt proved mistaken. Perhaps all the rebellious Germans had already left, and it needed another generation, which had grown up behind the Wall, to rise in wrath and demand its removal. In October 1973, while Willy Brandt was chancellor, the Federal Republic at last recognized the partition of Germany, and exchanged ambassadors with the DDR. Both states were then admitted to the United Nations, and the DDR was recognized by the rest of the Western alliance. The DDR was able to participate in the Olympic Games, where its elaborately trained (and drugged) athletes quickly won a pre-eminent position. Ulbricht, who was still president, had lived to see his creation, the Democratic Republic, firmly and, it seemed, permanently established.

By the 1970s, the DDR boasted that it was the Eastern bloc's second, Europe's sixth and the world's eighth largest industrial power, and alleged that its citizens enjoyed a higher *per capita* income than the British. Certainly its shops were brighter than those of Poland or the USSR, more East Germans owned cars, and the housing shortage was less acute. These claims were all lies – except the assertion that the DDR was second only to the USSR in the Eastern bloc. Its standard of living was not higher than that of Britain, and comparisons of its economy with those of Western Europe depended upon the DDR's own statistics, which were doctored, and the exchange rate of the *Ostmark*, which was preposterous. The East Germans claimed parity for their *mark* with the *Deutschmark*, but the reality – that is, the black market rate – was nearer 4:1 in 1970, and the disparity steadily widened, to about 10:1 when the Wall was breached. Indeed this steady loss in the value of its currency was a sign of the DDR's fatally weak economy. The World Bank abandoned offering figures for Eastern block economies in about 1980 because of the impossibility of making valid comparisons.

When the Wall fell and the DDR prepared to unite with West Germany, the falsity of its earlier claims became glaringly apparent. Its citizens 'enjoyed' a standard of living that was perhaps a third of that in the West, and even that level depended upon enormous state subsidies for housing and foodstuffs, which further weakened the economy. Furthermore, East German trade was still chiefly with the Soviet Union, which bought goods that would never pass muster in the West: the DDR's much-vaunted industrial strength consisted, for a large part, in producing goods that nobody wanted. East Germans had far more cars than other East Europeans, but they were small, under-powered and unreliable Trabants – Honecker had ruled that a people's democracy had no need for more modern vehicles. The DDR's apologists once boasted that it produced more lignite (a soft, brown coal) than any other country in the world. That was perhaps true, but the result was a wasteland of pollution stretching across the country; the DDR, like the rest of Eastern Europe, was an environmental disaster. The 'Eastern economic miracle' was no miracle; it was a swindle perpetrated upon a helpless population and on future generations, which will have to spend the next half century cleaning up Honecker's 'socialist paradise'.

The wall comes down

The reform movement started by Gorbachev in the Soviet Union took the DDR entirely by surprise. The Polish crisis came into the open in the autumn of 1988. By the following summer, the Polish government had been forced to allow new and relatively free elections, which Solidarity won by a landslide; in August 1989, a Solidarity government had taken power in Warsaw. Simultaneously, the Hungarian Communist Party was beating a precipitous retreat, surrendering every position to the opposition even before there was an opposition to attack it. The hurricane was approaching, and Honecker and his comrades were totally unprepared.

When these winds of change reached East Berlin, Honecker was faced with an intolerable dilemma. The main demand of the population was freedom to emigrate, to go West. If the government now attempted reform, such as opening the doors to the West, this would provoke irresistible demands for further reforms amounting to an abandonment of Communism and that would mean the end of the DDR. Its *raison d'être* was to be a socialist German state; without socialism, it must reunite with West Germany. On the other hand, by October 1989, it was apparent that the only alternative to reform was a new round of Stalinist oppression which, in turn, might provoke an uprising.

There was no strong, organized opposition in the DDR, like Solidarity in Poland, nor was there a strong reformist movement in the SED itself, as in Hungary. The few party leaders who could see the coming deluge lacked even the capacity to organize a party coup, like the one in Bulgaria, as a last, desperate measure to save the party.

Although there was no Solidarity, there were many dissidents – Greens, Christians, reform Communists or socialists – grouped in a body called the New Forum which met in churches to discuss reform. The absence of a German Lech Wałęşa or Václav Havel did not mean that the East Germans were any more satisfied with their government than the Poles or Czechs. On the contrary, the continued relative decline of the economy compared with the West, the claustrophobic effect of the ban on travel to the West and the perpetuation of a gerontocracy in the government, which consistently refused to follow Gorbachev's calls for reform, built up a steadily increasing frustration and despair.

In the summer of 1989, tens of thousands of East Germans went on vacation to Hungary, where they discovered the delights of a much more open society. Many stayed there, but about 6000 illegally crossed the border into Austria and presented themselves at the West German embassy in Vienna. Hundreds more camped out in the West German embassy in Budapest, demanding passage to the West, and later, others moved into the West German embassies in Prague and Warsaw. By the beginning of September, there were at least 3000 avowed refugees in Hungary – in camping grounds and a churchyard in Budapest – and another 100,000 extending their annual vacations, to see what would happen.

On 10 September, when Hungary declared its borders open, it also abrogated its treaty with the DDR, under which it had been committed to refuse East Germans permission to cross into Austria unless they had DDR exit visas. East Germans poured over the Austrian border, more than 30,000 in two weeks, and others packed into the West German and Hungarian embassies in Prague and Warsaw demanding exit visas. On 1 October, after frantic negotiations between East Berlin, Prague and Warsaw, 5500 embassy refugees from Prague and 800 from Warsaw were put on trains for the West; Honecker wanted the crisis settled before the glorious celebrations planned for the 40th anniversary of the DDR on 7 October. The trains passed through the DDR, and the regime called out the army to stop other East Germans joining them.

The crisis was not settled. East Germany banned its citizens from travelling to Hungary, but thousands went to Czechoslovakia and besieged the West German embassy anew. As a result, on 3 October, the DDR closed its borders with Czechoslovakia and Poland. It was now, like Albania, completely isolated from the world. Meanwhile, at home, mass demonstrations against the regime began in East Berlin, Leipzig and Dresden, and it became evident that the regime was losing control.

Gorbachev attended the anniversary celebrations, and was cheered in the streets by the crowds who conspicuously refused to cheer Honecker: 'Gorby, Gorby,' they shouted, to the Soviets' amusement and the SED's vast chagrin. There were violent clashes between demonstrators and police that evening, and again the next day, and some party leaders said ominously that they might follow the example of the Chinese in Tienanmen Square.

For some time, there had been large demonstrations every Monday in Leipzig, following meetings and services in the city's churches. On Monday, 9 October, two days after the dubiously triumphant parade in Berlin, Honecker ordered the police to disperse the weekly demonstration in Leipzig with whatever force was needed, including shooting. Various people have claimed credit for countermanding that order – including Egon Krenz, who later briefly succeeded Honecker as party leader, and the orchestral conductor Kurt Masur – but it is most probable that the army and police themselves refused to shoot other Germans. This demonstration was the largest yet, with 70,000 people parading around the city centre, and there were further huge demonstrations in other cities, including Dresden and East Berlin.

On 18 October, Honecker, having been abandoned by his colleagues, resigned and was replaced by Egon Krenz as party leader, head of state and head of the defence council. Honecker was followed into oblivion by a succession of other septuagenarian and octogenarian Stalinists who had governed the country undisturbed for 30 years and who were now witness to the complete collapse of their life's work. The demonstrators, seeing the regime in retreat, pushed harder, demanding free elections, an end to the Communist dictatorship and, above all, freedom to travel.

On 25 October, during a visit to Helsinki, Gorbachev gave the most categoric statement yet of the new Soviet policy. He asserted that the Soviet Union had no moral or politcal right to interfere in the affairs of its East European neighbours. He spoke appreciatively of Finland's neutrality, implying that 'Finlandization', so long feared as the Soviet recipe for Western Europe, was now the proper destiny of Eastern Europe. His spokesman, Gennadi Gerasimov, said flatly, 'I think the Brezhnev doctrine is dead' (*see* Chapter 9), and remarked that it had been replaced by the 'Sinatra doctrine'. 'You know the Frank Sinatra song, "I did it my way"?' he asked. 'Hungary and Poland are doing it their way.'

The new DDR government reopened its borders with Czechoslovakia, proclaimed an amnesty for all those who had left, and said that all travel restrictions would be greatly eased or abolished by Christmas, but its promises of reform were hardly heard. Thousands of East Germans continued to pour across the frontier, heading West. Three hundred thousand others demonstrated in Leipzig on 30 October, and five days later, half a million East Berliners showed their opposition to the regime. Power was now in the streets. The party could no longer control events, could not rely on the police or army to obey its orders, and when party leaders tried to address the crowds, they were shouted down.

On 7 November, the government resigned, and the following day, Krenz announced the resignation of the entire Politburo and the formation of a new leadership. On 9 November, the East Berlin party leader, Günter Schabowski, gave an evening press conference that was televised live. He announced that 'permission will be given at short notice for private travel and permanent emigration without the present preconditions having been fulfilled, across all border crossing points between East and West Germany and East and West Berlin.' People went to the Wall immediately and demanded to be let through. The border guards – perhaps under orders, perhaps swept by the tides of history – opened the gates.

By midnight, tens of thousands, then hundreds of thousands of East Berliners were pouring through the Wall to visit West Berlin, their first opportunity in 28 years. West Berliners rushed into the streets to welcome them, and there were immense traffic jams as East Berliners freely drove their cars through the Wall checkpoints. The DDR border police at first tried to check papers, then glanced at them, then stood back, smiling benignly. Young people from East and West climbed on top of the Wall and showered each other with champagne, revelling in the glory of the moment. Television carried the scenes live, and the world watched, astonished and delighted, as an unending flood of people poured through the gaps in the Wall.

Helmut Kohl, the West German chancellor, who was on a official visit to Poland, hurried to West Berlin on the 10th, where he stood ecstatic on the steps of the city hall with Willy Brandt (who had been mayor of West Berlin when the Wall was built). Kohl proclaimed, 'I want to call out to all in the German Democratic Republic: we're on your side, we are and remain one nation. We belong together!' Critics thought it demagoguery. In fact, it was a plain statement of the case: the Wall was down and reunification was inevitable.

East German visitors were each given DM100 'Welcome money', which they carried with them into the shops and boutiques of West Berlin, to be amazed at the opulence of the Christmas cornucopia spread before them. Five new crossings were opened in the Wall the next day, and in a few days, the first bulldozers started demolishing it.

Krenz announced that 'reunification was not on the agenda' – a sentiment which was echoed by several Western leaders, notably Margaret Thatcher. They were whistling in the wind.

The disintegration of the party continued. On 13 November, the *Volkskammer* (people's chamber) elected as prime minister Hans Modrow, the party leader from Dresden, who was one of the few Communist leaders who retained any popularity: he had kept up a dialogue with the opposition in Dresden, and had met the demonstrators there. A meeting of the *Volkskammer* was startled to hear details of the economy's difficulties: the former finance minister revealed that the budget deficit was 130 billion *Ostmark* ($70 billion at the official exchange rate); the efficiency of the country's factories had sunk by nearly 50 per cent in the previous nine years; and, according to outside experts, the inflation rate was well into double digits. The country's external debt was $20 billion.

The new government tried to regain control of the situation, Krenz calling a party congress for 15 December. On 17 November, Modrow introduced a new, rejuvenated cabinet, and asserted that his reforms would end 'unrealistic and dangerous speculation about reunification'. A week later, on the 22nd, the country was scandalized to discover the sybaritic lifestyle of Honecker and other party leaders, past and present. Reporters had been allowed to inspect the government compound at Wandlitz, north of Berlin, where 23 top leaders and their families had lived in luxury, each with two maids paid by the government. The compound included a small department store, beauty parlour, swimming pool, cinema and various other suburban amenities. The party leaders had also enjoyed hunting: one of them, the trade union leader, had kept for himself a 5000-acre preserve, a hunting lodge and a 200-acre farm to breed wild boars in Mecklenburg. True, all this hardly matched Western notions of conspicuous consumption, but to East German workers, after 40 years of endless exhortations to socialist restraint offered by their leaders, it was appalling.

Krenz, who had a house in Wandlitz, could not defend himself, and on 3 December, at an emergency Central Committee meeting, the entire government, Politburo and Central Committee resigned. Krenz lost all the offices he had won from Erich Honecker only six weeks earlier. The party congress was brought forward, opening three days later. It elected a new first secretary, Gregor Gysi, and a new government, headed by Hans Modrow, the only party leader to survive the cataclysm. Free elections were promised in the spring.

A ground-swell for reunification suddenly appeared, much to the dismay of many opposition intellectuals who distrusted the materialism of the Federal Republic. The new Communist leaders tried to restore their authority and to inhibit the formation of new parties, in the hope that they might still save the party and the DDR. However, by the end of the year, a total of about 350,000 Germans from the DDR had moved to the Federal Republic – and continued to do so at a rate of 1000 a day – as well as 225,000 Germans from Poland and 87,000 from the Soviet Union. The rate of emigration increased in the New Year, and the *de facto* reunification of the country also proceeded apace. Opposition groups, who had opened negotiations with the government, threatened to resume the street protests if the liberalization of the regime did not quicken. In January 1990, these groups discovered that Modrow had approved a plan to revive the secret police, the *Stasi*. The country was outraged, and demonstrators stormed *Stasi* headquarters and ransacked its files. Modrow was obliged to abandon the plan – striking proof that the Communist government remained in power only on sufferance.

The economy was disintegrating faster than anyone had anticipated, and the only salvation lay with the West. The party surrendered: it even changed its name – to the Party of Democratic Socialism. The West Germans pushed for rapid reunification, and the last diplomatic barriers were removed in February, when the Soviet Union bowed to the inevitable: Germany would be reunited as soon as possible.

East Germans had their first free elections since 1932 on 18 March 1990. West German politicians and parties played the leading role in the campaign, treating the DDR as though it were already part of the Federal Republic. The electorate evidently approved: the Christian Democrats and their allies won 48 per cent of the vote, the Free Democrats (Liberals) 5 per cent and the Social Democrats 22 per cent. The former Communist party, under its new guise, managed to win 16.33 per cent, considerably more than most people expected. However, none of these totals takes into account the hundreds of thousands of people who had already voted for reunification by moving West.

On 12 April, a new, non-Communist government took office in East Berlin. Lothar de Maizière, head of the Christian Democratic Union, became prime minister in a coalition government including Social Democrats and Liberals. The Communists were consigned to the opposition. Maizière's first act was to admit that all Germany was responsible for the Holocaust, saying, 'We feel sad and ashamed, and acknowledge this burden of German history.' The Communist leaders of East Germany, unlike the West Germans, had never recognized any guilt.

On 18 May 1990, the governments of East and West Germany

signed a treaty providing for a currency union to begin on 1 July, and at the same time, the DDR was to scrap central planning, price controls and all the other apparatus of a Communist state. All this meant that the *Bundesbank* (the West German central bank) was taking over the East German economy. The last step to reunification would be taken before the end of the year, when the five eastern *Länder* would vote whether to join the Federal Republic.

The two nations' allies were dragged along, bewildered and slightly nervous, in the wake of the Germans' rush to unity. What would they do with a country that was a member of both NATO and the Warsaw Pact? This, obviously, was the real sticking point. The question was what price could the Soviet Union extract from the West for removing its troops from eastern Germany and accepting that a united Germany would be a member of NATO alone.

Poland was less enthusiastic about German unity than other European nations. The Polish government demanded that West Germany commit itself to the post-war frontiers before proceeding any further, a step West Germany's Chancellor Kohl hesitated to take. There were enough survivors of the 10 million refugees from Silesia, Pomerania and East Prussia, and enough children of these refugees, to give any politician pause. But the allies insisted, and eventually the Federal Republic conceded the point – which, in fact, its government had never seriously contested. The eastern territories, including Breslau, Danzig and Stettin, were lost for good. There were last-minute disputes on the question of whether the two German states should settle their differences first, before meeting together with the four World War II allies (the United States, the Soviet Union, Britain and France) – the 'two plus four' formula – or whether the four would meet first: the 'four plus two' formula. It turned out to be a dispute without substance: the two Germanies pursued their negotiations for reunification without regard to the other four. The Poles were promised that all questions concerning Germany's eastern frontiers would be agreed with them.

There would, of course, be many difficulties in reuniting Germany, chiefly financial, and West Germans grumbled about the likely costs and East Germans about the disruptions. The latter would suffer the same shock endured by the West Germans 40 years earlier because of the Erhard reform: large numbers in the east would lose their jobs as their inefficient factories were faced with Western competition. But this time, they would have help: West Germany had an annual trade surplus of $70 billion, highly efficient and well-managed industries, and an experienced government, as well as the benefits of membership in the European Community. All that remained to be settled, for the Germans, were the practical details of currency reform and the dismantling of the Communist system.

It was quite clear that, well before the end of the century, East Germans would have caught up with their Western compatriots in virtually every respect. The long nightmare, which began with a mass rally of brownshirts in Berlin, on the night of 30 January 1933, was at last coming to an end.

2 Poland

The Polish Home Army rose against the Germans in Warsaw on 1 August 1944. They seized the centre of the city, on the west bank of the Vistula, and held it against 30,000 German troops for two months. By the end of the fighting, on 2 October, 200,000 people had been killed and over 90 per cent of the city was in ruins. On 15 September, the Soviet army had reached the Praga suburbs of the city just across the Vistula. There it remained, waiting for Warsaw to die.

The Germans moved through the devastation, block by block, killing those who resisted, those who surrendered and the wounded in the cellars. Andrzej Wajda's 1957 film about the Uprising, *Kanal*, ends with a series of images. Defeated fighters, emerging from the sewers, are lined up by the Germans and shot. A party of survivors escaping through the sewers to the river bank, find their way blocked by an iron grill; across the wide river they can see the Soviet troops, watching.

The Polish high command had miscalculated. They thought that the Germans were in full retreat, and that they could seize Warsaw and restore the national government in the capital before the Red Army arrived – just as the French Resistance did in Paris later that month. But Hitler was determined to hold Warsaw at all costs, and he ordered the city to be destroyed.

The Poles appealed to the Red Army. Stalin replied,

> Now, after probing more deeply into the Warsaw affair, I have come to the conclusion that the Warsaw action is a reckless adventure, taken without the knowledge of the Soviet command. So the Soviet Headquarters have decided to dissassociate themselves openly from the Warsaw adventure, since they cannot assume any responsibility for the Warsaw case.

The Communist Polish army, fighting under Soviet command, made a token sally across the river, and was driven back. Stalin then allowed the Germans to destroy the Home Army so that Polish Communists loyal to the Soviet Union would inherit the ruins. It was the last act of collaboration between those old allies, Joseph Stalin and Adolf Hitler.

In 1939, they had partitioned Poland. The Germans invaded from the west on 1 September, the Soviets from the east on 17 September. Agents of the *Gestapo* and its Soviet equivalent, the NKVD (now renamed the KGB), met at the new frontier to transact their business: German Communists who had taken refuge in the Soviet Union were handed over to the *Gestapo*, and Stalin's Polish and Soviet enemies, arrested in Poland, were sent east. Hitler incorporated most of western and central Poland into the *Reich*, driving out or enslaving the Polish inhabitants, and leaving only a truncated fragment from Warsaw to Kraków to be administered as a satellite. The Soviet Union annexed the eastern territories that Poland had seized from the USSR in 1920. They had been part of ancient Poland but now had a mixed population in which Poles were a minority.

In the first phase of World War II, Stalin killed more than Hitler did: of the 1.5 million soldiers and civilians deported to Siberia, up to 750,000 died of starvation or neglect, or were murdered. Among the dead were 100,000 Polish Jews, killed in a Soviet Holocaust two years before the German Holocaust began. In addition, 15,000 Polish army officers were murdered by the Soviet secret police in 1940. Three years later, the Germans found the bodies of more than 4000 of them buried in a mass grave in the Katyn Forest, near Smolensk in the USSR.

The balance was redressed later. The Germans eventually killed about 6 million Poles, half of them Jews, totalling 20 per cent of the population. When the Red Army drove out the Germans early in 1945, the killings continued: Poles who resisted the imposition of a Communist government were executed in their tens of thousands; survivors of the Home Army were systematically liquidated; thousands more, Poles and Germans, died as Stalin moved the Polish border 200 miles west, taking what had been the German *Länder* of Silesia and Pomerania. There was a merciless civil war in the forests for three years after 'peace' came to Europe.

This had been the history of Poland for over two centuries: a state repeatedly invaded and partitioned by Germans and Russians, a people subject to frequent massacre and constant tyranny. The counterpoint to this distressing story is that the Poles never surrendered; they always resisted, rose against their oppressors, defied them. The Warsaw Uprising was by far the bloodiest revolt against German occupation anywhere in Europe during World War II (though, over all, the Yugoslav resistance was more costly and more effective). And Polish resistance to Soviet oppression was the most consistent and determined in all Eastern Europe between 1945 and 1989.

For those 200 years, the Poles always and rightly feared and distrusted the Germans and the Russians. At the same time, they looked to the West for protection, usually in vain. In 1939, the West failed them, and in 1945 abandoned them to their enemies, pleading *force majeure* and weeping salt tears of pity. However, despite this, nothing has changed: Poles still distrust their neighbours and hope for Western support.

What is different today is that the great mix of populations in eastern Europe is much simpler than it used to be. The massacres and forced movements of millions of people between 1939 and 1950 have rearranged the nations. In 1939, 30 per cent of the population of Poland were not ethnic Poles; they were Ukrainian, Ruthenian, White Russian (Byelorussian), Russian, Lithuanian, German or Jewish. Today, Poland is probably 95 per cent homogeneous: Polish and Catholic. What is more, there are few Poles left in the Soviet Union. Wilno (now Vilnius, capital of Lithuania) and Lwow (now Lvov, in the western Ukraine), which were Polish cities for hundreds of years, have only small Polish minorities. On the other side of the country, former German cities are now Polish – Danzig (now Gdánsk), Breslau (Wrocław) and Stettin (Szczecin) – and although there are still a few Germans in Silesia and Pomerania, they are a small minority.

It does not follow that the 'Polish Question' has been settled permanently. Irredentist claims, both German and Polish, may easily be revived: early in 1990, when the West German government was agonizing over the need to recognize Poland's western frontiers, that most peaceful of men, Tadeusz Mazowiecki, prime minister of Poland, stated that the present frontiers could only be changed by war. It was the first statement of an independent Polish foreign policy since 1945, and a sudden reminder that the reconciliation between Germany and Poland has hardly begun.

The conquest

After Hitler and Stalin obliterated Poland in 1939, the Soviets assumed that Poland would never be restored, and Molotov told the Supreme Soviet, 'Nothing is left of that monstrous offspring of the Versailles treaty.' Eastern Poland was incorporated into the Soviet Union, which in 1940 also annexed the three Baltic republics. Then, on 22 June 1941, Hitler invaded the Soviet Union, and Stalin was obliged to ally himself with Britain and with Britain's ally, the Polish government-in-exile in London.

Although they resumed diplomatic relations with the USSR, the Poles never trusted Stalin. They remembered too well the events of 1939, and Polish prisoners who returned from Siberia recounted the horrors they had endured – shipped in cattle trucks from Poland to the Arctic and left to starve. The dispute over the frontier continued. Stalin acknowledged that the treaty with Hitler was void, but insisted that the Soviet Union would keep the territories it had annexed from Poland.

When the *Wehrmacht* was stopped outside Moscow in November 1941, Stalin could give thought to other matters. He changed his policy on Poland, deciding that it would not be swallowed up by the USSR, like the Baltic states, but would be restored after the war. He was determined that the Soviet Union would control it, and therefore, he had to find more malleable Poles than the intransigent exiles in London. Unfortunately, he had killed most of the Polish Communists – leaders and followers together – during the Moscow purges in 1938, and had dissolved the party: Władysław Gomułka survived only because he had been in a capitalist Polish prison at the time, not in the Socialist Motherland. The NKVD searched through the prison camps to find Polish men and women who were utterly loyal to Marxism, to the Soviet Union and to Stalin. A Polish Workers' Party (PPR) was formed on 5 January 1942.

Its first leaders inside Poland were caught by the Germans, and Gomułka took over in 1943. Real power in the party – that is, support from Stalin – remained with the leaders in Moscow: Boleslaw Bierut, later president of Poland; Jakub Berman, Stalin's chief political operative (first in Moscow, then in Poland); and Hilary Minc, later economics minister. When the Germans discovered the Katyn graves in 1943, and brought in the International Red Cross to examine them, the Polish government demanded an explanation from the USSR. Stalin blamed the Germans, and used the incident as an excuse to break relations with the London Poles. He had alternatives ready: a 'Union of Polish Patriots' (ZPP) was formed in Moscow, as well as a Polish Communist army, commanded by General Zygmunt Berling. When the Red Army fought its way into Poland in 1944, the ZPP formed a 'Committee of National Liberation' and, on 22 July, set itself up in Lublin as the nucleus of a new government of Poland.

The Home Army, the largest resistance movement in Europe after the Yugoslav partisans, was defeated in Warsaw. Elsewhere, as the Red Army advanced, Home Army units were forcibly incorporated into Berling's forces or were suppressed by the Soviets. The Red Army command in Poland then invited the senior leaders of the Home Army to discuss future arrangements. When they arrived, they were arrested, sent to Moscow and put on trial for treason, receiving relatively lenient sentences for this 'crime'.

The Polish government chose to make its last stand, not on the question of its own legitimacy, but on the question of frontiers, insisting that Lwow and Wilno must remain Polish. The British and American governments accepted the Soviet position that the frontier should be moved back to the 'Curzon line' which had originally been proposed at the Versailles conference in 1919, and approximately demarcated the territories containing predominantly Polish and predominantly Ukrainian or Byelorussian peoples. Poland had rejected the Curzon line and invaded the Soviet Union in 1919, seizing a great swathe of territory to the east. Then, at the Tehran Conference in November 1943 and again at Yalta in February 1945, Churchill, Roosevelt and Stalin agreed that the Curzon line should be the permanent eastern frontier of Poland and that Poland should be compensated with territory taken from Germany.

The Lublin Committee had proclaimed itself the 'Provisional Government of the Polish Republic' a month before Yalta. At the conference, the two Western leaders requested that representatives of the Polish government-in-exile in London should be admitted to this quisling institution, which they then recognized as the legitimate government of Poland. This betrayal still rankles with the Poles to this day.

Finally, at the Potsdam Conference in Berlin, in July 1945, the allied powers agreed provisionally that the new frontier between Germany and Poland should run along the Oder and Neisse rivers. The government-in-exile ceased to exist, and the one minister who joined the new regime, Stanislaw Mikolajczyk, leader of the Peasants' Party, became minister of agriculture. He escaped to the West in 1947.

In the early years, the Soviets governed Poland as though it were part of the Soviet Union. They looted German factories in the newly acquired western territories, in the name of reparations, and shipped them back to the Soviet Union. They supervised the mass deportation of people: Norman Davies, the leading western historian of Poland, has calculated that, between 1939 and 1956, over 23 million were forcibly deported into or out of Poland, or within the country, including the millions of Jews brought to Poland to be killed. In addition, the Soviets set up the new state with Soviet agents in key positions throughout government and party. For instance, Marshal Konstantin Rokossowski, who had been born Polish but served his entire career as a loyal soldier of the Red Army, became minister of defence.

From the start, the new regime was split between the Stalinists, led by Bierut, who returned to Poland in the baggage of the Red Army, and the partisans, led by Władysław Gomułka, who had remained inside the country throughout the horrible years of the occupation. Gomułka, though a dedicated, humourless Marxist, never trusted the Soviet Union. He was in a Polish prison in Lwow when the Soviets occupied the town in 1939, but instead of joining them, he escaped to German-occupied Poland. After the war, he became secretary-general of the Polish Workers' Party and presided over a great expansion of that organization: by 1948, it had over one million members and had eliminated its rivals. In that year, it merged with the Socialist Party to form the Polish United Workers' Party.

By then, Stalin had decided to impose his own brand of

Communism on Poland. (In 1944, he had remarked that introducing Communism to Poland would be 'like putting a saddle on a cow'.) The Cold War was getting under way, with the Berlin blockade, the Communist coup in Czechoslovakia and Tito's secession from the Eastern bloc. It was time for the 'people's democracies'. Gomułka opposed the idea at a party plenum (meeting of the Central Committee), but then was forced to recant, was accused of 'Titoism' and was replaced as secretary-general by Bierut, who was head of state. Gomułka was arrested in 1951, but in Poland, unlike the other satellites, disgraced leaders were not murdered. Gomułka, and later Jakub Berman, owed their survival to Bierut who remembered how many of his comrades had disappeared during the purges, and protected them. It became a Polish tradition: disgraced leaders were held in reserve.

Stalinist Poland

The Polish Communists did not seize power, as had the Bolsheviks in Russia. They were installed, protected and directed by the Soviet Union. The country had no hope of resisting the Red Army. Besides, in 1945 Poland was the most devastated country in all Europe, and the main concern of its people – a majority of whom had been displaced from where they had lived before the war and had been forcibly moved from one ruin to another – was their own survival.

The Polish Communists knew that they were unpopular and depended upon the Soviets for their existence: Stalin told them, 'When we go, they will shoot you like partridges.' But the Soviets would not leave. They believed that they needed a subservient Poland, as well as an occupied zone in Germany, to protect themselves from German revanchism, and therefore they needed the Polish Communists. Conversely, from 1945 to 1981, the Polish party defended its every betrayal of the country's sovereignty as a necessary concession to the USSR. If Bierut and Berman first, then Gomułka, Gierek and Jaruzelski in lamentable succession, did not bow to the repeated *diktats* from Moscow, they said, the Soviets would destroy Poland, make it the 16th Soviet republic or impose a new and even more repressive order upon the country.

The Polish party exploited its own weakness. In its uneasy

partnership with Moscow, the weaker of the two partners manipulated the stronger, threatening to collapse if it were not allowed
a slight measure of independence. It thus managed to protect
disgraced leaders such as Gomułka and survive the convulsion
of 1956, when the Hungarian party collapsed, and the upheavals
of 1970, 1976 and 1980–81. On each occasion, it offered itself to
the Soviets as the only alternative to a popular uprising, such as
had occurred in Budapest in 1956, and offered itself to the Polish
people as the only alternative to direct Soviet intervention – again,
like Budapest. The party was not finally overthrown until the Soviet
Union abandoned it in 1989.

In the years after 1948, the regime proceeded briskly to bring
Communism to Poland. The last traces of private property in
business and in the cities were suppressed. The collectivization of
agriculture was pushed boldly forward, and Poland was committed
to heavy industry on the Soviet model. Every priority was given to
iron and steel production: the ancient capital of Poland, Kraków,
was overwhelmed by the enormous steel plant at Nowy-Huta, one of
the largest and most polluting in Europe. The mines and industries
of Silesia, inherited from the Germans, were developed without any
regard to the environmental consequences, and a large shipbuilding
industry was built up along the Baltic, at Gdańsk, Gdynia and
Szczecin. The Roman Catholic Church was remorselessly attacked,
its property confiscated and its priests persecuted.

The tyranny was less extreme than in the other satellites, and
at the top of the party, all but a handful of Stalinist stooges
preserved a distinctly Polish attitude towards their masters in
Moscow. Dissidents were persecuted, but although some were
murdered, the purges never reached the intensity endured in the
other satellites. In Stalin's last years, as the 'anti-cosmopolitan'
campaign got under way in Czechoslovakia, Hungary and Bulgaria,
culminating in the show trials that resulted in the executions of
the Jewish members of those country's governments, the Polish
party fought a successful rearguard action against the encroaching
horrors. In Teresa Torańska's 1987 book of interviews, 'Them'
– Stalin's Polish Puppets, the Stalinists describe the deepening
nightmare of 1952 as Stalin launched the 'doctors' plot', which
was to turn into another mass purge. They could see the noose
tightening around them, and were only saved by Stalin's death.

At the same time, the collectivization of the land proceeded only slowly and, in the summer of 1956, was finally abandoned. The peasants then took their land back from the collectives. Poland was always poorer than East Germany, Czechoslovakia or Hungary, but life was easier.

The Poles were not satisfied with these small mercies. The first stirrings of rebellion followed immediately upon the death of Stalin in 1953. The East German revolt, in June that year, terrified the Polish leaders. Their first reaction was to clamp down on the opposition: the Roman Catholic primate Cardinal Wyszynski was arrested and imprisoned for 'anti-state' activities, and a number of dissident Communists and surviving Home Army men were shot. Later, the government began cautiously to introduce reform measures, starting with a comprehensive purge of the security services. Gomułka was released in 1954, and although he was not then restored to the upper ranks of the party, his influence spread rapidly and he quickly established a sort of loyal Communist opposition. The thaw was beginning.

In February 1956, Boleslaw Bierut, president and first-secretary of the Polish United Workers' Party, went to Moscow to attend the Soviet Communist Party's 20th Conference, at which Khrushchev delivered his 'secret speech' on Stalin's crimes. Everyone who heard it, of course, had known about the purges and murders, and knew that Khrushchev was revealing only a small fraction of the truth. But since this was the first time that anyone had told the truth in Moscow for nearly 30 years, the speech was a sensation, and it was Polish Communists who released copies of it to the West. When Bierut died immediately after the Conference, many Poles suspected suicide.

The 'secret speech' and Bierut's death spread chaos through the Polish party. Berman, Minc and other hardliners were purged, the last Polish prisoners were released from Siberia and returned home, and for a few months, Poles hoped for better things. Then they demanded reform.

The first explosion came in Poznań in June 1956. An international trade fair was taking place, and foreign delegates watched, astonished, as workers marched through the streets demanding 'bread and freedom'. Then a delegation was arrested by the security services, and the demonstrations turned violent. Crowds stormed party headquarters and the local prison, demanding the jailed delegates; there were running battles between militia and demonstrators. In the end, 57 people were killed, by the official count. The government, which had first blamed foreign provocateurs, admitted that the demonstrators had justifiable grievances that the party would try to satisfy. The same pattern was to be followed in all subsequent upheavals.

The October Revolt

The government crisis continued throughout the summer. The remaining hardliners were led by Rokossowski, who was still minister of defence and was supported by the Soviets. Gomułka's faction steadily increased its influence, offering itself as an alternative to a discredited and frightened regime. Party leaders could read the writing on the wall – an ability strikingly absent in the higher reaches of other Eastern European parties – and in October 1956, a plenum was called which restored Gomułka to power. It was a peaceful revolution, and its most striking innovation was that it was carried out without consultation with Moscow.

On 19 October, in the midst of the plenum, Khrushchev arrived at Warsaw airport, together with leading members of the Soviet government, and the plenum hastily adjourned so that Gomułka and other Polish leaders could meet them. Khrushchev was enraged that the Polish party had dared to change its leaders without permission, and he had ordered Soviet troops to move over the border from East Germany, from the Soviet Union itself, and from Czechoslovakia to the south. The tanks were converging on Warsaw.

Units of the Polish security forces, which were not under Rokossowski's command, took up defensive positions in the city. For a while, it seemed that another disaster was imminent. It was Gomułka's finest hour: he faced down Khrushchev in an all-night debate, convincing him that the Poles would rather fight than allow the Soviets to dictate to them again, but also reassuring him that Poland would remain Communist and a loyal member of the Warsaw Pact.

The Polish party, unlike the Hungarian party that capitulated a week later, was united behind its new leader. Gomułka was just as much a Marxist–Leninist as Khrushchev himself and believed devoutly in Poland's Communist destiny. Khrushchev accepted his assurances and flew back to Moscow on 20 October. Soviet troops returned to their barracks, and Rokossowski was removed as minister of defence. It was a great victory for Poland – it became known as 'The October' – and the Poles believed for a while that they had at last recovered their independence.

The Hungarian uprising three days' later was a direct consequence of the events in Warsaw. That tragedy showed the wisdom of Gomułka's policies, but it also demonstrated the limits that the Soviets set for the independence of their allies. Poland remained a satellite, and Communist, and all the euphoria of 'The October' was soon dissipated in drab reality.

There were no further extensive attempts to collectivize agriculture, but neither was there any money available to modernize the farms. Food prices were heavily subsidized, which in effect meant that farmers were not paid enough for their produce to make a decent living, let alone to invest to increase their productivity. Agriculture remained primitive, quite unable to feed the country adequately. The fundamental Stalinist error of industrial planning – the concentration on heavy industry – was repeated in Poland, as everywhere else in Eastern Europe. The environment was progressively wrecked, but nobody benefited.

The basic contradictions remained: in the circumstances of Eastern Europe, Poland could not be both prosperous and Communist, and it could not be independent. Gomułka was both a Polish patriot and a dedicated Communist; he was also increasingly authoritarian and finally unable to face the contradiction, much less resolve it. He was soon as unpopular as the Stalinist stooges he had replaced: his 'Polish way to socialism' was a failure from the start.

Gomułka never established absolute control in the party, and there were always dissident movements. Some were 'revisionists' – Marxists who wanted to revise Communist dogma and liberalize the system, the sort of people who directed the 'Prague Spring' in Czechoslovakia in 1968. A rival group, led by the interior minister, General Mieczyslaw Moczar, called themselves 'The Partisans'. They were super-nationalists, whose leaders were veterans of the Communist underground during the war. Another Communist faction was led by Edward Gierek, the party's leading 'technocrat'; they wanted to modernize the economy without loosening the political reins.

In 1967–68, the 'Partisans' launched a violent, anti-intellectual and anti-Semitic campaign in an attempt to overthrow Gomułka. He kept his position by mounting an anti-Semitic campaign of his own: as a result, most of the surviving Jews in Poland were driven out. It was the most disgraceful episode in post-war Polish history.

Gomułka survived challenges from every direction until the end of 1970. He suppressed the 'revisionists', outmanoeuvred the 'Partisans' and enthusiastically supported the Soviet invasion of Czechoslovakia in August 1968. He disposed of Moczar and accommodated Gierek, but none of his reforms restored the economy, which deteriorated steadily from the early 1960s. His greatest triumph occurred in December 1970, when the West German chancellor Willy Brandt came to Warsaw and at last recognized the Oder–Neisse frontier, abandoning a dogma that had dominated German foreign relations for 25 years. Brandt also knelt in penitence before the memorial to the Warsaw Ghetto, where, during the war, thousands of Jews had died and from which hundreds of thousands of others had been transported to the death camps.

Gierek and the rush to industrialization

Flushed with this diplomatic triumph, on Saturday, 12 December, the government announced steep rises in the prices of food and other commodities. It was two weeks before Christmas and the Poles were outraged. The following Monday, there was a demonstration by workers from the Lenin shipyard in Gdańsk. The next day, shipyard workers in Gdynia came out on strike, and the first real riots occurred in Gdańsk, during which 27 people were killed and the party headquarters were burned down. Riots spread along the Baltic coast and Gomułka ordered them suppressed by all means. Troops fired on workers, and by the end of the week, the whole area was in open insurrection. In a hastily called Central Committee meeting on 20 December, Gomułka was summarily dismissed, while still protesting vehemently, and Edward Gierek, party leader from Silesia and technocrat, took his place. He made conciliatory speeches and broadcasts, promising reform and calling on the workers to end their strikes, and sent the troops back to their barracks.

There were further disturbances after Christmas, and in January, the shipyards went on strike again. Once more, the situation was slipping out of control. On 24 January 1971, Gierek and his senior colleagues, including General Wojciech Jaruzelski, the minister of defence, arrived in Szczecin, driving to the shipyard in a taxi. For nine hours, they argued with the workers and at last persuaded them to end the strike. They repeated the same remarkable dialogue in Gdańsk the next day. The price rises were rescinded a month later, after a further strike by textile workers in Lodz.

These events were a stunning victory – not for the liberal Communist intellectuals who had supported Gomułka in 1956, but for the Polish working class. When the new regime failed to live up to its promises, just as the Gomułka regime had during its time in office (1956–70), the workers lost whatever illusions they had retained of the Communists' honesty and ability. They had also learned an important lesson, which was applied with dramatic success in 1980 and 1988–89: they could bring the government to its knees.

Gierek wagered his government on a rush to industrialize the country. Huge sums were borrowed from Western banks, and invested in factories of every description. In the short term, the policy appeared to work. The standard of living rose rapidly, and for a few years, Poland's growth rate was among the highest in the world. But in Poland, as in Latin America, the Philippines and much of Africa, foreign capital was wasted on prestige projects and badly planned or uneconomic industries, or was simply stolen. By the middle of the decade, it was becoming clear that much of the money had been wasted. The worldwide recession provoked by the rise in the price of oil hit Poland harder than any other country in Europe. There were shortages of the most basic consumer goods, pharmaceuticals, even coal. In Neal Ascherson's words, 'Through the sheer incompetence of its rulers, Poland was now entering the worst economic disaster suffered by any European country for over 30 years.'

In 1976, the government again announced steep food price rises. The cost of meat went up by 70 per cent, sugar 100 per cent, butter and cheese 30 per cent. Strikes swept the country, and party headquarters at Radom, south of Warsaw, were burned to the ground. The price rises were 'withdrawn for further discussion'. It was not only a political humiliation for the government, it was an economic disaster. By then, 70 per cent of the price of food was subsidy. In the aftermath of the 1976 crisis, workers who had played prominent roles in the strikes were sacked, including Lech Wałęsa, an electrician at the Lenin shipyard at Gdańsk. In response, a group of Warsaw intellectuals, led by Jacek Kuron and Adam Michnik, formed the Committee for the Defence of Workers' Rights (KOR).

There was a great shift in power in Poland on 16 October 1978, when Karol Wojtyła, the Cardinal Archbishop of Kraków, was elected Pope. The Polish Church had always been the most powerful institution in the country, after the Red Army. Now it suddenly received an enormous reinforcement: its head had become the Vicar of Christ on Earth. John Paul II instantly became the personification of the nation. When his coronation was televised, the Poles saw the power of their Church. The following year, in July 1979, the Pope returned in pilgrimage to Poland and was received rapturously by millions of his compatriots. All Poland was united for the first time, and Poles realized the strength that comes from such unity.

In December 1979, Wałęsa reappeared at the Lenin shipyard at an unauthorized commemoration of the men shot by security forces there in 1970. He announced that he and his friends would return to the same spot the next year to begin construction of a memorial to the dead – if necessary, they would each carry a stone to build it. No one paid much attention to him.

Solidarity

In July 1980 faced with a new economic crisis, the government again tried to raise food prices by as much as 100 per cent. There were increasingly frequent strikes in various parts of the country. Then the management of the Lenin shipyard in Gdańsk tried to sack a crane driver, Anna Walentynowicz, for agitation. On 14 August, her comrades called for her reinstatement, the shipyard closed – and Lech Wałęsa scrambled over the wall to take command of the strike committee. It was a strike–occupation: the workers locked themselves inside the shipyard. The strikes spread over the Baltic region, and then to the rest of the country, including the mining districts in Silesia and Warsaw itself. A group of intellectual dissidents from Warsaw, led by Bronislaw Geremek (a medieval historian) and Tadeusz Mazowiecki (a Catholic journalist), arrived in Gdańsk to help the strikers formulate their demands. On 21 August, the government sent a vice premier to negotiate with them, and the whole world watched and listened.

The talks were held in the works' recreation room and were broadcast live over a public address system. Press and television reporters watched through the room's glass walls – as did the workers outside and, at one remove, their families and supporters outside the gates. The vice premier was thoroughly intimidated.

The strikers made six general demands: free trade unions to be permitted; the right to strike to be guaranteed; freedom of the press to be restored; the students and dissidents who had been punished for their roles in the events of 1970 and 1976 to be compensated and those still jailed to be released; the strikers' demands to be published in the official press; and every section of society to be consulted on ways of extricating the country from its economic crisis. Beyond these six general points, the strikers also demanded an immediate wage rise of 2000 *zlotys*, and a long list of other economic reforms ranging from better distribution of food supplies to day care for children, from ending party leaders' privileges to the principle that all promotions should be made on the basis of ability, not party loyalty. They even demanded that Mass should be broadcast on state radio and television every Sunday. As for the Silesian miners, they demanded a five-day week.

The Warsaw group's influence was apparent in the way the demands were phrased: the right to free unions and the right to strike were buttressed by quotations from the relevant clauses of the International Labour Organization's convention, and freedom of the press by the Helsinki Final Act – to both of which Poland was a signatory. Furthermore, the strikers were, from the start, acutely aware of the danger from the east. An early bulletin stated:

Our demands are intended neither to threaten the foundations of the socialist regime in our country nor its position in international relations, and we would not support anyone who wanted to exploit the present circumstances to that end; on the contrary, we would oppose them.

It was the very voice of moderation. Events were to show that the aims of what was to become Solidarity and those of the 'foundations of the socialist regime' were incompatible.

On 31 August 1980, the government signed an agreement with the strike committee in Gdańsk, conceding all the union's demands. An agreement with shipworkers in Szczecin had been signed the day before, and on 3 September, the government reached agreement with the coalminers in Silesia. It was the greatest defeat of a Communist regime since Budapest in 1956. In the next few weeks, free trade unions were formed throughout the country, taking the collective name 'Solidarity' (*Solidarność*) after the title of a strike bulletin published in Gdańsk. They differed from Western unions, which tend to represent workers only in particular trades: in Poland, every worker, in every trade, was a member of Solidarity, which therefore more nearly resembled the mass political party that, in due course, it indeed became.

An emergency plenum was called in Warsaw to face up to the new situation. The entire Gierek team was swept away; Gierek himself had a heart attack on 6 September, and was thus spared the indignity of being fired. The party chose as general secretary Stanislaw Kania, a moderate and cautious *apparatchik* who tried to hold the party together while promising to concede Solidarity's most pressing demands. The promises were not always convincing, and the government repeatedly delayed implementing the promised pay raises. Solidarity suspected that the new government was trying to weasel out of the Gdańsk agreements, and called a nationwide one-hour general strike on 3 October to demonstrate its power. The country came to a complete halt. On 23 October, the judge designated by the government to register the union unilaterally altered its statutes so that they included a provision recognizing the 'leading role' of the Communist party. Solidarity threatened another general strike, and the government backed down; the offending words were withdrawn, and the union was registered on 10 November 1980.

Later that month, there was another crisis, provoked by the arrest of two Solidarity members in Warsaw. Two of the largest factories in the capital – the Ursus tractor plant and the Huta Warszawa steel works – came out on indefinite strike, and all Solidarity prepared to follow their example. The government once again capitulated and released the two men, but the workers were not satisfied. For the first time, Wałęsa and his colleagues had to go to the factories to persuade the members to call off their strikes.

The government was faced with the prospect that, whatever professions of moderation the Solidarity leaders offered, the avalanche of reform would sweep away the Communist regime. The danger was felt in Moscow, too, where Leonid Brezhnev, in his dotage, and fresh from the invasion of Afghanistan, set in hand preparations for an attack on Poland. In December, Soviet troops were massed on the border and the other Communist countries were lined up to join them. As in 1939, Poland was threatened with invasion from east and west.

At an unscheduled Warsaw Pact summit in Moscow, the leaders of East Germany and Czechoslovakia, Honecker and Husák, took the lead in attacking the Polish comrades for their weakness. If Solidarity were not stopped immediately, they said, its revolution would spread to the rest of the bloc and destroy the entire Communist order in Europe. As the events of 1989 were to show, they were right. The meeting ended with the ominous communiqué: 'The Polish people can firmly rely on the fraternal solidarity and support of the members of the Warsaw Pact.' NATO issued dire warnings of the consequences if the Soviet Union invaded Poland.

The Poles closed ranks: both Solidarity and the Church stressed their moderation; the party insisted on its Leninist purity and reformist intentions. They all came together on 16 December, outside the Lenin shipyard at Gdańsk, to inaugurate the memorial to the dead of 1970. Lech Wałęsa's promise a year earlier had been dramatically fulfilled, and the memorial was unveiled in the presence of the president and a slew of Communist and ecclesiastical notables – but Wałęsa himself lit the eternal flame.

There was much coming and going between Warsaw and Moscow before the threat of intervention subsided. In the New Year, the Polish government and Solidarity resumed their negotiations, but mistrust and suspicion grew steadily greater. Solidarity rapidly evolved from a trade union into a political movement, constantly probing the limits of its power. The government announced that it could not pay the wage raise nor permit the five-day week. On 11 February, the defence minister, General Jaruzelski, became prime minister.

The next crisis occurred in March. When a group of Solidarity activists were severely beaten by security men in Bydgoszcz, north-west of Warsaw, Solidarity assumed that this was a provocation by hardliners, designed to precipitate confrontation and martial law, and they called a four-hour protest strike on 27 March. By then, Solidarity had over 9.5 million members (out of a workforce of 12.5 million), and the strike was a dramatic show of strength: party members joined the strike as willingly as everyone else.

Solidarity talked about an indefinite general strike, with occupation of the factories. In response, there were renewed threats of Soviet intervention, and the government once again promised reforms, consultations, concessions of every kind. The most important of these last was permission for the formation of 'Rural Solidarity'. Peasants all across the country promptly took advantage of the new dispensation, and soon, in effect, recreated the old, pre-war Peasants' Party. The concessions persuaded Wałęsa and his associates to call off the strike.

Economic crisis and coup d'état

It was a turning point: Solidarity was never so united again, nor was the government ever so near total surrender. Militants denounced Wałęsa for timidity: if Solidarity stayed its hand and withdrew the threat of revolution, it could not force the government to make further concessions. The realists answered that they had reached the limit of Soviet toleration: if Solidarity overthrew the government, the USSR would intervene; so long as the Soviets remained determined to impose their terms, by any means necessary, Solidarity must bend.

The point was reinforced by developments inside the party. Subterranean battles were fought between the factions during the preparations for the party conference, to be held in July 1981. Members of liberal factions, conservative factions, anti-Semitic, Stalinist and military factions struggled to win election as delegates to the conference. The Soviet Communist Party sent a formal letter to the Polish comrades stating that 'enemies of Socialist Poland are conducting a struggle for power, and winning,' and singling out Jaruzelski and Kania for criticism. It was perhaps at this stage that serious planning began for the *coup d'état*, although the final decision was probably not taken before the autumn.

The party conference was held in July 1981, and most of the old guard was deposed, but the reformers were also eliminated. The conference selected a new Politburo which accurately mirrored the splits in the party: it included Stalinists and centrists, but no reformers. This meant that the party bureaucracy, the *nomenklatura*, remained in charge, closely allied to the Soviet party. Jaruzelski, who had won some popularity as minister of defence in 1980 by refusing to allow troops to be used against strikers, now emerged as the dominant figure. He succeeded Kania as secretary-general on 18 October, while remaining prime minister and minister of defence, thus bringing together the three most important offices of state.

There were further negotiations between Solidarity and the government. The country's economic condition was steadily deteriorating. The GNP, which had dropped by 2.3 per cent in 1979 and 5.4 per cent in 1980, fell by 15 per cent in 1981. Foreign debt totalled $25 billion, and much of Polish industry was shut down for lack of spare parts. Basic foodstuffs and consumer goods were in disastrously short supply: people had to queue for hours for rationed potatoes, bread and vegetables; there was seldom any meat. In these negotiations, the government side was led by Mieczysław Rakowski, who presented himself to the world as a reformer but was, in fact, the quintessential time-server, now doing Jaruzelski's dirty work. The negotiations made no progress.

After the Communist party conference, in September, Solidarity held its first national congress, the most representative assembly of Poles in decades. It gathered in Gdańsk, and the Soviet Union marked the occasion by holding naval manoeuvres outside the harbour. The movement had to consider its future role. Delegates had to decide whether to continue their 'self-limiting revolution' or take over the state. The government offered Solidarity responsibility without power: it wanted the union to support its austerity measures without playing any part in defining or administering them. It was an intolerable dilemma. The delegates in effect authorized their leaders to try once again to persuade the government to relinquish some of its power voluntarily, but they were not prepared to force the issue if the government proved recalcitrant. Lenin would have told them that this was no way to run a revolution.

Solidarity now demanded 'self-government' for industries, proposing to administer every factory in the country itself. The matter was taken to the *Sejm* (parliament). To the Communists' vast surprise, the Democratic and Peasants' parties (which had continued in existence – fictitiously independent – for the previous 37 years) turned against the government for the first time since 1947, when they had been forced into a coalition with the Polish United Workers' Party. Self-government was approved by the *Sejm* on 25 September.

The Solidarity congress also proposed a plan for economic reform – but took care not to challenge the fundamental tenets of the Communist state, the 'leading role' of the Communist party or membership in the Warsaw Pact. It was rather unreal: for over a year, the government had been smothering Solidarity with concessions and promising reforms, but in fact, it had been doing nothing to implement them. There was a new wave of strikes in October (which Wałęsa and other Solidarity leaders tried to stop), and another nationwide one-hour stoppage was called on 28 October, as a further show of force. But it seemed that all Solidarity could do was bring the country to a halt; it could not improve economic conditions in any way. It was a great democratic success, but it had neither restored democracy nor brought the economic crisis under control.

On the night of Saturday, 12 December 1981, Jaruzelski imposed a 'state of war' (the Polish equivalent of a state of emergency) and suppressed Solidarity. Solidarity and KOR leaders were arrested, most of them being picked up in their hotel rooms in Gdańsk where they had been attending yet another Solidarity conference. All civil liberties were suspended. Gierek was also arrested, together with many other former leaders. In all, some 10,000 people were arrested during the five months following the December coup.

The workers resisted as best they could, occupying their factories, shipyards and mines. The army sent tanks to smash through the gates of the Lenin shipyard and soldiers to drive out the occupying workers. The longest resistance was put up by coalminers in the Piast mine in Silesia, who stayed underground until 27 December before finally surrendering. A number of workers were killed: seven by official count, between 50 and 100 by Solidarity's estimate.

The Solidarity leaders refused to negotiate with the government, and those who had escaped arrest, led by Zbigniew Bujak, set up a provisional committee to represent the movement. The Church denounced the imposition of martial law, but by degrees, resistance was beaten down, and Poland relapsed into sullen apathy.

Jaruzelski's public justification for invading his own country was that Solidarity had brought Poland to a state of anarchy. The other side of the coin, of course, was that the crisis was the result of the government's refusal to give way to a democratic and popular movement. By the end of the year, the confrontation had become so acute that it could only end in revolution or civil war (which would both have led to Soviet intervention), and the only alternative for Jaruzelski was to suppress Solidarity.

The roughly ten-year cycle of post-war Polish history continued. In 1945, 1948, 1956 and 1970, new regimes had taken over the country, with greater or lesser optimism, and tried to solve its problems. They had all failed. In 1956, 1970 and 1980, the regimes had simply collapsed in the face of public disorder. Jaruzelski understood perfectly that, if he could not solve the problems that had defeated his predecessors, he, too, would be driven from office.

Military government

Solidarity survived as a sort of government-in-internal-exile – illegal, proscribed, but at any moment liable to rise from its ashes. In a typically Polish manner, the security forces made no excessive efforts to arrest those of its leaders who had escaped in 1981, and throughout the period of martial law, they continued to hold clandestine meetings and press conferences and publish *samizdat*. While Jaruzelski tried to patch together the Communist party, shattered by the events of 1980–82, the government was left in the hands of the military, who named themselves the Military Council of National Salvation. The party did not recover. When the next crisis came, in 1988–89, it had neither the will nor the leaders to attempt once again the Sisyphean task of restoring the economy.

The striking difference between Poland in 1980 and Czechoslovakia in 1968 and the USSR in 1988 was that, in Poland, the reform movement arose from among the workers, who then invited the intellectuals to join them. In Czechoslovakia, and in Gorbachev's Soviet Union, the radicals seized the commanding heights of the party and then appealed to the workers for support. It came too late in Czechoslovakia, and the verdict is not yet in for the USSR.

Soon after the military coup in Poland, in December 1981, the workers were ready to strike again. Time after time, from 1970 onwards, they had seen how effective strikes could be, and they did not now sink into melancholy resignation as the Czech workers had in 1968 – or as had most Czech intellectuals. Jaruzelski's government remained in power for eight more years because it was supported by the Soviet Union, but it never dared impose the same bitter repression upon the country that Husák inflicted on Czechoslovakia. There was constant tension between government and people: the government feared an explosion if it drove the people too far; while the people cursed the government, but assumed that, in a final crisis, the Soviet Union would intervene as it had in Budapest and Prague. Whatever happened in Afghanistan, the Balkans, or in Africa, the USSR would not permit Poland to escape.

Wałęsa and others were released in November 1982. Then, after Pope John Paul II visited Poland again the following year and urged conciliation, martial law was lifted, the Military Council was dissolved and an amnesty was granted to political prisoners and activists. In 1984, on the 40th anniversary of the People's Republic, 35,000 prisoners and detainees were released.

The situation remained tense, and almost reached breaking point in October 1984, when the secret police kidnapped and murdered Father Jerzy Popieluszko, a turbulent Warsaw priest who was an outspoken supporter of Solidarity. There was an explosion of outrage, and for a while, as the monument to the priest in Warsaw became the scene of enormous daily demonstrations, it seemed that the whole country was about to defy both the government and the Soviets and rise in revolt. The regime arrested the men responsible for the murder and put them on trial; they were convicted amid widespread suspicion that they had been acting on orders from senior ministers. After that, the regime and its police were much more cautious about harassing Solidarity and its leaders.

Jaruzelski managed to bring some improvement to the economy immediately after the coup: the worst of the shortages were dealt with, for a time; severe rationing and steep price rises were introduced; and Poland managed to roll-over some of its debts. The government promised to use the emergency to impose the first stage of a reform programme, which would be followed by a second stage, after the emergency was lifted. It managed neither, and overall, the economy continued to decline throughout the 1980s. The West, outraged by the 'state of war', imposed sanctions on Poland that severely affected its ability to recover. The underlying problems, which had brought down previous governments, grew steadily worse. By 1988, Poland's foreign debt had risen to $39 billion, the GNP had dropped 13 per cent in the previous decade and real wages were 20 per cent lower than in 1980. The government repeatedly offered to hold 'round table' discussions on the economic situation with the Church and other 'social forces' – though it would not admit that the only force that counted was Solidarity. Furthermore, its intention was always to co-opt the opposition as junior members of a ruling coalition, to offer responsibility without power. It was a technique the party had used when establishing itself after the war, and had tried to apply during Solidarity's heyday in 1980–81. As the government still refused to legalize it, the union flatly rejected the proposal.

In 1985, the government announced further steep price rises for many essential goods. The clandestine leaders of Solidarity issued a call for a general strike, and the government hastily backed down. The economic crisis continued, and worsened, and the government was incapable of dealing with it. Among other things, government policy was paralysed by institutional conflict between conservatives and radicals.

In October 1987, Jaruzelski announced another reform programme, and the Communist machinery set to work preparing draft legislation to expand the private sector and free industry from the bureaucratic control that was destroying it. As a first step, the government proposed steep increases in prices, and submitted the question to the nation in a referendum. At the same time, voters were asked if they approved of 'deep democratization' of the political system.

The referendum was held on 29 November 1987, and the government lost. Forty-four per cent of the electorate (a suspiciously high number) voted for the price increases and 46 per cent for 'democratization'. Under the constitution, the government needed a majority of voters to approve the proposals, which therefore failed. It was the first time on record that a Communist government had lost a vote. As for the rest of the reform proposals, by the time the *apparat* had finished its work, they had been so watered down that they were worthless. The government abandoned the programme in September 1988.

The debates over the Jaruzelski reforms, which were probably the Communist party's last hope of saving itself, were conducted amid steadily increasing labour unrest. By 1988, the government was living hand-to-mouth, buying off strikes by giving in to the workers' demands for higher pay. Since there was nothing to purchase with the money, workers steadily increased their demands, aided and abetted by Solidarity. The inflation rate began to rise rapidly. The government hesitated to rearrest Wałęsa and the others, and Solidarity showed its hand ever more openly. By then, government and opposition alike were talking of the inevitability of a new confrontation, like the one in 1980. Jaruzelski had wasted his seven years' rule. The only differences with the situation in 1980 were that everyone could see exactly what was going to happen – it would not be a surprise, as it had been at the Lenin shipyard in Gdańsk in August 1980 – and the attitude of the Soviet Union was much less clear.

In May 1988, there was yet another outbreak of strikes, which were put down with difficulty. In August, they began again, starting in the Silesian mines and spreading to Gdańsk, where the workers once again occupied the Lenin shipyard. On both occasions, strikers demanded the restoration of Solidarity.

To all appearances, the Soviet will to dominate and its preferred instrument, the Red Army, remained as formidable as ever. In fact, the strength of both had been sapped by the Soviet Union's own economic catastrophe and its government's mounting crisis of credibility. Soviet power had continued to grow in the 1970s on the strength of the oil boom (world oil prices rose 15-fold just as the big West Siberian oil fields began production), concealing the underlying economic disaster. When the price of oil dropped again, by 50 per cent, in 1982–83, the hollowness of the Soviet economy and Soviet power became apparent to the government.

After Brezhnev's death in 1982, his successor Yuri Andropov started the process of re-examination that became known as *perestroika*, and this continued and was expanded when Mikhail Gorbachev became party leader in 1985. The Poles were the first in Eastern Europe to sense what was happening in the Soviet Union and to draw the correct conclusion as it applied to their own situation: the USSR was losing the will to rule; its European empire was an intolerable burden on an economy that was heading inexorably towards bankruptcy. In April 1988, Gorbachev announced that the Soviet Union would withdraw from Afghanistan. It proved the first step in a retreat that rapidly turned into a rout.

Jaruzelski was perfectly aware of the dangers he faced. The domestic economic situation was even worse than in 1980, and he could no longer rely on the Soviet Union as the protector of last resort. On 26 August 1988, as strikes continued all over the country, he summoned a plenum of the Central Committee at which the party's failures were openly debated. The following day, Jaruzelski himself admitted his lack of success and called for 'a courageous turnaround' by the government. It was an extraordinary admission from a man who had been given dictatorial powers almost seven years earlier to resolve Poland's long-standing difficulties. He told the plenum – and the rest of the country (the speech was televised) – that solving Poland's problems demanded 'the courage to break with old stereotypes and barriers, the courage to use new and unconventional means, and, first of all, effective ones'. He invited Lech Wałęsa and other Solidarity leaders to 'round table' meetings with the government to consider possible reforms. It was the same offer as before – but this time specifically directed at Solidarity. Once again, the union replied that it must be legalized before it would participate in any negotiations with the government. At the end of August 1988, Jaruzelski at last conceded that he would discuss legalizing Solidarity, and Wałęsa then called on the strikers to return to work.

In September 1988, Jaruzelski appointed Mieczysław Rakowski prime minister. He tried to form a coalition government, holding a number of ministerial positions open for the official opposition, which declined to take up the offer. The government was bankrupt, and knew it. It needed Solidarity to help it escape from the crisis that its own failures had created.

The end of Polish communism

Unofficial negotiations between Solidarity and the government began. The government side was represented by General Czeslaw Kiszczak, the minister of the interior, who had directed the coup and the arrest of the Solidarity leaders in 1981; Solidarity was represented by Wałęsa. By November, matters had progressed so far that Polish television staged a debate between Wałęsa and the leader of the official union. Wałęsa demonstrated his dialectical and debating skills and won a smashing victory. It was the first time since 1981 that the Polish people had been allowed to see him, uncensored, and it dramatically reaffirmed his position as the dominant political figure of the opposition.

After protracted haggling, the official round-table negotiations between the government and Solidarity – involving the same principals – finally opened in February 1989, and continued until April. The government was forced to cede point after point to the opposition, starting with the legalization of Solidarity and Rural Solidarity, and the creation of an independent Students' Association. The decisive concession was the government's reluctant agreement to hold partially free parliamentary elections, the first anywhere in Eastern Europe in over four decades. Furthermore, the government promised wholly free elections in 1994. Poland was thus the first East European country to abandon – de facto, although not yet de jure – the 'leading role' of the Communist party, the essential pillar of any Communist system. The constitution would be amended to provide for a president, on the French model, who would be elected by the Sejm. The pre-war Senate (abolished in the Communist constitution) would be revived, and the new bicameral legislature would elect the government.

The first elections were to be held in June. All 100 Senate seats would be freely contested, as would 161 of the 460 seats of the

Sejm (now the lower house). The Communist party was reserved 173 seats, and 126 were set aside for the Peasants' and Democratic parties. The agreement also contained provisions to protect workers against inflation, mitigate press censorship (Solidarity would be allowed to publish its own newspapers again), and to allow Poles to form their own associations and clubs.

After 45 years of lies, trickery and betrayal, the Poles were deeply suspicious of these government concessions. Solidarity leaders, noting that the elections would be 35 per cent free, asserted that they trusted the government 35 per cent. In the event, the first round of the elections, on 4 June 1989, produced a Solidarity landslide – and within six months, the Polish Communist Party disintegrated completely.

Solidarity won 92 of the Senate seats outright, and picked up seven more in the run-off; the 100th was won by a millionaire, running as an independent Communist. Solidarity won all but one of the 161 freely contested *Sejm* seats in the first round, defeating many 'moderate' Communists and public figures put up against it by the party, as well as scores of independents, including candidates selected by the Catholic hierarchy; it picked up the remaining seat in the second round. The Communists were humiliated. They had been allocated 173 seats, but so few people voted for them, and so many others crossed the Communist candidates' names off the list, that only three won the necessary 50 per cent plus at least one vote to win in the first round. Worst of all, on a separate list of 35 unopposed official candidates – including the prime minister, the minister of defence, the minister of the interior, and five other members of the Politburo – only two were elected. A majority of electors had crossed their names off the ballot. Of the two who were elected, one was the leader of the Peasants' Party, and the other was a Communist called Adam Zielinski, whose name appeared last on the alphabetical list of the 35 on the ballot. Apparently a number of voters failed to get to the end as they worked their way through, crossing off the names. The 33 unelected Communists and their allies had to face a run-off on 18 June – and many of them were only elected when Solidarity instructed its supporters to vote for them.

Lech Wałęsa was not a candidate. He had decided to lead Solidarity from outside parliament, perhaps awaiting the call to assume the presidency.

The new parliament elected Jaruzelski president, with only a majority of seven: the Peasants' and Democratic parties, seeing the way the wind was blowing, had deserted the Communists. He was replaced by Rakowski when he then retired as general secretary of the party, and he nominated Czeslaw Kiszczak to succeed Rakowski as prime minister. For the first time in Communist history, the party had then to negotiate with the two official minority parties to build a parliamentary majority.

The Communists were in such obvious disarray that Lech Wałęsa floated the idea of Solidarity taking power. The small parties having abandoned the government altogether, it became apparent that Kiszczak's government could not win a majority in the *Sejm*. The government crisis, which had begun with the election on 4 June, progressed throughout the summer. In mid-August, Kiszczak finally submitted his government to the *Sejm* and was rejected. Jaruzelski bowed to the inevitable (and also, perhaps, to pressure from Gorbachev to end the crisis): Solidarity offered him the names of three of its leaders who might become prime minister, and on 19 August, he nominated Tadeusz Mazowiecki, editor of Solidarity's weekly magazine and one of Wałęsa's closest advisers. Mazowiecki was confirmed by parliament on 24 August and his cabinet was approved on 12 September. It was the first non-Communist government in Eastern Europe since 1948: Poland was the first domino to fall. The Communists kept the ministries of defence and the interior, as well as the presidency and a few minor ministries; the rest went to Solidarity and its new allies. Thus, the Communists believed, they retained the ultimate power in the state.

Suspicious Poles feared that the Communist party, whose members ran all the bureaucracies in Warsaw and the local governments throughout the country, would strangle the new central government. They were mistaken. The disintegration of the party continued rapidly, helped by events elsewhere in Eastern Europe. Mazowiecki's government proceeded to dismantle the Communist state, meeting little resistance even from Communist civil servants, whom it invited to change their ways and remain.

The party fell apart, and finally on 28 January 1990 at a conference, it voted itself out of existence – 'because of the impossibility of the party regaining the public's confidence'. Rakowski, in his last appearance as a political leader, admitted that 'the main weakness of the Communist movement and the source of all its failings was the abandonment of political democracy.' The conference resolution admitted that it bore the main responsibility for violating democracy and damaging the economy. Then they adjourned to form a new party, which they called 'Social Democracy'. However, a group of liberal ex-Communists broke away and formed their own new party, the 'Union of Social Democracy', charging the Social Democratic Party with being full of neo-Communists.

In May 1990, the local elections swept the newly renamed Communists out of their last bastions in town halls and village councils throughout the country. There was nothing left. The ministers of defence and the interior, who were meant to guarantee the party's hold on power, were no longer Communists, and Jaruzelski himself supported Solidarity. The government decided that it would hold new elections in 1991 at the latest, instead of waiting for 1994.

The economic crisis continued. Inflation was running out of control by the end of 1989, industrial production continued to drop and the country entered a severe recession. In December, the government – proclaiming that 'You cannot leap a crevasse in two jumps' – proposed a package of reforms amounting to a complete abandonment of Communism. Parliament approved the proposals just after Christmas, and on 1 January 1990, all price controls except rent were lifted, all restrictions on private property ended, state-owned companies were put up for sale and a first step was taken towards a convertible currency. Poland was no longer a Communist state, although it remained a titular member of the Warsaw Pact.

Living standards dropped sharply, from their already wretched levels. In ten weeks, real incomes dropped by 37 per cent, and prices rose dramatically: bread by 38 per cent, petrol 100 per cent, meat 55 per cent, electricity 400 per cent.

It became inevitable that many firms would go bankrupt and hundreds of thousands of people would lose their jobs. Perhaps the most dramatic sign of rapid change was the imposition by the government of a wage freeze and its abandonment of the wage–price regulator that Solidarity had extracted from the previous regime during the 'round table' talks that had concluded in April 1989.

Solidarity was no longer an opposition trade union movement with political aspirations; it was now a responsible government, with a popular mandate.

The medicine worked: inflation was brought under control. Food appeared in the shops – but many people could no longer afford to buy it. Farmers struggled to bring their crops to market (there was soon a glut of potatoes) but had to cope with the old, inefficient transport system. It would take a while before private transport companies could set up delivery systems, and before private shops started to compete, to bring prices down. Entrepreneurs were given a free rein, but without an adequate banking system, without even the most rudimentary knowledge of how to run a business, it was inevitable that the new system would initially produce little but confusion and misery.

In the beginning, the Polish people accepted these privations, which, in fact, were far more severe than those that had been proposed by earlier, Communist governments and which had been met with riots in the streets and revolution. The new reforms were offered by a democratic government, and because almost all Poles, at last, wanted an end to Communism, they were willing to pay the price. However, the Poles eventually did protest: the first strikes occurred in May 1990, as workers rebelled against the new wave of austerity. The Solidarity government (and Lech Wałęsa, outside the government) had to devote themselves to persuading the strikers to return to work – without the pay raises they demanded.

Salvation lay with the West. West Germany, the European Community and the United States all promised help. Poland was, in effect, relieved of the need to pay interest on its $39 billion in foreign debt, a concession worth $4 billion in the first year. The International Monetary Fund (IMF) and other Western financial organizations made $2.3 billion in credits available at the beginning of 1990, with more to come. Western entrepreneurs flooded into the country to examine the new situation. Most of them concluded that it was too soon, and Poland's situation was too dire, to make any large investments, but a few hardy companies started joint ventures, or invested directly in the country. Soon a familiair and reassuring pattern emerged. Poland's problems were now just those of underdevelopment, and the West knows how to solve them. The Poles have the added advantages of a well-educated work force and, *mirabile dictu*, a stable political system.

Their relations with the Soviet Union remained amicable. The Soviets agreed to remove all their troops shortly, and showed no interest at all in interfering in Polish affairs. In March 1990, in a concession of major symbolic importance, the Soviet Union at last, after 50 years, admitted that its secret police had been responsible for the 1940 Katyn massacre of over 4000 Polish officers taken prisoner by the Red Army.

Things were not so clear to the West. Poland remained most sensitive about its western borders, and was of all nations the one most opposed to German reunification. The Poles' worries were somewhat allayed by assurances from all German politicians that the first act of the newly united Germany would be to sign a peace treaty with Poland, recognizing the border.

In the longer term, Poland believes that its future lies with the West. Along with the other newly liberated countries of Eastern Europe, it began negotiations in Brussels to become an associate member of the European Community, and sought advice and help from Western Europe, the United States and Japan to revive its economy. It is the largest, the most important but also the most backward country in northeast Europe. East Germany will be absorbed into the Federal Republic within five years, Czechoslovakia and Hungary may hope to recover and to join the Community by the end of the century, but Poland faces far greater difficulties because of its lamentable inheritance of economic incompetence. Paradoxically, it draws strength from its weakness. There can be no stability or progress in north-central Europe, in the whole region from the Baltic to the Balkans, unless Poland's stability and economic recovery are assured. Europe – and, above all, Germany – cannot allow chaos and ruin in Poland, and they have the resources to rescue it from its miseries.

3 Czechoslovakia

The Communist regime in Czechoslovakia, with all its paraphernalia of army, police and workers' militias, was swept away in
a week. First, there was a students' demonstration in Prague on 17
November 1989, and on the 24th the government and party leadership all resigned together. It has been called a 'velvet revolution':
no one was killed, and when the Czech and Slovak people took
their destinies into their own hands, they exacted no revenge on
their oppressors. It was a revolution led by intellectuals, and its
spokesman was the dramatist Václav Havel who had been released
from prison only six months earlier. The intellectuals discovered to
their delight that they had the support of the workers, who joined
enthusiastically in the demonstrations against the Communists. It
was a striking contrast to the situation in the country in 1948, when
the Communists had used the workers to suppress the republic, and
in Romania, where violent hostility persists between workers and
intellectuals.

As late as August 1989, the state appeared so solid, so strong,
that Havel recommended against a demonstration on the 21st
anniversary of the Soviet invasion of 1968. No one really knew
what the Czechoslovak people thought. They appeared contented
with their lot: their standard of living was clearly higher than in
Poland or the Soviet Union, though lower than in West Germany;
and although they suffered under the pervasive oppression of the
state police, they did have fully stocked shops, motor cars and many
of the other ordinary comforts of life. Later, Havel observed that
one of the worst results of Communism was universal hypocrisy –
everyone said one thing while thinking another. Nobody believed
in Communism any more, but everyone pretended to believe, and
the dissidents feared that their fellow citizens were too sunk in

despairing apathy ever to recover their independence. Then the East Germans rose in revolt, overthrew their government and smashed the Berlin Wall. Eight days later, the students of Prague took to the streets.

Czechoslovakia was created in 1918 from the debris of the Austro-Hungarian empire. Bohemia and Moravia – the western provinces – had been ruled from Vienna since the 16th century; Slovakia, to the east, had been ruled by the Hungarians for almost as long. The western territories were the most advanced economically in the empire, and their industries were as modern and profitable as any in the rest of Europe. The Czechs were firmly anchored in western Europe. Their factories making glass, shoes and armaments (e.g. the Skoda works), as well as the most famous breweries in the world, at Plzeň (Pilzen) and Budweis, gave them a solid bourgeoisie and a large working class. They formed an equally solid democratic state, which showed all proper respect to the susceptibilities of the numerous minorities, and it survived through the Fascist 1930s until the German occupation. The state reappeared undamaged in 1944, only to be suppressed again, by Stalin, four years later.

Czechoslovakia's minorities were its undoing. There were over 3 million Germans living in communities along the frontiers with Germany and Austria, and in isolated pockets in and around Prague and scattered across the rest of the country. The border territories – collectively known as the Sudetenland – were the most advanced industrially in all Czechoslovakia, and the Germans resented their sudden minority status, after centuries of domination. The Weimar Republic had accepted the frontiers and rejected all irredentist temptations, but in January 1933, when Hitler took power, he proclaimed his determination to reunite all scattered Germans into the *Reich*.

There were other dissatisfied minorities: 100,000 Poles in Těšín (Teschen); half a million Hungarians in districts in Slovakia near the border with Hungary; and 400,000 Ruthenians occupying the easternmost section of the country, Trans-Carpathian Ruthenia. There was also continuing tension between Czechs and Slovaks. Czechoslovak politics throughout the First Republic (1918–39) consisted of a balancing act between these groups.

Czechoslovakia's foreign policy between the wars consisted of building up alliances with France and the Soviet Union; and with two other vulnerable Eastern European countries – Romania and Yugoslavia – to form the 'Little Entente'. Poland, coveting Těšín, refused to join. The Czech army built elaborate fortifications in the Bohemian mountains to defend itself against Germany. In March 1938, Hitler annexed Austria, turning the Czech fortifications, and announced that he had no further territorial ambitions in Europe. Everyone knew what that meant.

The Sudeten Nazi leader, Konrad Henlein, stepped up his demands that the Sudetenland be united with Germany. The crisis came in September, with Hitler poised for war. The British and French offered to mediate, and following a series of conferences with Hitler, culminating in Munich, an agreement was produced that aimed to avoid war at the price of dismembering Czechoslovakia: the Sudetenland was ceded to Germany. About a month later, the Hungarian districts of Slovakia were annexed by Hungary. The Czechoslovak government, headed by Eduard Beneš, was forced to accept. The only country to offer any assistance was the Soviet Union, and Beneš thus learned a distrust of the West and a faith in Stalin that finally betrayed him ten years later.

Hitler annexed the rest of Bohemia and Moravia in March 1939. Hungary took Ruthenia, and the Poles Těšín. Slovakia was set up as a semi-independent, Catholic dictatorship, similar to Croatia in 1941, but less vicious.

Czechoslovakia suffered less than any other European country involved in World War II except Denmark. Its greatest atrocity was the 1942 massacre of the entire adult population of Lidice, a town of about 10,000 people near Prague; the children were sent to German orphanages. This was in revenge for the assassination of Reinhard Heydrich, governor of Bohemia and Moravia, who had also been Himmler's principal deputy and had presided over the Wannsee Conference in January 1942, which had decided on the extermination of the Jews. In Czechoslovakia, only about 25,000 Jews out of a pre-war population of 180,000 survived.

The Soviets liberated the eastern part of Czechoslovakia at the end of 1944, and promptly annexed Trans-Carpathian Ruthenia to the Ukraine. The following spring, the Soviet and American armies raced towards Prague. The US commander, George Patton, would have won the race if Eisenhower had permitted it, but as the Americans reached Plzeň, just west of the capital, they were ordered to pull back and leave Prague to the Soviets. Prague itself was liberated by a Communist-led resistance, which then welcomed the Red Army.

In later years, the children of Plzen were taught that their city had been liberated by Soviet soldiers wearing American uniforms.

The allies had declared the Munich agreement null and void in 1942, and Beneš's government was recognized as the legitimate government of Czechoslovakia. From exile in London, Beneš went to Moscow in 1944, where he was persuaded to admit Communists into the government, and when the Red Army reached eastern Czechoslovakia, he announced the new 'National Front', including a large number of Communist ministers; the prime minister, Zdeněk Fierlinger, was a fellow-travelling Social Democrat. There was no opposition to the new coalition government, and the elections that it organized in 1946 were completely free. The Communist party won the largest number of votes (38 per cent), giving it 114 deputies out of 300; the Social Democrats won 39 seats, and joined with the Communists to form a majority government. The 'National Front' coalition continued in office, but the Communist party's leader, Klement Gottwald, became prime minister and other Communists took over all the essential ministries: Václav Nosek, the minister of the interior, who controlled the police; the minister of finance; and the minister of information, who controlled the radio and the allocation of newsprint to newspapers throughout the country, and thus controlled the press. The minister of defence General Ludvík Svoboda, ostensibly non-party, was a fellow-traveller. The one major figure in the government to be independent of the Communist party was the foreign minister Jan Masaryk, son of Czechoslovakia's founder Tomáš Masaryk.

The 'bourgeois' parties (i.e. the democrats) were evidently in grave danger. As well as holding the main offices of the state, the Communists were busily setting up workers' militias in the factories around Prague. Furthermore, the party had the support of the Soviet Union, while the Western powers, who should have supported the democrats, were preoccupied with other matters. It was only later that the Czechoslovak Communists, including most notably the party's secretary-general Rudolf Slanský, would discover just how costly Stalin's support could be.

The first order of business was to expel the Germans living in the Sudetenland, in Prague and in other parts of the country, and over 2 million were driven out in the 18 months after the liberation. They had been the fifth column which had provided the pretext for Hitler to dismember Czechoslovakia in 1938 and 1939, and many had remained loyal Nazis until the bitter end. It seemed a justifiable case of corrective surgery at the time, and there was no dispute between the democratic and Communist leaders on the need for the expulsions. It was, however, like the eviction of Germans from Silesia, Pomerania and East Prussia, an act of great cruelty, causing tens of thousands of deaths and great misery. After the revolution of 1989, Václav Havel publicly acknowledged the expulsions as a crime.

The new government launched a programme of rapid nationalization of industry and land redistribution. The bourgeois parties, who opposed these policies or tried to limit them, were constantly outvoted in the cabinet. In June 1947, the Americans announced the Marshall Plan to restore European economies, and the Czech government, like the Polish, at first welcomed it. Then Stalin decided that this was an imperialist plot to reduce Soviet influence in Eastern Europe, and he instructed his allies to refuse American aid. The Polish Communist Party, without any popular support at all, had no choice but to fall into line immediately. Some of the Czech Communist leaders, conscious of the enormous advantages of American aid, wanted to accept, but they were overruled by Gottwald, who never hesitated to obey Stalin's direct orders.

It proved a turning point. From 1947 onwards, apart from the brief moment of revolt in 1968, the Czechoslovak Communist Party was the willing slave of the USSR. It subordinated Czech economic and political interests to those of the Soviet Union, despite the fact that it had considerable popular support and great industrial resources. The population was educated, disciplined and apparently ready to try the socialist experiment. Like Britain and France, Czechoslovakia was one of the few major industrial countries in Europe whose industries had survived the war more

or less intact. In fact it was in many ways better prepared for
the post-war world than either of the others: its industries were
more modern and adaptable than France's; and it had none of
Britain's imperial pretensions and responsibilities. If the Marxist
theory were correct, the party had the opportunity to establish an
independent and prosperous Communist nation in the centre of
Europe; alternatively, they might have made their country into the
Sweden or Finland of Central Europe. However, the Communist
Party of Czechoslovakia, unlike Tito in Yugoslavia (*see* Chapter
5), never considered the possibility of independent prosperity. It
remained loyal to international socialism, to the Soviet Union and
to Stalin.

The coup

The National Assembly, elected in 1946, had a two-year mandate
to direct the first phase of the nation's recovery; then there were to
be fresh elections. Although the Communists succeeded in pushing
Czechoslovakia far down the road of state socialism, their objective
was to win full control of parliament and to establish a fully fledged
'people's democracy'. To this end, they constantly attacked and
harassed the democratic parties. On one occasion, there was an
attempt to assassinate Jan Masaryk, Prokop Drtina, the minister
of justice, and another democratic politician by sending them parcel
bombs, but the bombs were discovered before they exploded. They
were traced to a noted Communist extremist, Alexej Cepika, whom
Drtina tried to prosecute. After the coup, Cepika himself became
minister of justice – and jailed Drtina for 'false accusation'.

In February 1948, the Communist minister of the interior, Václav
Nosek, dismissed eight non-Communist police chiefs. The democratic ministers protested volubly and, for once, won a vote in the
cabinet, ordering the men to be reinstated. Nosek refused to obey,
and 12 non-Communist ministers, in a moment of folly, resigned in
protest: Beneš had promised them that he would not accept their
resignations, and would use the crisis as a lever to break up the
Gottwald government and replace it with one less dominated by
the Communists.

The Communists responded with resolution and skill, helped by
Valerian Zorin, a senior member of the Soviet government, who

came to Prague to direct the coup. There was a series of mass rallies in the capital, at which the democrats were denounced for treason. The Communist workers' militias flooded into Prague and occupied public buildings and strategic points throughout the city. The army remained benevolently neutral, but the police – whose senior ranks had by then been thoroughly purged of non-Communists – supported the Communists and when they occupied opposition party headquarters, they claimed to have discovered a plot to overthrow the government. The same thing happened in Slovakia. In Bratislava, operations were directed by Gustáv Husák, who had led the Slovak resistance during the war and had been one of the heroes of the 'Slovak Uprising'.

The Communists scheduled a one-hour national strike on 24 February. It was a complete success, the country coming to a stop while demonstrators everywhere denounced the democrats. The democratic parties vacillated and hesitated. The Social Democrats threw in their lot with the Communists, and police and militia occupied opposition party headquarters outside Prague and seized their newspapers. The next day, Beneš capitulated. He accepted the democrats' resignations and allowed Gottwald to appoint their successors. The Communist triumph was complete.

Drtina attempted suicide on 27 February; Masaryk died on 10 March. With Beneš, Masaryk had been the best-known Czechoslovak leader, son and heir of the republic's founder, and himself one of the founders of the United Nations. Deeply depressed and uncertain, he had remained in the government after the coup, but had not used his immense prestige in the fight between the Communists and democrats, and perhaps regretted his inactivity. His body was found in the courtyard below his apartment in the foreign ministry building: he had jumped, or he had been pushed, out of the bathroom window.

There has been much debate ever since whether his death was suicide or murder. On the one hand, his motives for killing himself were quite as strong as Drtina's, and the Communists had no particular need to do away with him – they had won the battle, and Masaryk was a useful prisoner, or hostage, as titular but powerless foreign minister. On the other hand, there were many suspicious circumstances surrounding his death, all sedulously covered up by the authorities. An enquiry was opened in 1968, but it was suppressed after the Soviet invasion, before it could reach any conclusion. Masaryk was given a state funeral, and 200,000 people turned out to mourn him and their lost democracy.

The Communist coup of February 1948 was the tocsin that announced the Cold War. In the rest of eastern and southeastern Europe, the Communist regimes were installed by the Red Army or emerged from the chaos of wartime resistance. In Czechoslovakia, a democratic regime of unquestioned legality was overthrown by the Communist party, aided by street demonstrations and the moral and political collapse of the 'bourgeois' parties. This was the way the Fascists had taken over central, eastern and southern Europe in the 1920s and 1930s – all except Czechoslovakia. Indeed, the Prague coup closely resembled Mussolini's 'march on Rome' in 1922 and Hitler's triumph in Berlin in 1933. In all three cases, the democrats surrendered without a fight. In 1948, the surviving democracies in Europe, and their American allies, justifiably feared that the same thing could happen in France or Italy, and took the necessary precautions. The Iron Curtain came down across the Continent, each side determined to protect itself from contamination and danger, and the division remained until 1989.

Stalinist Czechoslovakia

In the beginning, no doubt, large numbers of Czechoslovaks welcomed the revolution. It was not an alien tyranny imposed upon them by the Soviet Union, as in Poland or Romania where there were no national Communist parties to speak of and strong traditions of hostility towards the Russians. There had been an active Communist party in Czechoslovakia between the wars, and the party was well represented among the intelligentsia and the workers. In this respect, Czechoslovakia was like France or Italy. In addition, there was in Czechoslovakia, as in most of Europe, a strong move to the left immediately after the war, a reaction against the right-wing regimes that had produced that catastrophe. The nationalizations, the redistribution of land, the dispossession of the upper classes and the bourgeoisie (now much reduced because of the murder of most of the Jews by the Nazis), the expulsion of over 2 million Germans – all these proved largely popular. In the short run, in Czechoslovakia as in other newly Communized countries, the sudden redistribution of power and resources benefited large numbers of people. Although the Communists were never in a majority – they had won only 38 per cent of the vote in 1946 and would probably have won considerably less in 1948 if the elections had been free – they were undoubtedly a considerable political force.

Eighteen months after the coup, the party learned the price it had to pay for its subservience to Moscow when a purge began of those members whose loyalty to the Soviet Union might be questionable. The same thing happened in the other Soviet satellites and for the same reason: after Tito was expelled from the bloc in June 1948, Stalin required absolute and slavish obedience from all the others to ensure against further defections. Some of those accused might indeed have put their own nation's interests ahead of the Soviet Union's; others were accused, tried, convicted and executed simply as a warning. The Communists chosen for disgrace or death were mostly those with connections with the West, those who had fought in Spain, those who had fought in the resistance movements instead of waiting for the Red Army victory – or those who were Jews. Some met all these criteria.

Surviving Marxists, for many years afterwards, denounced Stalin for perverting the basic Marxist doctrine that each country would chose its own path to socialism. Until 1948, it had seemed self-evident that different economic and social policies would be appropriate in countries as diverse as Albania, Czechoslovakia, Poland, China and the USSR itself. Stalin decreed otherwise. Furthermore, he imposed upon the satellites his own odious doctrine that class war intensifies after the revolution – the theory he had used to justify the killing of the Old Bolsheviks in the Soviet Union. These theoretical considerations should not be taken too seriously. Stalin's concerns – in the Soviet Union in 1937 and in Eastern Europe in 1948 – were power and paranoia, not Marxist theory. He killed his rivals, as well as those he thought might become his rivals, and then he thought up a suitable justification.

The purges in Czechoslovakia were conducted on the Soviet model, with the Czechoslovak security services under the direct control of the MVD (the immediate predecessor of the KGB). Eugen Loebel, the first deputy minister of foreign trade and one of the survivors of the Prague show trial of 1952, described how he was interrogated by two men – one Russian, one Ukrainian –

who were clearly in charge of the whole process; the Czechoslovak prosecutors attended Loebel's sessions simply as subordinates. These MVD agents were known to Czechoslovak security men as the 'Teachers'.

The man who began the terror, on Stalin's order, was Rudolf Slanský, secretary-general of the party and the official in charge of security. It was he who ordered the arrest of the foreign minister Vladimir Clementis, his deputy Artur London, Eugen Loebel and a string of other officials. Thousands of lesser Communist officials were arrested, tortured, forced to confess their non-existent crimes, tried and sentenced. Hundreds were executed. Among those who escaped with a life sentence was Gustáv Husák, party chief in Slovakia.

Slanský had been Gottwald's closest associate in organizing the subversion and overthrow of the Second Republic (1946–48) and in the subsequent Communization of Czechoslovakia. He had supervised the persecution of non-Communist government officials after the coup and had established the first Czech concentration camps, in September 1948. A year later, on Beria's orders, he started the purge, declaring, 'The enemy is penetrating our ranks: it is necessary to examine every party member. Our party must pass through a purification process.' He is reported to have remarked that it was necessary to find a senior scapegoat – a 'Czechoslovak Rajk'. László Rajk, the Communist minister of the interior in Hungary, had begun the purge there in 1948, and was then himself arrested, tried, convicted of espionage and hanged. Beria, indeed, needed a 'Czechoslovak Rajk': he chose Slanský.

Loebel, who in September 1949 was the first of the defendants at the Prague trial to be arrested on Slanský's orders, was initially accused of plotting against the party leaders, Gottwald and Slanský. He was therefore stupefied to be told suddenly, in March 1951, that he had so far concealed his greatest guilt – his collaboration with the party's greatest enemy, the imperialist agent Slanksý.

Slanský was probably unaware of the noose tightening around him. In the summer of 1951, even while the security services prepared their case against him, he was showered with honours to mark his 50th birthday: a special edition of his works was published, and Gottwald and other comrades issued statements of fulsome praise. He was arrested in November.

Eventually, 14 senior members of the government, party and security apparatus were put on trial in Prague in November 1952. The principal defendants were Clementis and Slanský, but those charged also included the deputy head of security who had arrested Loebel. They were all charged as

> Trotskyite, Titoite, Zionist, and bourgeois-nationalist traitors [who] created, in the service of the US imperialists and under the direction of Western espionage agencies, an anti-state conspiratorial centre, undermined the people's democratic regime, frustrated the building of socialism, damaged the national economy, carried out espionage activities and weakened the unity of the Czechoslovak people and the Republic's defensive capacity in order to tear the country away from its close alliance with the Soviet Union, to liquidate the people's regime in Czechoslovakia, to restore capitalism, and to drag the Republic into the imperialist camp once again and destroy its national sovereignty and independence.

All the accused pleaded guilty to every charge, however ridiculous. Slanský, for instance, confessed that he had publicly shouted 'Long live Trotsky!' in October 1927.

Two of the survivors, Loebel and London, published their memoirs in 1968, at the time of the Prague Spring. Their books revealed at last, after 30 years, how the NKVD (the KGB's predecessor) had obtained the confessions of Bukharin, Zinoviev, Radek and the other Old Bolsheviks – as well as that of the former head of the NKVD itself, Yagoda. In his 1940 novel *Darkness at Noon*, Arthur Koestler had advanced the romantic notion that these old revolutionaries had agreed to admit to the most extreme treason for the sake of the party: the party needed their confessions and deaths, and these men, who had devoted their lives to the Communist cause, at the end devoted their deaths to it, too. Loebel and London showed that the reality was quite different. Their party loyalty was, indeed, used against them. They were told, 'What the party needs, in the present situation, is not heads but a well-organized political trial,' and if they cooperated in the show trial, their lives would be spared. But that was not how these Russians, who had survived Tsarist prisons, or these Czechs, some of whom had survived the *Gestapo*, were persuaded to confess. They were tortured – Bukharin, Radek, Slanský, Rajk, all of them – until

they were incapable of resisting, until all their courage, all their
individuality, all their intelligence were destroyed and they were
ready to grovel to their prosecutors. London was told that Radek
had resisted for three months – and had then confessed everything.
London, too, they said, would confess everything. He took this as
proof that the whole operation was being directed by the KGB, for
who else knew about Radek? For the first time, loyal Communist
though he was, he realized that the Moscow show trials had all
been lies.

The defendants were not physically abused directly: the
'Teachers' only used beatings when they needed immediate
results. The preferred method was to interrogate the defendants
(who had to stand at all times) for 16 hours a day (with two hours
of breaks) using a series of interrogators, for weeks or months on
end. During the six hours of sleep that the defendants were allowed,
they were interrupted by a guard every ten minutes and forced to
stand and say: 'Detention prisoner 1473 reports. Number in cell:
one. All in order.' According to Loebel, the interrogation

> was conducted by three men, each taking his turn and consisted
> of a never-ending flood of insult, humiliation and threats . . .
> I was not allowed to sit. I even had to eat standing up. You
> could not even sit on the toilet, since what was provided was a
> so-called 'Turkish closet'. Walking for 16 hours a day, however
> slowly, meant covering 15 or 20 miles – on swollen feet. Such
> a day seemed endless and the prisoner could scarcely wait for
> night. Yet lying down caused more pain than anything else. The
> sudden change in pressure brought such violent pain to my feet
> that sometimes I had to scream out.

Every so often, the prisoners were taken out for a mock execution,
and some of them were fed drugs. Loebel wrote: 'Suddenly I had
a feeling as if a hand had thrust itself through my forehead into
my brain . . .' No wonder that, at their trials, they confessed to
everything. Their testimony, the questions put to them and their
answers were all written in advance, and they had to learn their
lines by heart. London relates: 'I once again rehearse my text. I
also know by heart at what precise moment I will be interrupted
by the prosecutor and by the judge, and what their questions will
be.' The trial was pure theatre.

It opened on 20 November 1952. Czechoslovakia was by then

in the grip of Gottwald's egomania, just as the Soviet Union was prisoner of Stalin's. The prosecutor declared:

> Thanks to the vigilance, the clear-sightedness and the decisiveness of Comrade Klement Gottwald, guide of the Czechoslovak people, thanks to the unity and the fraternal cohesion of the Central Committee of the Communist Party, firmly united around Comrade Klement Gottwald, thanks to the unshakable fidelity and the attachment of the whole Czechoslovak people to the party, to the government and to Comrade Klement Gottwald, thanks to the unalterable faith of our people in the Soviet Union, the conspiracy has been broken and the attacks of the criminals annihilated. Faithful to the people, to the government, to the party and to Comrade Klement Gottwald, the organs of state security stopped in time the criminal hands of the conspirators.

The prosecutor, denouncing the plots of 'imperialist agencies', continued:

> Little by little, these agencies, which had implanted themselves in the very heart of the Communist and workers' parties which were in power in the people's democracies, were finally unmasked. Thanks to the vigilance of the working people and of the Communist parties, the band of traitors was unmaksed and made harmless: László Rajk in Hungary, Traicho Kostov in Bulgaria, Kotchi Dzodze in Albania, as well as the band of Patrascanu in Romania and Gomułka in Poland . . .

In addition, he said:

> The danger with which the Zionist organizations threaten the world has become greater since the establishment of the American protectorate, the so-called State of Israel . . . The principal centre of Zionist organizations is still in America, where the Zionists count numerous supporters among the American monopolists which decide the whole aggressive policy of the United States . . .

In their memoirs, Loebel and London tell how their interrogation and indictment and the trail itself showed continuing, virulent anti-Semitism, although the preferred terms of abuse were 'cosmopolitan' and 'Zionist'. Indeed, 11 of the 14 defendants were Jews, including Slanský.

The only light moment in the trial came during the testimony of one of the accused who had lost a great deal of weight during his imprisonment: his trousers suddenly fell down. His fellow prisoners, the prosecutors and the judges were completely overcome with hysteria; Slanský wept with laughter. The session had to be adjourned.

Eleven of the prisoners (eight of them Jews) were sentenced to death, three to life imprisonment. In one last act of torture, they were all made to appear before the court to accept their sentences and to refuse their right of appeal. Years later, in a Czech newspaper published during the Prague Spring, London learned the end of the story.

> When the 11 condemned men had been executed, Interrogator D. found himself, by accident, in Ruzyn prison with the Soviet counsellor Galkin when he received the report of the driver and two interrogators who had been charged with disposing of the ashes. They announced that they had put them into a potato sack and set out into the countryside near Prague intending to scatter the ashes in the fields. Seeing that the roads were covered with ice, they had the idea, instead, of spreading the ashes on the road. The driver was laughing in recounting that he had never before carried 14 people in his little Tatra, three living and 11 in the sack.

The thaw

Hubert Ripka, one of the democratic leaders in 1948, wrote in his memoirs:

> During the first few days following the *coup d'état*, people of all circles, from Prague and from the provinces, friends, acquaintances and unknowns, came to see me. Routed and beaten, they came to ask me to explain to them what had happened; they wanted to consult me especially to know how they ought to act in face of the Communist threats. Many of them felt the need to strike back, and seemed disappointed when I told them that, in the present situation, any active resistance would be suicidal. I advised them to help one another in a spirit of fraternal solidarity, to remain dignified but prudent, to await the time when the situation became favourable. I stressed that, as had been the case after Munich, everything would depend on the international situation.

For 41 years and nine months, from February 1948 until November 1989, most Czechoslovaks followed his advice. They were dignified but prudent, and they waited for the international situation to change. It was a grey, grim, persecuted country. The one democracy in Central Europe that had rejected all forms of Fascism until it was destroyed by Hitler, a country that had always been part of the Western political tradition, was swallowed up by the Stalinists from the East.

With the magnificent exception of 1968, Czechoslovakia remained remarkably stable throughout those 41 years. Thanks to the Soviet intervention, government and party survived intact and unchanged, a sort of mummified relic of the 1940s. It was quite unlike Poland, Hungary or even East Germany. The differences between those countries, over two generations, is quite enough to prove that there is such a thing as national character, whatever the Marxists say.

Czechoslovakia entered the post-Stalin years without its leading Stalinists: Slanský had been hanged and Gottwald conveniently – or dutifully (there were rumours of suicide) – died a week after Stalin himself. The purge continued. There were trials of economists, Slovak nationalists (Husák was the principal victim), security officers, officials of the foreign ministry. The trials followed the usual pattern: everyone confessed, some were executed, all the others were sentenced to life imprisonment.

The Czechoslovak Communist Party remained united throughout the 1950s, unlike the Polish and Hungarian parties which suffered catastrophic splits, and the new leaders showed no mercy to their opponents or alleged opponents. Even after Beria had been executed in Moscow, together with his most notorious accomplices, and the Czechs were at last able to dispose of the KGB agents and stooges who controlled the security services, the persecutions continued. The men most responsible for extorting the false confessions of the defendants at the Prague show trial were themselves accused and sentenced to short prison terms for that crime in 1955 – but the three of their victims who were still alive were not released until the late 1950s, and all of them, executed and living, were not rehabilitated until 1963. The Czechoslovak Communist Party was as reluctant to admit to its past crimes as the Soviet Communist Party, because it was the leaders themselves who were responsible. Antonín Novotný, who became the Czechoslovak party's first secretary in 1953 and president of the republic in 1957, had played a leading role in the purges and had no intention of admitting the error.

He had other concerns. In Czechoslovakia, as in East Germany, economic conditions deteriorated in the early 1950s, with the same result. The government introduced severe labour laws, imposing a Draconian discipline on all workers, and on 1 June 1953, a few weeks after Stalin and Gottwald died, it declared a currency reform which at a stroke wiped out all personal savings. During the same period, the East German government increased the workers' 'norms' and provoked the July riots. In Czechoslovakia, riots broke out in Plzeň in Bohemia (the country's brewing and armaments centre), which were ruthlessly crushed by the police. The government, seeing the writing on the wall, briskly reversed itself. The labour decrees were repealed and the Stalinist insistence on heavy industry was somewhat relaxed, to permit a better supply of consumer goods.

In 1956, the year of the Hungarian Uprising, there were a few demonstrations against the regime by students, but the workers never stirred. The Czechoslovak party was delighted by the Soviet intervention in Budapest. It showed that the USSR was a reliable ally, and that any 'democratic' nonsense among Czechs or Slovaks would be firmly repressed. The country drew the same conclusion: revolt against the government was hopeless. Czechoslovakia remained quiet through all the upheavals in Poland and Hungary – until 1968.

There were two centres of unrest in the party: among the intellectuals and in Slovakia. The Prague Spring grew out of an alliance of these two. Novotný was a rabid Czech chauvinist who despised and detested the Slovaks. From the time the two nations were federated by Tomáš Masaryk in 1919, there had always been a great deal of tension between them. Czechs treated Slovaks with much the same contempt that the English showed for the Scots after the Act of Union united England and Scotland in 1707. The Slovaks, of course, resented this treatment, and in the 1960s, the party in Slovakia formed a united front against Novotný. Although Husák was rehabilitated in 1963, he was not then restored to his party functions. (Clementis, the other leading Slovak victim of the purge, was rehabilitated posthumously.) However, the Slovak party managed to get rid of its leading Stalinists and appoint Alexander Dubček, an obscure bureaucrat, as first secretary. Novotný allowed his promotion because he seemed much less dangerous than other party leaders in Slovakia.

Dubček was born in 1921. His father had been one of the founders of the Communist party in Slovakia, and had taken his family to the Soviet Union to help build socialism there, first in Central Asia, later in Gorky, east of Moscow. Dubček therefore grew up in the USSR and, until August 1968, was probably the most genuinely pro-Soviet of all Czechoslovak leaders. Returning to Czechoslovakia, he took part in the Slovak Uprising against the Germans in 1944 (during which his older brother was killed), and afterwards devoted himself to party work.

Dubček was much more dangerous than Novotný realized. For all his good nature and honesty, he was also devious, manipulative and ambitious. He steadily built up his influence in Slovakia, and encouraged party dissidents to express their views in local newspapers. Circumstances helped him. In the mid-1960s, yet another economic crisis developed in Czechoslovakia with the failure of the Soviet model imposed after 1948. The country had abandoned its traditional light industry in favour of heavy industry – whose products had to be shipped East to pay for the raw materials which that same heavy industry needed. The Soviet Union, under the pricing system it imposed on its satellites through Comecon, benefited hugely from both transactions, and Czechoslovakia was progressively impoverished. In 1967, as so often in Poland, Hungary and elsewhere – and in the USSR itself in 1990 – the party tried to reform the economy by altering the domestic pricing system. The economics minister, Ota Šik, introduced a 'New Economic Model' with the support of the entire government, but local bureaucracies sabotaged it and it failed completely. (Soviet reformers are suffering the same frustrations today.) The Czechoslovak reformers blamed Novotný.

Novotný's position continued to weaken throughout 1967, and in October, Dubček felt strong enough to attack him openly. The alliance of Slovaks and party intellectuals proved irresistible. The party opposition demanded that Novotný renounce either the position of first secretary or the presidency. Novotný appealed to Leonid Brezhnev (who was also both president and general secretary), but the Soviet leader declined to interfere. Novotný contemplated a military coup against his colleagues, but was faced down by Dubček and the others, and after a prolonged party crisis, he was forced to resign as first secretary on 5 January 1968. Dubček succeeded him.

The Prague spring

The reform movement in Czechoslovakia – Dubček's 'Communism with a human face' – provided the greatest inspiration for the European Left since World War II. For a few heady months, it seemed that Communism could evolve peacefully into a more egalitarian social democracy than had been achieved by the British Labour Party or the French Socialist Party. If Czechoslovakia could become democratic while remaining socialist, then the same thing could happen elsewhere – and perhaps the democracies might become socialist. If the Soviet Union permitted it, then there might even be hope for Soviet Communism. Perhaps Western socialists were about to escape from the burden of the Soviet example which had weighed so heavily upon their electoral chances for so many years.

In the event, the suppression of the Prague Spring, on 20/21 August 1968, killed Communism in Europe. The Dubček experiment was the last time democrats, East or West, were ever willing to give Communists the benefit of the doubt. The retreat from socialism that was to become a worldwide phenomenon began in Prague. When the type of 'international situation' that Hubert Ripka had looked forward to in 1948 at last occurred, and the Soviet Union decided to abandon its satellites to save itself, the Communist regimes in Prague and everywhere else were swept away beyond all hope of recovery.

The reforms of 1968 started quietly enough. For one thing, Dubček and his colleagues had no very clear idea of where they were going. They knew that they wanted to dispose of Novotný and push ahead with Šik's economic reforms, but that was all. For the first two months after Dubček's accession to power, while the new team considered its strategy there were no striking changes in party practices. Then the party published its 'Action Programme', which, 22 years later, looks a very tame document. The reforms of 1989–90 in the Communist parties of Eastern Europe, and in the Soviet Union itself, went much further than Dubček ever imagined – but in 1968, the Action Programme was revolutionary.

It dealt with the accumulated grievances of Slovakia, proposed to rehabilitate all those who had been persecuted during the 'violation of socialist legality' between 1949 and 1954 and announced rather vague plans to reform the relationship between the party and the government. Although there was no question of the party abandoning its 'leading role', the other subservient parties making up the National Front were to revive and the government was to escape from its absolute dependence on the Communist party. All these reforms had been tried, or at least discussed, in other Communist countries, including the USSR. What was new, and dangerous, was the Action Programme's explicit admission that sweeping reforms were needed.

By that time, the party had abandoned press censorship. Journalists began writing what they wished, and soon a full-scale press campaign against the former regime was under way. Novotný and his supporters were still conducting a rear-guard action against Dubček, but then, in March, a leading hardline security official, General Jan Sejna, defected to the West and broadcast incriminating accounts of corruption in the Novotný regime, and revealed details of the contemplated Stalinist coup the previous year. Sejna himself had escaped to avoid arrest on charges of embezzlement. Novotný's own son was implicated, and the president was forced to resign on 22 March. The landslide was gathering momentum.

The next day, the Warsaw Pact hastily convened a summit meeting in Dresden to discuss the Czechoslovak situation. It was the first meeting of a series in which Brezhnev, Gomułka of Poland, Ulbricht of East Germany and Kádár of Hungary tried to bring Dubček under control. The assembled Pact heavies berated him for the excesses of the Czechoslovak press, and Dubček assured them of his fidelity to socialism and to the alliance with the Soviet Union. When he returned home, he tried ineffectually to rein in the press, but for the next five months, he never imposed censorship.

Dubček's critics later pointed to a series of errors which left him naked in the face of his enemies. First, he should have purged the party leadership of all Novotný's supporters. The most notorious were removed, but most survived, and they abandoned Dubček the moment the Soviet tanks entered Prague. He should also have called the 14th party conference immediately, to elect a new Central Committee and Praesidium. Finally, he should have played as hard as Brezhnev – or as hard as Gomułka in Poland in 1956.

He was, it appears, too nice to do any of these things. Quite adept enough a politician to outmanoeuvre Novotný's band of thugs, and strong enough to hold fast to his reform programme until the Soviet troops came to arrest him, he was not tough enough to win the sort of bare-knuckled fight that soon broke out around him. He was also, apparently, too kind – he hated hurting people – and too democratic to purge the party and government of his enemies without going through the due democratic process first. His opponents were not so moderate when they took power – and neither was Mikhail Gorbachev, in the USSR, 20 years later.

As the spring wore on, the press used its new liberty to examine every corner of recent Czechoslovak history, to debate every aspect of current policy – from economic reform to the need for the country to remain in the Warsaw Pact. They paid particular attention to the abuses of Gottwald and Novotný. The Prague show trial was examined in detail, and the whole dossier of Stalin's crimes was reopened. Nothing was sacred, including the persons of Alexander Dubček, who did not mind ridicule or criticism, and Leonid Brezhnev, who did.

Party political life abruptly revived. The rumps of the Socialist and Peasants' parties, which had been wholly subservient to the Communists since 1948, suddenly demanded that they be allowed to recover their independence. Communists as well as opposition figures began to demand that the party give up its 'leading role'. The Action Programme was soon left far behind.

Abandoning the doctrine of the party's 'leading role' would be to abandon one of the basic tenets of Leninism, and the warnings from Moscow, Warsaw, Berlin and Budapest grew ever shriller. In response, Czechoslovak reformers demanded that Dubček advance the reforms further and faster than he had planned. Dubček needed their support against the conservatives who were still entrenched in the Central Committee and in the government, not to mention in the bureaucracy, so he allowed himself and his programme to be pushed along by the reformers. On 30 May, Novotný and several of his closest associates were expelled from the Central Committee and from the party. The reformers then demanded that Dubček convoke an extraordinary party conference. After prolonged hesitation, he finally agreed, and the electoral process got under way. The Slovak party was to hold its conference on 26 August and the Czechoslovak party on 9 September, and both looked certain to be triumphs for the reformers. One reason for the Soviet invasion was to forestall them.

In May and June, the Warsaw Pact held military manoeuvres of unprecedented scope in Czechoslovakia. Described as 'limited staff exercises', they amounted to a full-scale invasion. Hundreds of thousands of Soviet and other Pact troops moved into the country to practise defending it against Germany – and they stayed after the manoeuvres were over.

On 27 June, Ludvík Vaculík published his 'Two-Thousand Word Manifesto', signed by 70 leading writers and intellectuals, sports personalities, artists and other public figures. They all pledged their full support for the reform programme and urged the government to accelerate it. The manifesto said:

> There has been great alarm recently over the prospect of foreign forces interfering in our development. Whatever superior forces may face us, all we can do is stick to our own positions, behave decently and start nothing ourselves. We can show our government that we will stand by it, with weapons if need be, if it will do what we give it a mandate to do.

The appearance of this manifesto was probably the most significant cause of the Soviets' invasion of Czechoslovakia. Although it was couched in terms of support for Dubček, it was also a warning that this support depended on a continuation of the reforms. Clearly, its signatories expected these to go much further, and the Soviets, probably rightly, saw it as an incitement to counter-revolution. The manifesto was reprinted in papers throughout the country and was hugely popular.

Ten days later, the Warsaw Pact summoned Dubček to answer for his sins at a summit in Warsaw on 15 July. He declined politely, citing previous engagements and the pressure of work. So the Pact sent him a letter:

> The development of events in your country deeply disquiets us. The rise of reaction against your party and the bases of the social system in Czechoslovakia, supported by imperialism, threaten to lead your country away from the path of socialism, and, as a consequence, is a danger to the interests of the whole socialist system.

The letter went on to say, 'We have no intention to intervene in such matters as are the purely internal concern of the party and of your state' – but the real meaning was clearly just the opposite. It was a most extreme warning, and Dubček took it most seriously.

The Soviets then invited the entire Czechoslovak Praesidium to Moscow, but Dubček and his colleagues once again declined: Daniel would not go willingly into the lion's den. Finally, since Dubček would not go to Brezhnev, Brezhnev was constrained to come to Dubček. The three-day meeting began on 27 July at Čierna nad Tisou, a railhead just inside the Czechoslovak border with the Soviet Union.

Brezhnev submitted Dubček to a torrent of abuse, accusing him of every crime from treachery to counter-revolution. Dubček resisted the bullying as best he could, supported by his colleagues – including the president, Ludvík Svoboda, a general who had served in the Red Army during the war, and whom the Soviets had expected to take their side. The two delegations failed utterly to agree on anything, except to hold a Warsaw Pact meeting in Bratislava a week later. That meeting also failed to resolve the differences between the two sides, though the Soviets finally agreed to pull their troops out of Czechoslovakia.

The Čierna confrontation was reminiscent of the dramatic events of 19 October 1956, when Khrushchev had flown into Warsaw to berate Gomułka and the Polish Politburo for defying the Soviet Union (*see* Chapter 1). Dubček was a much less forceful personality than Gomułka. He never thought of defying Brezhnev (although this Soviet leader was less formidable than Khrushchev), nor did he order the army to defend the country. He was more like Hungary's Imre Nagy in 1956, who until the last moment refused to believe that the Soviets would invade and did nothing to stop them (*see* Chapter 4).

The invasion of Czechoslovakia occurred during the night of 20/21 August 1968. About 400,000 troops were involved, including contingents of 50,000 Poles, 20,000 East Germans, 20,000

Hungarians and 10,000 Bulgarians. A 100-man task force that had flown in the night before seized Prague airport, and then giant An-12 cargo planes, one landing every minute, delivered an armoured division to the capital. Three columns of tanks were sent into Prague: one occupied the party headquarters, one the prime minister's offices, the third surrounded the residence of the president, the Hradčany Castle. A meeting of the Praesidium was in session there when the Soviets entered. The troops made them all, including Dubček, lie on the floor; one Praesidium member commented later, 'For some time, all we could see of our allies was their boots.'

Prague Radio broadcast a statement by the invaders:

> Responding to the request for help from leading party and state leaders of Czechoslvakia who have remained faithful to socialism, we instructed our armed forces to go to the support of the working class and all the people of Czechoslovakia, to defend their socialist gains, which are increasingly threatened by plots by domestic and foreign reactionary forces. This action is based on the collective commitment that the Communist and workers' parties of the fraternal countries adopted at Bratislava, and on the commitment to support, strengthen and defend the socialist gains of every nation and to stand up to imperialist plots.
>
> Counter-revolutionaries incited and supported by imperialists are grasping for power. Anti-socialist forces that seized positions in the press, radio and television have attacked and smeared everything created by the hands of industrious Czechs and Slovaks in the 20-year-long struggle for socialism . . .

On the afternoon of 21 August, Czechoslovak security men came to arrest Dubček and his colleagues; they were taken to the airport and loaded into a Soviet plane. Through the windows, they observed four men apparently carrying a corpse towards the plane, and concluded that their turn would be next – until the 'corpse' started struggling. It was Oldřich Černík, the prime minister, who had been arrested at the government building but had refused to move. The prisoners were first flown to Poland, where they were incarcerated for 60 hours without being allowed to wash, shave or change. Then they were flown on to Moscow. They had assumed that they would be shot, but instead they were driven straight to the Kremlin and taken to a large room, where they waited. Then Brezhnez marched in, followed by the Soviet Politburo, and said, 'How nice to see you gentlemen.'

President Svoboda, whom the Soviets wished to retain in office, had been brought to Moscow separately. He refused to talk to them without Dubček and the others, a refusal they believe saved their lives.

In fact, they were saved by the Soviets' incompetence: the invasion had been launched without any political preparation. The Tass statement announcing the invasion had been even more categoric than the one broadcast in Prague:

> Tass is authorized to state that party and government leaders of the Czechoslovak Socialist Republic have asked the Soviet Union and other allied states to render the fraternal Czechoslovak people urgent assistance, including assistance with armed forces.

Everyone suspected that this statement was true, that a number of old-line party leaders had indeed offered their services to the Soviets – but then when they saw the unanimity of the people's opposition, they changed their minds. Even the most reactionary party leaders declined pressing invitations by the Soviets to form a new government, which was intended to resemble the Kádár clique they had installed in Budapest in 1956. It was a major defeat for the Soviets.

It was evident that the USSR had either to deal with Dubček or to impose a military government, occupying Czechoslovakia like Hitler 30 years earlier. The choice was put to Dubček and his colleagues, and they were browbeaten into signing a 'Moscow protocol' approving the invasion. It preserved the appearance of national independence and Dubček's Action Programme. The prisoners were then to be sent back to Prague. One of their colleagues, František Kriegel, a Jew and a dedicated reformer, was detained by the KGB, which intended to put him on trial. The others refused to leave without him, and the Soviets grudgingly released him.

The Czechs and Slovaks put up an astonishing resistance to the occupiers. Radio stations stayed on the air by moving their studios around the country and using army transmitters; newspapers continued to appear. The occupying armies were confused and harassed: every street sign and house number was removed; shops and farmers refused to sell supplies to the invaders; and railway workers so tied up the rail network that all supplies had to be transported by road or air. Václav Havel recounts that, in the provincial city where he was caught by the invasion, the 'Tramps' – a 100-strong gang of local thugs who had been terrorizing the populace for months – put themselves at the service of the local authorities and provided security for the mayor and other officials.

Two days after the invasion, the elected delegates to the national party conference met clandestinely in a factory in Prague, guarded by the workers' militia. That was another sign of the times: the militias had been reputed to be completely loyal to the Stalinists. A new Central Committee was elected, and the delegates restated their complete loyalty to Dubček and his government.

For a while, it was possible to hope that Dubček would out-manoeuvre the Soviets. It was not to be. The clandestine radio stations and newspapers were closed down, and the Stalinists resumed ccontrol of local government and industry. Over the next eight months, Dubček was progressively worn down, forced to cede position after position. His closest collaborators were removed one after another, to be replaced by party leaders who were prepared to do the Soviets' bidding. The people's resistance was steadily eroded, and by the end of the year, there was very little hope left.

On 16 January 1969, a young Czech student, Jan Palach, set himself on fire at the Wenceslas statue in the central square of Prague, in protest against the occupation. He died three days later, and his funeral, like Masaryk's in 1948, was marked by an immense, mournful demonstration. At the end of March, a Czechoslovak ice-hockey team beat the Soviet national team in a European tournament in Stockholm, and sports fans seized the occasion for a riot, looting the Aeroflot office in Wenceslas Square. Two weeks later, on 17 April, Dubček was removed from office and given the position of chairman of the National Assembly (a post he returned to in triumph in 1989); he was replaced as party leader by Gustáv Husák.

The sad decline continued. On the first anniversary of the invasion, 20/21 August 1969, huge demonstrations in Prague were broken up by police with great violence. Tanks patrolled the city, and the next day, the government published emergency laws suspending all civil rights and giving police unlimited power. In a final humiliation, Dubček, as chairman of the National Assembly, was obliged to sign the decrees.

He was removed from the Praesidium of the party on 25 September but still refused to recant, and three weeks later, he lost his job as chairman of the parliament. Sent to Turkey as ambassador in January 1970, possibly in the hope that he would defect, he stayed there until the end of May and then returned home. He was finally expelled from the party on 27 June and was later given a menial job as a forestry worker in Bratislava. There he remained, ignored but not forgotten, for 19 years.

The Brezhnev doctrine

The Soviets' justification for the intervention was the 'Brezhnev Doctrine', which stipulated that if a Communist government gets into trouble, other Communist states may come to the rescue. The doctrine was greeted with much indignation in the West, although Western powers had enforced their own versions – the Truman Doctrine and the Monroe Doctrine – on numerous occasions: in Greece in 1944 and 1946, for instance, and in the Dominican Republic in 1965, three years before the Soviet invasion of Czechoslovakia. President Bush enforced the Monroe Doctrine again, in Panama, in 1989.

Brezhnev spelled out his doctrine a month after the event:

> The weakening of any of the links in the world socialist system directly affects all the socialist countries, which cannot look on indifferently when this happens. Thus, with talk about the right of nations to self-determination, the anti-socialist elements in Czechoslovakia actually covered up a demand for so-called neutrality and Czechoslovakia's withdrawal from the socialist community. However, the implementation of 'self-determination' of that kind, or, in other words, the detaching of Czechoslovakia from the socialist community, would have come into conflict with Czechoslovakia's vital interests and would have been detrimental to the other socialist states. Such 'self-determination', as a result of which NATO troops would have been able to come up to the Soviet borders, while the community of European socialist countries would have been rent, would have encroached, in actual fact, upon the vital interests of the peoples of these countries and would be in fundamental conflict with the right of these people to socialist self-determination.

That doctrine remained in force for the next 20 years, until it was abandoned by Mikhail Gorbachev.

The lost years

Gustáv Husák had become first secretary of the Communist party, and took over the presidency when Svoboda retired in 1975. He purged the party, national government, local government, the police, the army, the unions, every professional association, every newspaper, radio and television service, the management of every company and every authority of any description. For Husák, those who were not for him were against him. Czechoslovakia was governed by timid mediocrities, who directed every aspect of national life. Only Romania was more venal, more terrorized.

Husák ensured that there were sufficient consumer goods and foodstuffs in the shops. Czechoslovak industry, inherited from the old republic, was still efficient enough to provide something approaching a tolerable life for the people, and the government, terrified of a new uprising, put consumerism ahead of the usual Stalinist objectives of industralization. The ploy was effective: Czechs and Slovaks, apart from a handful of brave and gallant rebels, remained quiescent for 20 years.

Czechoslovakia had a more modern economy than Poland or Hungary, and after East Germany, it was the most prosperous of the Communist states within the Eastern bloc. However, it suffered from severe environmental pollution, and its industries, once the equal of those in Austria and Germany, fell steadily behind. Consumerism cannot be sustained indefinitely without investment, and Czechoslovakia did not invest. Like Hungary and the Soviet Union itself, it was declining into a Third World economy.

The Czechoslovak government remained wholly subservient to the USSR after 1968, obeying the Soviets in all things, suppressing dissidents and praising the great Soviet Motherland on every occasion. Dubček and the other leaders of the Prague Spring played little part in the dissident movement between 1968 and 1989 – they were too closely watched. The torch was carried by non-Communist intellectuals – Czechoslovakia's most prominent artists, writers, journalists and film makers – who protested against the regime's abuses of human rights. Their gospel was the Helsinki

Final Act, signed by every nation in Europe (except Albania) in 1975, which proclaimed the whole panoply of democratic rights.

The dissidents were constantly harassed, jailed, stripped of their positions and forced to work at menial jobs. In 1977, a group of them (and Prokop Drtina, the former minister of justice in the government of 1946–48) issued a statement of principle that they called 'Charter 77'. It was largely the work of the playwright Václav Havel who, refusing to leave the country, eventually served a total of five years in jail for dissidence.

In *Disturbing the Peace*, a book of interviews with his translator Paul Wilson, prepared before the revolution of 1989, Havel describes this period:

> None of us knows all the potentialities that slumber in the spirit of the population, or all the ways in which that population can surprise us when there is the right interplay of events, both visible and invisible. Who would have believed – at a time [in 1967] when the Novotný regime was corroding away because the entire nation was behaving like Svejks* – that half a year later [during the Prague spring of 1968] the same society would display a genuine civic-mindedness, and that a year later this recently apathetic, sceptical and demoralized society would stand up with such courage and intelligence to a foreign power! And who would have suspected that, after scarcely a year had gone by, this same society would, as swiftly as the wind blows, lapse back into a state of deep demoralization far worse than its original one! After all these experiences, one must be very careful about coming to any conclusions about the way we are, or what can be expected of us ... People withdrew into themselves and stopped taking an interest in public affairs. An era of apathy and widespread demoralization began, an era of grey, everyday, totalitarian consumerism.

The velvet revolution

Husák retired as party general secretary at the end of 1987, though he remained president, and was replaced by Miloš Jakeš, one of the small group of party leaders who had welcomed the invasion in

* The eponymous hero of *The Good Soldier Svejk* by Jaroslav Hašek (1883–1923) is variously interpreted as a Czech patriot making fun of the Austrian rulers and as the 'little man' struggling against bureaucracy and surviving adversity by bending with the winds.

1968. The regime was more than a little surprised when Gorbachev was cheered in the streets during a visit to Prague early in 1988. When his spokesman was asked, 'What is the difference between the Prague Spring and Gorbachev's *glasnost*?' he replied, 'Twenty years.'

During the 1980s, there was a revival of Catholicism in both the Czech and Slovak halves of the country. The Church had been ruthlessly persecuted since the Communist coup, but it remained one of the centres of opposition to the regime. It was never as important as the Church in Poland, but it played a considerable role, and that role increased while dissidents were harassed and jailed.

Despite the continuing changes in Gorbachev's Soviet Union, the Czechoslovak government had no intention of loosening the reins. In October 1988, the prime minister Lubomír Štrougal was forced to resign. He had been the leading advocate of economic reform in the government, and although he never proposed to go as far as Hungary (*see* Chapter 4), his suggestions were rejected by the Politburo. Štrougal had been one of the senior quislings in 1968, one of the handful of Czechoslovak leaders ready to betray nation and party from the beginning. His newly discovered 'reformist' intentions were therefore a significant development. He was replaced by Ladislav Adamec, who later claimed to be a reformer himself.

On 21 August 1988, there was a small organized demonstration in Prague commemorating the 20th anniversary of the invasion. It turned into a march of about 20,000 people, but was firmly repressed by the police. On 28 October – the 70th anniversary of Czechoslovakia's independence from Austria – there was a demonstration of about 5000 people in the capital, called by Charter 77; police dispersed it with tear gas, water cannon and riot clubs. On 10 December, International Human Rights Day, Charter 77 organized yet another demonstration, and this time the police did not interfere. Havel told the crowd optimistically, 'Our government has finally recognized that it has to be more tolerant.'

The government itself had marked the 20th anniversary of the invasion by publishing virulent attacks on Dubček, evidently fearing that some new upheaval might bring him back to power. However, the following November, he was allowed to travel abroad for the first time in years, to accept an honorary degree at the University of Bologna in Italy. During his stay there, he gave several newspaper interviews and made a speech at the degree ceremony in which he vigorously defended the policies of the Prague Spring and, by implication, attacked everything that had happened since.

In 1989, the Czechoslovaks watched astonished as Poland voted out the Communist party and Hungary rehabilitated Imre Nagy, prepared for free elections and, in September, threw open its borders, permitting East Germans to travel freely to Austria. These events led to a series of ever-larger demonstrations in East Germany and, in early November, the collapse of the DDR government and the opening of the Berlin Wall. Throughout all this, Czechoslovakia remained quiet. As late as 20 August, the government was so firmly in control, and public apathy so great, that Havel and other Charter 77 leaders advised students against demonstrating on the anniversary of the 1968 invasion, and absented themselves from Prague, to avoid arrest. There was a small demonstration, all the same: students lit candles at the foot of King Wenceslas's statue, and the police briskly moved them on.

Then on 17 November, 25,000 students, inspired by the fall of the Berlin Wall, demonstrated in Prague. The crowd was broken up by police with considerable violence, and many demonstrators were beaten and arrested. Rumour had it that one, called Martin Smid, had been killed. The next day, there was a rally against police brutality, and the demonstrations continued every day thereafter. On 20 November, 200,000 demonstrators of all ages and classes massed in Prague demanding the government's resignation. Schools and universities closed, and a new phenomenon appeared: the crowds avoided attacking the police; and the police and military forces, large numbers of whom were guarding bridges and public buildings, conspicuously refrained from trying to break up the crowds. For the first time, too, the demonstration was properly reported on television. There were also demonstrations in Ostrava near the Polish border, in Brno, the capital of Moravia, and in Bratislava, the capital of Slovakia.

The government vacillated. It produced two Martin Smids, both alive and well, and was able to prove that nobody had been killed on the 17th. The crowds were not mollified. The party could no longer count on the police and army to suppress the demonstrators, and every day the crowds in Wenceslas Square grew larger. Havel and other dissidents, who had established their headquarters in the Magic Lantern theatre on Wenceslas Square, addressed the crowds from a balcony. They formed a committee of opposition groups which they called 'Civic Forum' and modelled on the New Forum in the DDR. A priest who had been imprisoned by the regime appeared on the balcony to read a letter from Cardinal Tomášek: 'There can be no confidence in the leadership of a state that refuses to tell the people the truth and give them the rights and freedoms that are common even in Third World countries. We can wait no longer.' Miloš Jakeš went on television on the 21st to appeal for calm and to warn that 'there are boundaries that should not be overstepped.' Then, in a first concession by the government, Prime Minister Adamec met some of the Civic Forum leaders.

Civic Forum called a two-hour general strike for 27 November. On the 22nd, the crowd in Wenceslas Square had grown to 250,000, and in Bratislava, Dubček addressed a rally. Two days later, he boarded a bus and travelled to Prague, joining Havel on the balcony to address a crowd of 500,000 and demand the immediate resignation of the government. It was his apotheosis or, rather, his resurrection. He told the crowd that he still held to 'socialism with a human face', that he could see that the ideals of the Prague Spring were still alive, and that he loved them all. He added: 'An old wise man said, "If there once was light, why should there be darkness again?" Let us act to bring the light back again.' The whole scene was televised live: the government had lost control of the media.

Victory came that evening: first, Miloš Jakeš, the party secretary, resigned; then the entire Politburo; then the government. They had hoped that these changes would save the party; they were mistaken. The Communist state withered away – though not in the manner Marx had predicted. The Communists deluded themselves with the belief that the opposition was limited to the intellectuals and students in Prague, that the mass of the population in other towns and in the countryside would not join the movement, would prefer the certainties of 'totalitarian consumerism' to the uncharted waters of democracy and a market economy. It was, after all, the workers' militias from factories in the Prague suburbs which had marched into the city centre in February 1948 to ensure the success of the Communist coup. Civic Forum and its supporters were quite aware of the danger; students from Prague University fanned out into the factories, mines and collective farms to persuade the workers to join the strike.

On 25 November, an opposition rally was held that the authorities numbered at between 500,000 and 800,000 people. Havel and Dubček addressed the crowd again. But this time so did Adamec (still acting prime minister), promising dialogue between the government and Civic Forum. The next day, there was a further purge in the party Politburo: three surviving hardliners were dropped. It was much too late. On 27 November, the whole of Czechoslovakia came to a halt for Civic Forum's two-hour strike, and immense demonstrations were staged to denounce the government. The party's hope was in vain: it was repudiated by the entire country.

A reformist Communist, Karel Urbanek, was named general secretary. Adamec promised a new coalition government and, the day after the strike, opened formal negotiations with the opposition; he also promised free elections, an end to the party's 'leading role' and a host of other reforms. The Politburo then declared that the Soviet invasion in 1968 had been wrong. On 4 December, at a Warsaw Pact meeting in Warsaw, the organization itself and the Soviet Union formally admitted that the invasion had been an error, and agreed to begin negotiations with Czechoslovakia on the withdrawal of Soviet troops. It was not enough.

The day before, on Sunday, 3 December, Adamec had announced his new government, consisting totally of Communists or fellow-travellers. Civic Forum rejected it at once and threatened a new strike, and on the 4th, 200,000 people demonstrated again against the government, demanding its resignation even before it took office. The party's prevarications had by now provoked Civic Forum to turn into a political party, and it published a programme that proposed the restoration of Czechoslovakia as a democratic state.

The government resigned on 7 December. A minor functionary from Slovakia, Marian Calfa, became prime minister and opened negotiations with Civic Forum on forming a real coalition. Its members were announced three days later: of the 21 ministers, only ten were Communists – and several of those were only nominal party members, reformers acceptable to Civic Forum. A leading member of Charter 77, Jiří Dienstbier, became foreign minister; another, Jan Carnogursky, who had just been released from prison, became first deputy prime minister; and the minister of finance, Václav Klaus, was a noted radical. The ministry of the interior was abolished; and the police placed under the jurisdiction of a ministerial committee including Civic Forum. The Forum's last demand was that President Gustáv Husák resign, which he did immediately after he swore in the new government on 10 December. Although the Communists kept the premiership and the ministries of defence, trade and economic planning, their position was so weak that they had, in fact, lost all control of the government.

The movement that had begun with a students' demonstration on 17 November, ended in victory 23 days later. No one had been killed, and after the first night of police brutality, everyone – police and opposition together – comported themselves with absolute propriety. Havel called it the 'velvet revolution'.

Parliament met to repeal a host of repressive legislation, amended the constitution to end the leading role of the Communist party, expelled former government leaders and co-opted a number of prominent opposition figures, most notably Alexander Dubček. Prime Minister Calfa was a Slovak and so, under a national convention, the president had to be a Czech. Dubček was a Slovak and therefore ineligible. Instead, parliament elected him chairman – and Václav Havel became president.

Czechoslovakia had rejected Communism, and the former dissidents were now in a position to ensure that the transition would be rapid and honest. Free elections were promised for the spring of 1990, and Havel took up his duties with a New Year's Day speech setting out the country's economic difficulties, and with a call for national unity.

> For the past 40 years on this day you have heard my predecessors utter different variations on the same theme, about how our country is prospering, how many more billion tons of steel we have produced, how happy we are, how much we trust our government and what beautiful prospects lie ahead of us. I do not think that you put me into this office so that I, of all people, should also lie to you.
>
> Our country is not prospering. The great creative and spiritual potential of our nation is not being used to its full potential. Whole sectors of industry are producing things in which

no one is interested, while the things we need are in short supply.

The state, which calls itself the 'state of the working people', is humiliating and exploiting the workers. Our outdated economy is squandering energy, of which we are in short supply. A country which could once be proud of the standard of education of its people spends so little on education that today it occupies 72nd place in the world. We have laid waste to our soil and the rivers and the forests that our forefathers bequeathed to us, and we have the worst environment in the whole of Europe today . . .

The worst thing is that we are living in a decayed moral environment. We have become morally ill, because we have become accustomed to saying one thing and thinking another. We have learned not to believe in anything, not to have consideration for one another and only to look after ourselves . . .

When I talk about a decayed moral environment . . . I mean all of us, because all of us have become accustomed to the totalitarian system, accepting it as an unalterable fact and thereby kept it running. None of us is merely a victim of it, because all of us helped to create it together . . .

It would be very unwise to see the sad legacy of the past 40 years as something alien to us, handed down to us by some distant relatives. On the contrary, we must accept this legacy as something we have brought upon ourselves. If we can accept this, then we will understand that it is up to all of us to do something about it. We cannot lay all the blame on those who ruled us before, not only because this would not be true but also because it could detract from the responsibility each of us now faces – the responsibility to act on our own initiative, freely, sensibly and quickly . . .

Havel announced that Czechoslovakia would abandon the arms trade, and it immediately stopped exporting Semtex, a brand of plastic explosive much favoured by terrorists. In January 1990, the Communist collapse accelerated again: Calfa and two of the other Communist ministers resigned from the party, and the party was obliged to give up 90 of the seats reserved for it in parliament. Czechoslovakia – like Poland but unlike the other East European countries – was now effectively non-Communist. The party, like others in Eastern Europe, held a congress which purged those hardliners who had not already resigned.

In February 1990, Havel visited Moscow on a state visit, as president of the republic. The Soviets agreed to withdraw all their 73,500 troops by July 1991, 24 years after they had first arrived. Previously, Havel had often joked about his first 'meeting' with Gorbachev: he had been walking his dog in Prague when Gorbachev visited the city in 1988, and he had watched the Soviet leader drive by. After he told this story to Gorbachev himself in Moscow, Havel reported: 'He laughed and told me that, at that time, he did not feel good in Prague. He felt the air was suffocating. He felt the manifold attention and hopes pinned on him. He was aware of the deep dissatisfaction of society with the regime.' It is the nearest Gorbachev has come to admitting that he had anticipated and welcomed the overthrow of Communism in Eastern Europe.

Political problems between Czechs and Slovaks re-emerged. They had never disappeared, of course: the fight between Novotný and Dubček in the mid-1960s had been partly due to the old dispute. When, in 1990, parliament decided to change the country's name, abandoning the designation 'Socialist Republic of Czechoslovakia', Slovaks demanded that the hyphen be restored, that the country be named the 'Republic of Czecho-Slovakia', as it had been before the war. In the end, parliament voted for the 'Czech and Slovak Federative Republic'. This debate was a first sign of the strains that the country would face: many Slovaks want independence. The Poles in Těšín and the Hungarians in southern Slovakia also remain potential sources of irredentist trouble. The federation is not as shaky as Yugoslavia's, but its survival is not assured.

A further question was whether to punish the men who had invited the Soviet Union to invade Czechoslovakia in 1968, the police who had tortured and the judges who had imprisoned dissidents – the people responsible for the long tyranny that the country suffered from 1948 to 1989. What about the police, judges and politicians who had directed the Slanský trial in 1952? Slanský was perhaps a criminal and a murderer himself, but his trial and execution had been a judicial murder, and most of his fellow-defendants had been innocent of all crimes. Slanský's son is now Czechoslovakia's ambassador to the Soviet Union: can he not demand that justice be done and his father's murderers prosecuted? On 12 May 1990, a demonstration of 100,000 people in Prague, the largest since the revolution, demanded such justice on past oppressors. It is worth noting that Gustáv Husák, the principal leader of the regime from 1968 to 1988, was himself a victim of the purges, and had spent ten years in prison.

In the parliamentary elections in June 1990, Havel's Civic Forum and its Slovak ally won a large majority in both parts of the country. The Slovak nationalists were roundly defeated, and so were the Slovak Christian Democrats, who had hoped to build on Slovakia's Catholic traditions. The Communists were reduced to an inconsequential minority.

Czechoslovakia's new leaders could see that the post-Communist era was going to be difficult. To begin with, Czechoslovakia's industrial position was much weaker than it looked. The statistics showed that, although the gross national product was relatively high and its industrial production relatively impressive, its industries, like those of East Germany, were in fact outdated, inefficient and badly managed. They were fit only to produce goods for export to the USSR, and even the Soviets were beginning to reject the shoddiness, the lack of variety and, often, the complete unsuitability of the goods sent to them. Czechoslovakia had to turn to the West, if only to earn enough hard currency to pay for its essential imports, including oil, but it had very little to sell.

Some economists proposed that the country should simply revert to pre-war practices, and two major industries were offered as models. Before the war, one of the most important manufacturers and exporters of shoes in the world was at Zlin, in Moravia, founded by Tomáš Bata in 1894. His son fled the country in 1938 and, after the firm was nationalized in 1945, moved the company headquarters to Canada, where it continues to thrive – the largest shoe company in the world, selling more than 300 million pairs a year. The Communist government did everything in its power to eradicate the memory of the Bata family, even, in 1948, changing the town's name to Gottwaldov, after the party leader. (It was changed back to Zlin immediately after the 'velvet revolution'.)

In December 1989, Bata's son returned to Zlin for the first time in 50 years, a demonstration that the Communist reign in Eastern Europe (unlike in the Soviet Union) had not lasted long enough to eradicate memories of earlier times. He opened negotiations with the government to recover the company, which fervently hoped that he would bring capital and competence back to Zlin.

The second example was the brewing industry. Two brewing centres in Czechoslovakia, Plzeň (Pilsen) and Budweis, have given their names to beers sold throughout the world – or at least, in the case of Budweis, throughout North America. Anheuser Busch, of St Louis, Missouri, which derived from Budweis in the 19th century, still honours its founders' agreement with the original firm and does not sell Budweiser in Europe. Communist Budweiser and Pilsener beers are just as good as they ever were, but their marketing leaves much to be desired. Now, perhaps in association with their American relatives, they may reform themselves.

Czechoslovakia will face even more difficulties coping with the environmental disaster of the Communist years. Open-pit lignite and uranium mining in the northwest of the country, formerly the Sudetenland, has devastated the landscape, as it has over the border in East Germany and Poland. Power plants burning brown coal pollute the atmosphere and destroy vegetation. The incidence of lung disease and cancer is far higher in these mining regions than anywhere else in Europe – except in the mining and industrial zones of East Germany, Poland and Romania. It will be years before Czechoslovakia recovers.

4 Hungary

For 12 days in 1956, Budapest lived through one of the great dramas of 20th-century Europe. The city had seen revolution and conquest before, and Russians had fought Germans through the city as recently as 1944, but that was in a time of war. The atrocity in the Budapest of 1956 was that these were times of peace, and the uprising was a people's revolt. The Soviets suppressed the Hungarians as the Germans had suppressed the Poles in Warsaw in 1944.

The Hungarian uprising and its ending were the central events in Eastern Europe between 1945 and 1989. What happened in Hungary reaffirmed the power and utter ruthlessness of Soviet Communism and demonstrated that, unless the USSR itself changed beyond recognition, the Soviets would not allow the countries conquered by Stalin to recover their independence. This was later called the Brezhnev Doctrine (*see* Chapter 3, p. 102), but that dull *apparatchik*, who sent the tanks into Prague in 1968 and Kabul in 1979, was following faithfully in the footsteps of Stalin and Khrushchev.

Another lesson was learned in Budapest, which was to be repeated in Romania in 1989. Without Soviet protection, the Communists and their police had the choice of surrendering unconditionally to a popular uprising – or being torn to pieces by the mob. In October 1956, scores of Hungarian secret police were shot or lynched by demonstrators. Photographs of the killings haunted Communist officials, and in 1989, in Eastern Europe, the regimes and their police all preferred surrender, except Ceauşescu's *Securitate* in Romania. The people of Bucharest, in December 1989, avenged the Hungarians who had overthrown their own, odious tyranny, and then succumbed to the overwhelming force of the Red Army.

The conquest

Hungary suffered frightful losses in the Second World War. The army lost 400,000 dead, and scores of thousands of civilians were killed as the *Wehrmacht* fought its last battles across the Hungarian plain. The Germans made their last stand in Budapest, which was besieged from November 1944 until February 1945, when the Red Army finally fought its way into the ruined city. Hungary already knew the atrocities of occupation: in four months during the summer of 1944, Eichmann had shipped 437,000 Hungarian Jews to Auschwitz. When the Soviets at last conquered the country, a further 250,000 Hungarians were carried east to Siberia, half of them never to return.

It was a heavy price to pay to defend the Holy Crown of St Stephen, the patron saint and first king (997–1038) of the Magyars. Until the disaster of 1945, Hungarians believed and taught their children that medieval Hungary at its fullest extent and all the country's subsequent conquests still belonged to them, whatever those territories' inhabitants might think. St Stephen's crown is the symbol of this mystic imperium.*

Hungary was a partner with Austria in the Austro-Hungarian empire from 1867 until its dissolution in 1918, ruling Slovakia as well as northern Yugoslavia and half of what is now Romania. Magyar rule over the various Slavs was oppressive and unpopular; the governing hereditary aristocracy treated their vassals as serfs or cattle.

Impelled by its dreams of ancient glory, Hungary played a leading role in starting both world wars. In 1914, the Hungarians wished to extend their empire over the southern Slavs by conquering Serbia, and lost everything in their defeat. In the Treaty of Trianon in 1920, they were restricted to their ancestral heartlands, and 3 million Magyars in Romania, Czechoslovakia and Yugoslavia were abruptly subjected to foreign rule.

Hungary was proclaimed a republic, independent of Austria, in the general collapse of 1918. It then became the second European

* At the end of the war, the crown, a medieval treasure of incalculable value, fell into American hands and was locked up in Fort Knox. It remained there until President Carter had it returned to Budapest in 1978.

state, after Russia, to suffer a Communist revolution: Béla Kun set up a Hungarian Soviet in Budapest in 1919, which survived precariously for only 133 days, when it was overthrown by the Romanians. Later, in 1921, the last Habsburg king, Charles IV twice tried to recover his throne. He was defeated both times, but there remained sufficient monarchical sentiment in Hungary for the political parties to agree to a bizarre compromise: Charles was deposed but the monarchy was not abolished; instead, a regency was proclaimed. The regent was Admiral Miklós Horthy who ruled the country until he was deposed by the *Gestapo* in the last months of World War II.

Between 1919 and 1938, Hungary was one of the principal sources of instability in Europe. It became a thoroughly Fascist dictatorship in the 1920s, and ceaselessly plotted to recover the lands lost in the war. To contain Hungary, Tomáš Masaryk, the president of Czechoslovakia, formed the 'Little Entente', an alliance with Romania and Yugoslavia, which was in turn allied with France. Hungary was thus isolated and resentful, and saw Hitler as its natural ally.

In 1938, following the first partition of Czechoslovakia, Hungary annexed southern Slovakia, an area principally inhabited by Magyars. In March of the following year, when Hitler occupied Bohemia and Moravia and set up Slovakia as a semi-independent client state, Hungary seized Trans-Carpathian Ruthenia, the easternmost Czechoslovak province. In 1940, after the defeat of France, Stalin (then Hitler's ally) claimed Bessarabia and Bukovina from Romania, and Hungary then demanded the return of Transylvania, lost in 1920. Hitler instructed his foreign minister, Ribbentrop, to adjudicate the dispute, and the Hungarians were awarded the northern half of the territory. Finally, when the Germans invaded Yugoslavia in 1941, Hungary annexed the western Banat and some territory on the border with Slovenia. Hungary thus recovered half the lands lost in 1920, as well as 5 million people, only 2 million of whom were Magyar. Hungary's subsequent sufferings under the Communists have doubtless redeemed the country, but its neighbours, formerly its victims, have not forgotten its ruthless aggression of 50 years ago.

Hungary did not enjoy its recovered empire for long. Having endorsed the German–Italian–Japanese treaty in November 1940, it was forced to declare war on the Soviet Union in June 1941, and to send its armies into battle. They were reluctant warriors. The Hungarians lost 130,000 troops at Stalingrad, and as the Red Army drove west, Horthy engaged in frantic secret negotiations with the allies in an attempt to escape going down to defeat with the Third Reich. The *Gestapo* was well informed, and in March 1944, Hitler ordered the occupation of Hungary. Horthy remained regent, but the Nazis installed a pro-German government. Until then, the Jews had escaped the Holocaust, Horthy's government having refused to deport them, but now Eichmann came to Budapest, and 70 per cent of the Hungarian Jewish population were sent to their deaths before Horthy succeeded in stopping the deportations.

The Soviet army crossed the border in October 1944, and Horthy asked for an armistice. The Germans then organized a coup in Budapest, neutralizing Horthy by kidnapping his family and threatening their lives, and appointing Ferenc Szalasi, the head of the Fascist party, the Arrow Cross, as prime minister. The Red Army reached Budapest in December, and the city was under siege until February 1945, German and Soviet troops fighting through the ruins as they had in Stalingrad. Budapest was one of the most badly damaged cities in Europe, its landmarks – such as the parliament and the royal palace – reduced to shells and the centre of the city devastated. The Soviets completed the conquest of Hungary in March. Szalasi escaped with the Crown of St Stephen to Austria, and surrendered to the Americans, who sent him back to face trial (he was executed) and kept the crown. Horthy was allowed to end his days in exile.

The Communist party in Hungary, as in Poland and Romania, was a small and inconsequential organization. Béla Kun and other senior members of the Budapest Soviet had escaped to Moscow but had perished in the purges. Those who had survived were completely loyal to Stalin but were not united among themselves. A Jewish group, led by Matyas Rákosi (who had escaped Kun's fate because he was in a Hungarian jail from 1924 to 1940), was dogmatically Stalinist; its members included Ernö Gero, Milhaly Farkhas and Gábor Peter, who were all from the professional classes.

Imre Nagy, from a peasant family, was far more pragmatic. He had survived the Moscow purges, and then had worked at a

Soviet radio station. László Rajk, a fanatical and ruthless Stalinist, and his deputy János Kádár headed the small Communist resistance movement inside Hungary. None of these last three was Jewish.

Following their usual practice, the Soviets established a 'Hungarian National Independence Front' as soon as they reached Hungary. Although the Communists had little or no public support inside the country – indeed, the memory of the 1919 Budapest Soviet meant that they were even more unpopular in Hungary than they were elsewhere – they were supported by the Red Army, and that was enough. They took only a few positions in the new government, but from the start, they dominated it completely. By the same token, the handful of exiles from Moscow, carried in the baggage of the Red Army, instantly took over the reunited party, relegating the 'insiders' to junior positions.

Imre Nagy, the only leading Communist with any knowledge of rural Hungary, was given the post of minister of agriculture, and he immediately set about redistributing the land. In March 1945, he expropriated Church estates and those belonging to the Esterházy family and other magnates, and handed them over to the peasants. There was, at that stage, no attempt to force them into collectives, and the redistribution made Nagy exceedingly popular.

Stalin had ruled that the Communists in newly liberated Eastern Europe were not to seize power immediately; he preferred coalition governments. The first disagreement between Rákosi, who always conformed to Stalin's wishes, and Rajk, who wanted to establish the party dictatorship immediately, arose at this point. Rákosi prevailed. In December 1945, Hungary held its first completely free elections: the Smallholders' Party won 57 per cent of the vote, the Social Democrats 17.4 per cent and the Communists 16.9 per cent.

A member of the Smallholders' Party, Zoltán Tildy, was made president and another became prime minister; Imre Nagy was appointed minister of the interior, Rákosi was deputy prime minister, and Gábor Peter became head of the security police. A few months later, as Nagy was judged insufficiently ruthless for his job, he was replaced by Rajk. This government had to cope with economic catastrophe. In June 1946, Hungary attained the world record in inflation: the 1931 gold *pengo* was valued at 1.3 quintillion paper *pengos* – that is 1.3 followed by *30* zeros. The government waded through crisis after crisis as the country starved: since the currency was worthless, farmers would not sell to the cities, whose inhabitants survived only by barter.

In 1947, Hungary, like other European countries, was offered Marshall Aid by the United States. Like Poland and Czechoslovakia, Hungary welcomed the offer until Stalin explained that it was an imperialist plot to subjugate the free states of Eastern Europe. The future satellites all declined the aid, and their Communist parties set about consolidating their positions, Rákosi making the celebrated comment that he would apply 'salami tactics' to Hungary – the Communists would take power one slice at a time. Rajk, as minister of the interior, arrested party leaders who opposed him, established a Communist secret police to do his bidding and took complete control of the national police.

New elections were held in August 1947. The Communist party's vote rose to 22.3 per cent, but the Smallholders' Party, which was now little more than a Communist front, lost disastrously. (It got 15 per cent.) Democratic parties won the majority of votes (and seats), but the composition of the parliament was as irrelevant as that of the Constituent Assembly in Russia in 1918. Rákosi in Hungary, like Lenin in Russia, had no time for such things.

In the year following these elections, the last traces of opposition were mopped up, Rajk taking particular care to dispose of all Social Democrats. By the summer of 1948, the Communists controlled everything, and it was time for a purge. First, László Rajk was demoted from minister of the interior to foreign minister; then he was arrested in May 1949, and was tried and hanged the following October. At his trial, he confessed to being an American spy and a traitor.

There has been much debate on the question why Rákosi purged his party and executed Rajk. The initial impetus is clear enough: in June 1948, Stalin had expelled Tito's Yugoslavia from the Cominform, and orders came from Moscow that any Communist leader whose loyalty was in any way suspect should be purged. However, there was no reason why Rajk, a man of great charm and self-assurance who was also a dedicated and ruthless Stalinist, should have been suspected of 'Titoism' except for the fact that he was not a 'Muscovite' – had not spent years in Moscow, like the other party leaders.

The man who arrested Rajk and supervised his trial and confession was his successor as minister of the interior, János Kádár. He visited Rajk in prison and, in a conversation that was recorded, offered him a deal: if he would confess, his life would be spared and he would be allowed to retire in the Soviet Union. Kádár would later betray Imre Nagy in much the same way.

There is no need to weep for László Rajk. If Rákosi had been chosen as the sacrificial victim, like Rudolf Slanský, Czechoslovakia's most prominent Jewish Stalinist, Rajk would have had him tried, convicted and hanged with equal enthusiasm. In the *New York Review of Books* (18 August 1988), István Deak wrote:

> After the revolution of 1956, an exiled Social Democrat – so the anecdote goes – returned to Hungary and met with Mrs Rajk, herself an old Bolshevik, who had been arrested along with her husband (whom she called 'Laci') and spent many years in jail. Rajk's widow talked about the past and about the fate of socialist comrades in the antifascist struggle. One comrade, it turned out, had been killed by the Hungarian fascists, another had died in Auschwitz, and a third had fled into exile in 1956. 'And what about Comrade K?' the Social Democrat inquired. 'Oh, poor Comrade K,' Mrs Rajk answered. 'He was hanged by my poor Laci.'

In 1951, there was a second purge in the party, and this time Kádár was its chief victim. He was arrested, tortured and, though imprisoned, was lucky to escape with his life. Rákosi began planning a third purge in 1952, on Stalin's orders, which this time was to be an anti-Jewish purge, to follow the 'doctors' plot' in Moscow. Its intended victims were saved only by Stalin's death in March 1953. Since Rákosi himself and most of his surviving senior colleagues were Jewish, the identity of those victims must have been a matter of much nervous speculation.

The terror in Hungary was far more violent than anywhere else in Eastern Europe, and proportionately, it was almost as severe as Stalin's purges in the 1930s. Up to 40,000 people were tortured and executed or given long terms of imprisonment, and far larger numbers were persecuted and robbed of their property and livelihoods. The Catholic Church was subjected to particularly ferocious persecution. The primate, Cardinal József Mindszenty, was arrested, tortured, forced to confess to most improbable crimes and sentenced to life imprisonment for treason in 1949. Although he was German, not Magyar, having been born Josef Pehm in 1892, Mindszenty became a symbol of nationalist resistance to Communism. After ridding themselves of this turbulent priest, the Communists set up a subservient Catholic organization, which they called *Pacem in Terris*, and handed over most of the bishoprics to its members.

Matyas Rákosi was Eastern Europe's leading Stalinist. He was a man of enormous ability (for instance, he spoke nine languages), had worked in London, had taken part in the October Revolution in Petrograd and had survived 16 years in Horthy's jails with his faith intact. His position in Hungary was solidly based on his close association with Stalin – and when Stalin died, his power began to fade rapidly.

The economy was by then in serious difficulties. Rákosi had imposed a Soviet model of rapid industrialization upon the country, and he had also begun collectivizing agriculture. Imre Nagy had been removed from the government in 1948, before the Rajk purge, which he had escaped, presumably because Moscow judged him a loyal 'Muscovite'. He protested bitterly at the government's policies, in furious conflicts with Rákosi. Then in June 1953, Rákosi was summoned to Moscow and told to bring Nagy with him.

The Hungarians were confronted by the new Soviet leadership: Beria, Malenkov, Khrushchev, Molotov and Kaganovitch. Beria, the KGB chief, upbraided Rákosi bitterly, denouncing his policies and the fact that he was both prime minister and first secretary of the party. Rákosi tried to defend himself, but was overruled by the Soviet comrades. He was told that he must give up the premiership – and Nagy was to have the job.

It was a striking example of how complete the Kremlin's control of Eastern Europe was. Rákosi did as he was told, and Nagy immediately started reversing his policies. Further collectivization of agriculture was suspended, and when Nagy announced that peasants could take their land back from collective farms if they wished, they promptly did so. The relentless push for heavy industry was also stopped, and it became government policy to improve the standard of living. The Central Committee loyally did an about-face and voted unanimously for these new policies.

Nagy lasted 18 months. Rákosi intrigued ceaselessly in Moscow to regain power. He was helped by the sudden disappearance of Beria: he had taken the lead in overturning Rákosi's government, and since he was now exposed as an American spy and traitor, his policies could now be reversed. A more probable reason for Rákosi's success was that he was able to form an alliance with Khrushchev against Malenkov. These two were the main rivals in the Kremlin, and Malenkov was in favour of economic reform of the sort that Nagy was pursuing in Hungary.

In January 1955, Nagy and Rákosi were once again summoned to Moscow. In the time-honoured tradition, Malenkov, the Soviet reformer, was designated to attack Nagy, the Hungarian reformer, for carrying out the 1953 instructions of the Soviet Politburo. Nagy was berated for causing confusion and unhappiness in the party and told to resign. Back in Budapest, the loyal Central Committee once again reversed itself: Nagy was dismissed – and expelled from the party.

This episode was probably the most important single cause of the 1956 explosion. Hungarian workers and peasants were bitterly angry about the government's sudden reversal. They blamed Rákosi, and cherished the memory of Nagy as the one honest Communist minister. At the same time, a number of the surviving victims of Rákosi's purges returned to Budapest. Nagy had ordered their release though he succeeded in actually freeing only a minority of them, including János Kádár. The former police chief, Gábor Peter, was tried and imprisoned as a scapegoat.

Hungary is a small country and its intellectuals form a small and homogeneous class. Soon all of them had met and heard the purge victims and finally understood that the Rajk trial had been a complete fabrication. They could no longer deceive themselves on the nature of the regime. The chief culprit, Rákosi, was still in power and the ghosts came back to haunt him.

In February 1956, after Khrushchev denounced Stalin in his famous 'secret speech' to the Soviet party's 20th conference, Rákosi's position became rapidly untenable. The crisis deepened progressively, and in July 1956, after the riots in Poznań and the upheavals in the Polish party, Rákosi was removed as first secretary and sent into exile in the soviet Union. He was replaced by Ernö Gero. Nagy demanded that he be restored to the party and his condemnation reversed, but since he refused to recant or to admit any error, the months passed in fruitless negotiation until, in October, the Central Committee at last restored Nagy to his party membership.

At the same time, the party posthumously rehabilitated Rajk, putting all the blame for his murder on Rákosi. On 6 October, after some trouble finding Rajk's body, which had been buried in a remote forest clearing, he was given a state funeral, huge crowds turning out for the occasion and treating the detestable Rajk, in death, as a martyr. It was an ominous event for the regime – as the reburial of Imre Nagy in 1989 was to be – but for the moment, all seemed well.

A week after the funeral, Gero set off to Belgrade, to mend fences with Tito.

The uprising

The climax of the Polish crisis (*see* Chapter 2) occurred on the night of 19 October 1956, when Soviet tanks surrounded Warsaw and Khrushchev flew into the city to confront Gomułka. The Poles were prepared to fight, and at the last moment, Khrushchev backed down. His decision was announced on Sunday 21 October. Two days later, Budapest exploded.

On Monday, 22 October, Hungarian students gathered in their universities to celebrate the Polish victory. They concluded that they, too, should demand reforms from their government, and began to prepare lists of demands. The most comprehensive list was put together by the Technological University for the Building Industry in Budapest, where the students proclaimed a mass demonstration for the next day.

There were 16 points in the students' manifesto, starting with the most fundamental of all: 'We demand the immediate evacuation of all Soviet troops, in conformity with the provisions of the Treaty of Peace*.' The students called for a complete reform of the

* Hungary signed its peace treaty with the allies in Paris in February 1947, accepting the 1920 frontiers, and then ceased, in theory, to be an occupied country.

Communist party and the formation of a new government headed by Imre Nagy, and for Matyas Rákosi, Milhaly Farkhas (another leading Stalinist) and other 'criminal leaders of the Stalin–Rákosi era' to be put on trial. They also demanded free elections, freedom of the press, the restoration of Hungary's traditional emblems and the removal of Stalin's statue overlooking the city. It was a revolutionary manifesto, and even to discuss it meant favouring the overthrow of the regime.

To begin with, the government failed to realize what was happening. Ernö Gero had been in office for just three months. He was another fanatical Stalinist, brilliant, humourless, ruthless and vindictive. Ferociously hardworking, his stomach eaten by ulcers and his eyes failing from overstrain, he had first made a mark for himself during the Spanish Civil War, when he had directed the purge of Trotskyites and other Communists in Catalonia whose loyalty was in doubt. The Kremlin had appointed him to succeed Rákosi because he was absolutely trustworthy, unlike Nagy who showed signs of nationalist heresy. Gero's first major initiative as leader was a formal visit to Yugoslavia in the third week of October, to end the quarrel with Tito (*see* Chapter 5). Khrushchev had made his pilgrimage to Canossa the previous year, but Hungary had held aloof: Rákosi had been the Cominform's hatchet-man in the attack on Tito in 1948, and no reconciliation was possible until he had been removed from office. Gero's timing was off – his trip was quite overshadowed by events in Warsaw and in Budapest.

On this disastrous Tuesday, 23 October 1956, he returned from Belgrade to find crowds gathering in the centre of Budapest. The historian Ferenc Vali has suggested that Gero had already planned to crush all opposition by provoking a demonstration against the regime and suppressing it with overwhelming force; he would then arrest Nagy and other opponents inside and outside the government. The confused situation on the 23rd apparently lent itself to such a provocation. At 12.53 p.m., the radio broadcast that the proposed students' demonstration would not be permitted. The crowds already present and those coming into the city centre paid no attention. An hour and a half later, the ban was lifted, and it was announced that Gero would deliver a speech at 8.00 p.m. Special troops and police contingents were moved into the city, and Gero possibly concluded that the moment was come to crush the opposition with 'a whiff of grapeshot', like Bonaparte in Paris in 1795.

If this were indeed Gero's plan, it failed calamitously. The demonstration rapidly turned into a series of enormous mass rallies outside the parliament building and elsewhere in the city. Nagy appeared briefly on a balcony, and delivered a short speech. Crowds spread through the city denouncing the regime, while police and army were conspicuous by their absence. Thousands of people gathered to demolish Stalin's statue: its overthrow was one of the great symbolic moments of the revolt.

Gero's speech turned riot into revolution. It was harsh and uncompromising, and infuriated everyone who heard it. Gero denounced the demonstrators as Fascist counter-revolutionaries and said that they would be crushed mercilessly. A column of students marched off to the radio station to have the Technological University's manifesto broadcast. The authorities refused the students' demand, and they started to pound on the doors, trying to break in. The first shots were fired from the roof of the radio station – by the secret police, the AVO* – and several students were killed.

The crowd attacked the building with every weapon they could find. The regular police, the army and even the party militia joined the rioters, and within hours, the demonstration had emptied armories all over Budapest. The government's authority collapsed completely, and if the Soviet army had not intervened that night, the regime would have been swept away within 24 hours. It was – like the taking of the Bastille in 1789 and the overthrow of the Romanovs in 1917 – a sudden, wholly spontaneous and unexpected uprising by the whole country together against the detested government.

The party's Central Committee assembled in panic that evening. News was coming in from all over the city and country that the army and police would not obey orders to disperse the crowds. There were pitched battles between demonstrators and the AVO – and the security police were losing. Gero, presumably after consulting Moscow, instructed the Central Committee to appoint

---

* The AVO had been formed by Rajk in 1946. In 1949, under Kádár, they were reorganised and given a new acronym, AVH, but the old detested name stuck.

Nagy as prime minister. He was the most popular man in Hungary, indeed the only popular Communist, and his influence might help to restore order. He was persuaded to broadcast an appeal for calm, and promised an amnesty for those who had been involved in the fighting. He was then incarcerated in the party headquarters for the next two days. Gero intended that Nagy would be a figurehead, retained to pacify the mob but unable to exercise any authority at all. Undoubtedly, Gero meant to purge him yet again, once the situation calmed down.

Nagy's broadcast had no effect on the demonstrators. The government was obviously losing control by the hour – and so the Soviets intervened. Early on the morning of 24 October, the first of 400 tanks rumbled into Budapest. The Soviets claimed that they had been summoned by the Hungarian government, but it is clear that the movement of the tanks had started the previous afternoon as the demonstrations were beginning. The tanks were immediately attacked by young Hungarians – who had by now acquired the title of 'freedom fighters'. The battle continued for four days. It was episodic and confused. The freedom fighters had no central command and no strategy. They never attacked parliament or party headquarters, the only two buildings in Budapest still controlled by the government – something that an organized revolution would have done immediately. Instead, they fought the AVO wherever they found them and, on at least two occasions, shot or lynched dozens of AVO prisoners.

An army colonel, Pál Maleter, defected to the rebels and took charge of the fighting in the centre of the city. He set up his command in the Kilian barracks there and fought off Soviet tanks sent to attack it. Elsewhere, other soldiers or former soldiers directed the fighting. Some Soviet tank crews fought viciously, blasting buildings containing snipers, shooting back at the freedom fighters who attacked them. Other crews, possibly sympathizing with the rebels, merely took up position in public squares or street intersections and did nothing. They had been told that Fascist counter-revolutionaries had seized the city, and when they were confronted with Hungarian workers and students, they lost all enthusiasm for the fight.

In four days of fighting, the Soviets lost about 200 tanks. Many Hungarians knew from their time as army conscripts how to handle anti-tank weapons, and there were soon hundreds of specialists making and using Molotov cocktails. It was a curious conflict: violent battles occurred in one street while, 100 yards away, people went peacefully about their business. The worst episode occurred outside parliament on 25 October, when AVO snipers started firing on Soviet tank crews fraternizing with the crowd; the Soviet troops then fired indiscriminately at buildings and at the crowd. Between 100 and 200 people were killed.

On Wednesday, 24 October, two senior Soviet officials, Anastas Mikoyan and Mikhail Suslov, arrived in Budapest. They found the Hungarian party in the process of dissolution, controlling little more than its own headquarters and rent with disputes between the Gero, Kádár and Nagy factions. The next day, following the massacre outside the parliament building, the Kremlin's emissaries concluded that Gero was incapable of restoring order, and he was removed from office and replaced by János Kádár. Nagy, at last released, was allowed to direct the government. Gero continued his plots against Nagy for another 24 hours, before being spirited away in an armoured car to the airport and flown to the Soviet Union.

Nagy moved to the government building. As he walked through the city, he noticed with astonishment the symbol of the revolution: the national flag with a hole in the middle, where the red star had been torn out (a symbol that was to be copied by the Romanians in 1989). He plunged immediately into his last fight – a war on two fronts. He had to contend with the Soviets and the remaining Hungarian Stalinists, while trying to recover control of a nation now demanding that Hungary immediately withdraw from the Warsaw Pact, that all Soviet troops leave the country at once, and that Communism be abandoned. He discovered too late that he had a third and most deadly enemy: the 'centrist' Communists led by Kádár and Ferenc Munnich, who were prepared to sell their souls to the Soviets to obtain power.

In frenzied negotiations with Mikoyan, Suslov and Yuri Andropov, the Soviet ambassador (and later, KGB chief, Soviet party general-secretary and president), Nagy insisted that the Soviet troops must be pulled out of Budapest. Tanks are quite unsuited to holding a city: they can demolish its buildings but cannot occupy it. Sending only tanks into Budapest on 24 October had been an act of military folly; presumably Gero and the Soviets had thought that they would suffice to overawe the demonstrators. When the mistake became obvious, the Soviets agreed to withdraw the tanks and Nagy made the announcement on 28 October. Although this in itself was a huge victory for the freedom fighters, they mistakenly believed that they had defeated the Soviet Union.

The pressures on Nagy for revolutionary change increased dramatically. In the countryside, the peasants summarily disbanded the collective farms; in industrial centres, workers took over their factories and expelled Communist functionaries. 'Revolutionary committees' sprang up everywhere to administer every organization in the country, from local schools to huge industries. All over Hungary, the party organization and government collapsed. The most hated officials were hunted down and many were killed; others went into hiding. The official police and the army went over to the rebellion *en masse*, and even some of the AVO surrendered; the rest hid themselves.

There were a few instances of great brutality. On 30 October, after the Soviet tanks had withdrawn from Budapest, freedom fighters discovered a band of 47 AVO men hiding in the Budapest Party Committee building. They laid siege to it, and AVO gunmen fired on the crowds from the rooftop. A photographer for *Life* magazine, John Sadovy, arrived in time to watch and photograph the battle. At least 30 people lay dead in the square in front of the building after the crowd had stormed it. Now they brought out the AVO men.

> The first to emerge from the building was an officer, alone. It was the fastest killing I ever saw. He came out laughing and the next thing I knew he was flat on the ground. It didn't dawn on me that this man was shot. He just fell down, I thought. Then the revolutionaries brought out a good-looking officer. His face was white. He got five yards, retreated, argued. Then he fell forward. It was over for him. Six young policemen came out. Their shoulder tabs were torn off. Quick argument. 'We're not so bad as you think we are; give us a chance,' they said. I was three feet from that group. Suddenly one began to slouch forward. They must have been close to his ribs when they fired. They all went down like corn that had been cut. Another came out, running. He saw his friends dead, turned, headed into the

> crowd. The revolutionaries dragged him out . . . I could see
> the impact of bullets on clothes. There was not much noise.
> They were shooting so close that the man's body acted as a
> silencer . . .

One of the AVO officers was strung up from a tree, doused in petrol
and set alight; others were beaten to death. Sadovy's photographs
are among the most dramatic scenes of revolution ever recorded.

The conflict subsided over the next few days. Communism had
been swept away in one sudden burst of energy, and it was
time to rebuild the country. Shops reopened, as did cafés and
restaurants, and the city appeared to be returning to normal.
Rebels liberated the prisons of the tens of thousands of political
prisoners – Communists, democrats and even Fascists – who had
been imprisoned since the war. Cardinal Mindszenty was released
and returned to Budapest, where he made a broadcast welcoming
the revolution and calling for national reconciliation. Meanwhile
the Soviet Union was evacuating its embassy – Soviet civilians lined
up by one of the bridges, waiting to be taken by ship down the
Danube – and a number of leading Hungarian Stalinists followed
Gero to safety in the Soviet Union.

A heated debate was under way in Moscow on the question
whether or not to accept what had happened in Hungary. After
his apparent political defeat in Poland, Khrushchev was unwilling
to accept an even more serious setback in Hungary. Nagy was
demanding that all Soviet troops leave the country, and had
promised free elections; there could be little doubt that the next
government would pull the country out of the Warsaw Pact.
Khrushchev feared the 'domino effect' – that Hungary's defection
would be followed by that of the other satellites.

Khrushchev's memoirs include a detailed account of the discussions the Soviets had with other Communist leaders, including the Chinese. Mao Tse-tung sent Liu Shao-chi, who recommended Soviet intervention, which was also the opinion of the East
European Communist leaders that subsequently visited. Gomułka,
a mere ten days after avoiding a Soviet invasion of Poland, showed
his true colours by denouncing Nagy as a counter-revolutionary
traitor. Khrushchev took Malenkov with him to visit Tito on his
island retreat of Brioni in the Adriatic. The weather was very rough,
and Malenkov, who suffered badly from air and sea sickness, had a

terrible trip. Tito, too, advised the Soviets to intervene. Khrushchev in his memoirs admits that, in fact, the decision had already been taken.

On 28 October, the Soviets had agreed to pull its tanks out of Budapest and then out of Hungary. The withdrawal took several days: the last units left the capital on 30 October. Soon there were reports from the frontiers that large columns of Soviet troops were moving into the country, and Nagy urgently summoned Andropov to demand an explanation. The ambassador assured the prime minister that the troops were simply coming across the border to help their comrades leave. On Thursday, 1 November – the day, apparently, that the Politburo in Moscow formally decided to invade – 3000 Soviet tanks crossed the border and started to surround Budapest and other major cities. Three army corps took part in the invasion, including eight tank and armoured divisions and two infantry divisions, as well as artillery, air force and other units.

By the afternoon of 1 November, it was quite clear that a full-scale invasion was under way. Nagy summoned his cabinet and played his last card: Hungary formally withdrew from the Warsaw Pact. Andropov was summoned to a meeting of the Hungarian Communist Party's Praesidium to be informed of this decision, which had been agreed unanimously: both Kádár and Ferenc Munnich, who together defected to the Soviets two days later, had approved it. Kádár melodramatically declared, 'What happens to me is of little importance, but I am ready, as a Hungarian, to fight if necessary. If your tanks enter Budapest, I will go into the streets and fight against you with my bare hands!' The decision to leave the Pact was taken after the invasion had begun, and as a reaction to it. It was not the cause of the invasion.

Nagy sent off an urgent appeal to the United Nations, but it was lost in the confusion there: it had arrived at the height of the Suez crisis.

Israel invaded Egypt on 29 October. On the 30th, Britain and France issued an ultimatum to the two countries, demanding that they both pull back from the Suez Canal (only Israel agreed). The next day, the British and French bombed Egyptian air bases, and the invasion fleet set out. It was the last great fiasco of the

British empire, an act of supreme folly that turned the Arab world violently anti-Western. As the Hungarians were to observe with great bitterness, the West passed up an opportunity to liberate Eastern Europe because of a quarrel over a canal that no longer mattered very much. The United States, which was in the throes of a presidential election, took the Suez affair far more seriously than the Hungarian revolution. Eisenhower saw it as a personal affront. As a further complication, on 3 November, the US secretary of state, John Foster Dulles, was taken to hospital and operated on for stomach cancer.

It does not follow that, if there had been no Suez crisis or American election, or if Dulles had not been ill, the West would have been able to protect Imre Nagy. The Americans could not have sent troops to Budapest: Hungary was isolated behind neutral Austria and Communist Yugoslavia. Nor could the United Nations have helped directly: the USSR would certainly have vetoed any proposal to send UN forces. But at the very least, a vigorous Western declaration of support and threats of severe economic and political sanctions against the Soviet Union might have given Khrushchev pause and strengthened the hands of those members of the Politburo who opposed intervention. In the event, seeing the West wholly preoccupied by Suez, Khrushchev concluded that he could do as he liked.

Andropov did not protest when he was told of the Hungarian Praesidium's decision to leave the Pact. Instead, he calmly proposed that two committees be established, one military and one political, to discuss the details. A first meeting with a Soviet military delegation was held at the Ministry of Defence. Nagy promoted Pál Maleter to general and made him minister of defence, and sent him to represent the government at the talks. The Soviets demanded that their war memorials be respected, and the Hungarians agreed at once. It was arranged that a further meeting would be held, at Soviet headquarters outside Budapest, on Saturday evening, 3 November.

For a last brief autumn day, the Hungarians thought they had won. Nagy, who was under no such illusions, extended his government by including ministers from other political parties, miraculously revived after a decade of persecution. Among them was Zoltán Tildy of the Smallholders' Party, the first post-war president. By then, Kádár and Munnich had disappeared: they were flown to Ushgorod in Soviet Ruthenia, where they met the Soviet leaders and agreed to form a quisling 'Hungarian Revolutionary Worker–Peasant Government'.

From its studios in Munich, Radio Free Europe cheered the victory and urged Hungary to purge the last Communists from the government. On Saturday evening, General Maleter led his delegation to Soviet headquarters. The talks went well for the first hour; then General Ivan Serov, head of the KGB, burst into the room and arrested the Hungarians.

Early on the morning of Sunday, 4 November 1956, Soviet tanks again entered Budapest. At 5.20 a.m. Nagy broadcast to the nation.

> This is Imre Nagy, President of the Council of Ministers of the People's Republic of Hungary speaking. Today at dawn, Soviet forces launched an attack against the capital with the obvious purpose of overthrowing the legal Hungarian democratic government. Our troops are fighting. The government is at its post. I notify the people of our country and the entire world of these facts.

Half an hour later, there was another radio broadcast:

> *Attention! Attention! Attention!* Premier Imre Nagy calls Minister of Home Defence Pál Maleter, the chief of our General Staff, István Kovács, and the other members of the military delegation who went yesterday at 22.00 hours to the headquarters of the Soviet Supreme Command and who have not returned until now, to come back without further delay in order to take over their respective offices.

An hour later, the playwright Gyula Hay made a last broadcast:

> This is the Hungarian Writers' Association speaking to all writers, scientists, writers' associations, academics and scientific unions of the world. We turn to leaders of intellectual life in all countries. Our time is limited. You all know the facts. There is no need to expand on them. Help Hungary! Help the Hungarian writers, scientists, workers, peasants and intelligentsia. Help! Help! Help!

At six o'clock, Soviet radio broadcast a recording made by János Kádár announcing the new pro-Soviet government:

> *Attention! Attention!* Comrade János Kádár speaking. The Hungarian Revolutionary Worker–Peasant Government has been formed. The mass movement which started in our country on 23 October had the noble aim to remedy the anti-party and anti-democratic crimes committed by Rákosi and his associates and to defend national independence and sovereignty. Our socialist achievements, our people's state, our worker–peasant power and the very existence of our country has been threatened by the weakness of the Imre Nagy government and the increased influence of the counter-revolutionary elements who edged their way into the movement. This has prompted us, as Hungarian patriots, to form the Hungarian Revolutionary Worker–Peasant Government . . .
>
> Our nation is passing through difficult days. The power of the workers and peasants, and the sacred cause of socialism, are in danger . . . The counter-revolutionaries are becoming more and more impudent. They ruthlessly persecute the followers of democracy . . . We know that many questions are still awaiting a solution in our country and that we have to cope with many difficulties. The life of the workers is still far from what it ought to be in a country building socialism . . . The Rákosi and Gero clique has committed many grave mistakes and gravely violated legality. All this has rightly made the workers dissatisfied . . .
>
> Exploiting mistakes committed during the building of our people's democratic system, the reactionary elements have misled many honest workers, and in particular the major part of the youth, which joined the movement out of honest and patriotic intentions . . .

Kádár went on to say that he would be prime minister as well as party first secretary. 'Acting in the interest of our people, working class and our country,' he said, '[we] requested the Soviet Army Command to help our nation smash the sinister forces of reaction and restore order and calm in the country.'

The Soviets were now in the centre of the city and threatening to attack the parliament building. Nagy, a number of his colleagues and their families took refuge in the Yugoslav embassy; Mindszenty went to the American embassy (where he was to remain until 1971). The Soviets smashed resistance in Budapest in one vast paroxysm of fire power. Everyone in the Kilian barracks was killed, and whenever a sniper opened fire, the Soviets blasted away the entire building. There was no organized resistance by the Hungarian armed forces, but for several days, the workers in their factories and districts put up a valiant, futile struggle. The most sustained resistance was offered by workers in a group of factories on Csepel Island in the Danube, below Budapest, who manufactured their own weapons, dug trenches, built gun emplacements and defended themselves against the Red Army for a week before they were overwhelmed. Resistance elsewhere in Hungary was crushed with equal thoroughness and speed. A general strike was called, which was gradually suppressed, the last strike committee dissolving itself in January 1957.

Nagy was lured out of his refuge on 22 November by Kádár's promises of security. He was arrested by Soviet troops and carried off to Romania. For the next 18 months, the Soviet and Hungarian governments alike tried to persuade him to recant, admit his errors and thus legitimize the invasion. He steadfastly refused. Tito tried to protect him, but after a further deterioration in relations between Yugoslavia and the Soviet Union in the spring of 1958, Nagy and his colleagues were tried in secret.

On 16 June 1958, first Moscow and then Budapest announced that all of them had been convicted, and that Nagy, Pál Maleter, Miklós Gimes, a journalist and friend of Nagy's, and József Szilagyi, the former head of the prime minister's office, had been executed. Another of Nagy's advisers, Geza Losonczy, died of maltreatment in prison, and Nagy's other close colleagues received heavy prison terms.

By official count, 4000 people were killed in the uprising and 13,000 were injured. There is no reason to believe these figures, nor any means of knowing what the true totals were. Opposition exiles insist that about 2000 people were executed in the terror that followed in 1957–59 and a further 20,000 were imprisoned. About 200,000 people escaped over the border into Austria.

The Hungarian revolution was by far the most violent event in Europe since 1945, and it followed political purges and an institutionalized terror more severe and more prolonged than any other European Communist country suffered, apart from the Soviet Union itself. For the next 34 years, all Eastern Europeans –

Hungarians, East Germans, Poles, Czechoslovaks and Romanians – submitted to the indignities of foreign occupation and inefficient and detested government for fear of suffering the same fate. Czechoslovakia did not resist the invasion of 1968 and Poland accepted martial law in 1981 because of the spectre of another Budapest. At the same time, the hatred of the Soviets and of Communism induced by the invasion did not wane with the years, and when the Soviet threat was lifted, the captive nations seized their freedom again. There were other effects: Communist parties in Western Europe never recovered from the shock, and the Soviet Union itself remained a prisoner of its own empire until it could no longer bear the strain. But the chief result, and the one that Khrushchev intended, was to impose tyranny upon Hungary and the rest of Eastern Europe for another generation.

The Kádár years

> *'Whereas the Rákosi regime used to say, "He who is not for us is against us," we say, "He who is not against us is for us, and welcomed by us."'*
>
> *János Kádár, January 1962*

No government in Europe ever took office in less auspicious circumstances than did János Kádár on 5 November 1956. He arrived in Budapest as the Red Army was still smashing its way through the city, much as it had in 1945, its tanks blasting buildings apart, its soldiers shooting everyone on sight. For days and weeks afterwards, Kádár and his handful of colleagues, brought to the government building in an armoured car, depended upon the Soviet Union for their very survival.

The administration had collapsed completely, both in Budapest and throughout the country. The Soviet army directed everything, as in a conquered country, and it was months before enough loyal Communists, opportunist fellow-travellers, and intimidated citizens could be recruited to provide the minimum of public services. Kádár tried to win the people's confidence by promising them free elections, prosperity, a general amnesty for all former rebels and a rapid reduction in Soviet influence. It was all lies. In the first elections after the uprising, the Patriotic People's Front, dominated by the Communist party, won 99.6 per cent of the vote on a 98.4 per cent turnout.

Kádár followed Rákosi's tactics at first, cutting the salami very fine, stripping away every concession the government had made between 1953 and November 1956, one at a time. Collectivization of the land was resumed, and by 1961, 95 per cent of it was under the control of state farms. The purge of all those who had taken part in the revolt began early in 1957 and grew steadily more severe, until some 20,000 people had been arrested. There was a reign of terror, comparable to Rajk's and Rákosi's purges in the 1940s. By 1960, Kádár and his Soviet masters had reduced the country to abject subservience and terror and obedience.

Then began a most remarkable transformation. The 'Kádár experiment' was imposed upon the party by the desperate state of the economy after the revolution and the disruption caused by the flight of hundreds of thousands abroad. The country could not recover under the old system. Reform was essential and was possible now that the terror had reduced the Hungarians to abject obedience. Starting in about 1960, Kádár began loosening the reins. A few former rebels were given amnesty in 1961, many more the following year, and by the end of 1963, the jails had been cleared completely. Those released were 'counter-revolutionaries', 'murderers' and 'terrorists' who had been lucky to escape with their lives in 1957, including senior officials who had been tried with Imre Nagy. Press censorship was slackened, restrictions on the import of foreign books and newspapers were scrapped and restrictions on foreign travel were progressively lifted. In 1960, 35,000 Hungarians were allowed exit visas; in 1967, 143,000 were given them, and in the 1970s, over one million Hungarians a year visited the West. No other Eastern bloc country was so liberal.

At the same time, Kádár began to relax the rigidities of Stalinist economic policy. He was never able to follow a consistent line: when the Kremlin allowed him, he permitted private enterprises to flourish, and encouraged consumer industries rather than the mammoth steel mills and engineering plants of the Rákosi years; when the wind from Moscow blew cold, he closed down private companies and encouraged heavy industry. His purpose was to improve Hungarians' standard of living and to put goods in the shops, particularly the food shops. Budapest was never as prosperous as Vienna, but it offered a recognisably Western standard of living. Khrushchev called it 'goulash Communism'.

Kádár remained steadfastly faithful to the Soviet line in foreign affairs. When the Kremlin said, 'March!' he marched. When it said, 'Stand still!' he froze at attention. In 1967, he broke relations with Israel, and in 1968, he sent two divisions to invade Czechoslovakia along with his Warsaw Pact allies. It was the least he could do, to return the favour: Czechoslovakia had cooperated enthusiastically in the invasion of Hungary 12 years earlier.

Kádár's economic reforms brought the country greater prosperity than that found in Romania, Poland or Yugoslavia, but the changes soon ran out of steam. The productivity of the collectivized farms was less than half that of Western European farms, and the quality of Hungarian goods was never high enough to sell to the West. Hungary was still tied to Comecon, which meant trading the great majority of its exports with the Soviet Union and the other satellites, whatever the economic incentives. In addition, Hungary, like the rest of Eastern Europe, was severely affected by the recession caused by the oil crisis in 1973, and it began to run up debts to the West: in 1980, it already owed over $8 billion to Western banks, and the debt kept growing.

Kádár retained his popularity. In elections in 1975, the Patriotic People's Front won 99.6 per cent of the vote, and in 1980, 99.3 per cent. No one, of course, takes these figures seriously, but it would be fair to say that Kádár finally won at least a measure of grudging respect from his fellow-citizens. He was never loved and he was never forgiven his role in 1956, but Hungarians recognized that things could have been a lot worse. For one thing, the Soviets could have returned Rákosi to power.

Hungary now claims to have inspired Mikhail Gorbachev's *glasnost* policy. Certainly, Hungarians had long enjoyed certain freedoms before Gorbachev introduced them in the USSR, but there were limits to their liberties, and the relatively liberal economic policies followed since the early 1960s still failed to bring Hungary up to Western levels of prosperity. Because they could visit the West freely and read Western books and newspapers, Hungarians could see for themselves how rapidly they were falling behind.

The peaceful revolution

Kádárite liberalism failed to modernize Hungary economically, but it rotted the Communist party from within and prepared the ground, albeit unintentionally, for revolution. It was now possible to debate every question of politics and economics more or less in public without getting arrested (though there remained a few taboos governing printed matter), and all but the most obdurate were forced eventually to recognize that Marxism was a failure. None of the Communist officials who availed themselves freely of their right to visit Vienna for the weekend or Italy for the summer could deny that liberal capitalism was a dramatic success. By the 1980s, therefore, nobody – save for a few elderly relics grouped around Kádár himself – still believed in Communism. All that sustained the government was the threat of Soviet intervention.

Reform Communists were barely even socialist, and everyone else was vehemently anti-Communist. What is more, everyone knew it. There was none of the pretense and hypocrisy of Poland and Czechoslovakia, none of the terror of Romania, none of the residual Communist faith of Bulgaria. There were no delusions. The party leaders' loss of faith in Communism was so complete that when their power was challenged, and the Soviet Union abandoned them, they gave up without a struggle.

In 1988 and 1989, as the news from Moscow contained ever increasing evidence of *glasnost*, Hungarians who were not part of the *apparat* started demanding ever greater liberties for themselves. They discovered that they were pushing against an open door. At the same time, there was the economic crisis, which became a major contributory factor to the new revolution. The economy had gone into deep depression by the mid-1980s, and with a heavy burden of foreign debt (the highest *per capita* in Eastern Europe) and no means of paying it or of obtaining further credit, Hungary could not continue to modernize.

In May 1988, a party conference swept away the old leadership. Kádár was pensioned off, becoming party president, and was replaced as general secretary by Károly Grósz, who was a reformer and chose reformist colleagues. Within a year, he was overtaken by events and joined Kádár in oblivion.

The Grósz government proposed sweeping new reforms under

which a third of the economy would be turned over to free enterprise and a new political structure, separating the Communist party from the government, would be introduced in 1990. In November 1988, one of the new regime's leading reformers, the 40-year-old economist Miklós Németh, who had studied at Harvard, was appointed prime minister. He proposed to carry the reform movement even further, insisting that change was inevitable and must include the legalization of opposition parties and trade unions, as well as free elections under a new constitution, which would be introduced in 1990. He and his comrades expected a decorous reform process, like Gorbachev's *perestroika*. Instead, they presided over the rapid dissolution of the Communist party.

A split in the party developed between the moderate reformers, led by Grósz, and the radicals, led by Németh, Imre Poszgay and Rezso Nyers. The key symbolic issue was whether the uprising in 1956 had been a 'counter-revolution' or a genuine 'people's revolt'. Grósz still insisted that Nagy was a 'counter-revolutionary', but Poszgay and his friends could see the way the tide was running and, hoping to salvage the party, conceded that 1956 had been a national and popular revolution. On 8 May 1989, in a victory for the radicals, Kádár was retired. Nyers became party president in his place, and although Grósz remained general secretary, he lost control of the party. Poszgay, Németh and Nyers then set about preparing Hungary for a return to a mixed economy, without price controls and with private property and a stock market. They decreed freedom of the press and various other liberties, and contemplated free elections – and for the first time admitted the possibility that they might be voted out of office.

They also agreed that the bodies of Imre Nagy, Pál Maleter and the three others executed at the same time – Losonczy, Szilagyi and Gimes – should be exhumed from their unmarked graves in a paupers' cemetery and given a proper burial. The statue of Lenin outside the parliament building, which had replaced the one of Stalin demolished by rioters in 1956, was tactfully removed – 'for repairs' – before the funeral.

On 16 June, the 33rd anniversary of the announcement of Nagy's execution, he and the others were given a formal funeral in a ceremony in front of parliament. There was also an empty coffin to represent the thousands who had been executed without trial.

Németh, Poszgay and two other reformers laid wreaths in front of Nagy's coffin. That was their only role: they left before Nagy's friends delivered eulogies that contained bitter condemnations of the Soviet intervention and the role of János Kádár. One of them said of the party that it was 'fearfully clinging to power', and that 'what it failed to achieve in 44 years cannot be achieved now. They are responsible for the past. They are responsible for the damaged lives of Hungarians.'

The funeral had been organized by the opposition – veterans of 1956 and their youthful successors – and the ceremony at the parliament building was directed by László Rajk, son of the Stalinist minister of the interior who had been hanged by Rákosi in 1949 – and who had been rehabilitated, and given a state funeral, just before the revolution in October 1956. The ministry of the interior said that 100,000 people attended the ceremony, the organizers claimed 250,000. Whatever the exact figure, it was an enormous crowd – and all Hungary watched the ceremony, which lasted all day and was televised live.*

It was the first of the great demonstrations of people's power in Eastern Europe in 1989, just as the Polish elections, which had taken place less than two weeks earlier, had been the first comprehensive rejection of Communism. That June was a month of stirring events: on the 4th, the day of the Polish elections, Deng Xiao-ping sent tanks to crush the student rebels in Peking's Tienanmen Square. In Hungary, the Communist party leadership no longer had the power, and certainly lacked the will, to call in the tanks to save their positions and they watched helplessly as power slipped from their hands. They remained in office, but on sufferance, their only hope of survival was to join the reformers.

Over the next three months, Poland and Hungary advanced in tandem towards democratic government, Hungary following Poland's example and instituting 'round table' discussions with six opposition parties. Then, on 10 September, it opened its border with Austria to the thousands of East Germans who had been camped in Hungary all summer. It was the key gesture that

* Four of the dead, and the symbolic empty coffin, were buried in a new shrine constructed for them in the cemetery. Nagy himself, at his family's request, was returned to his original grave in the corner of the cemetery where 260 other victims of the Soviets' revenge are also buried.

precipitated the collapse of the East German government two months later (*see* Chapter 1). On 19 September, a week after Solidarity took power in Poland, the Hungarian 'round table' agreed on a schedule for reform. The government's most important concession was to permit independent political parties to contest the next parliamentary elections, which were promised for the following year.

The agreement also provided that a new office of president should be established, and that a presidential election should be held before the parliamentary elections. Two opposition parties – the Alliance of Free Democrats and the Association of Young Democrats – which had not formally joined the talks, refused to approve the agreement, objecting to the proposed presidential election.

A new Communst party congress was called in October. János Kádár died just before it opened. The radicals took over. Before them was the example of Poland, where the party was rapidly disintegrating, and East Germany, where there were increasing signs of dissolution. Grósz was summarily deposed on 11 October, to be replaced by Poszgay. The party then dissolved itself, reconstituted itself as the 'Socialist Party' and handed over all its assets to the state. It was the first European Communist party to vote itself out of existence. Later, the country's name was changed, from 'People's Republic' to simply the 'Republic of Hungary'. The party militia was disbanded, the 'leading role' of the party was abandoned, the electoral law was officially amended to allow free elections, and opposition leaders were invited to join the government in the run-up to the elections. The anniversary of the 1956 uprising – 23 October – became a public holiday.

Poszgay was nominated as the party's candidate for the presidential election which the government wanted to hold immediately. The opposition, however, insisted that it should wait until after the legislative elections, and the matter was submitted to a referendum on 26 November, the first completely free vote in Eastern Europe in over 40 years. Only 54 per cent of the electorate turned out – and rejected the proposed presidential election by a large majority.

By then, the whirlwind had swept away the East German and Czechoslovak regimes, the Berlin Wall had collapsed and the powder train in Romania had been lighted. Hungary, which had led the way in the reform movement, was now bringing up the rear. On 10 March 1990, the Hungarian and Soviet governments agreed that Soviet troops would withdraw from the country by the middle of 1991, ending an occupation that had begun in 1944.

This was the last act of the new 'Socialist Party' in government. On 25 March, in the first round of the parliamentary elections, the right-wing Democratic Forum won a decisive majority, beating the Alliance of Free Democrats into a poor second place. The 'Socialists' who had been quite unable to escape from their Communist past, won only 11 per cent of the vote, and Imre Poszgay, the party's leader, had even failed to win a seat. The second round, on 8 April, confirmed the results. It was less than a year since the funeral of Imre Nagy.

The election campaign was not entirely free of mud-slinging, demagoguery and dishonesty, but considering the background, it was astonishing that the Hungarians managed to elect a government with a comfortable majority in parliament as well as a coherent political and economic programme. The old divisions between town and country had re-emerged, there were traces of anti-Semitism and, above all, Hungary faced a period of exceedingly painful adjustment. But it had managed the transition from a Communist to a democratic system peacefully and rapidly, and had switched its allegiance from East to West with a minimum of difficulty. Its new government announced that Hungary intended to leave the Warsaw Pact immediately, and it started negotiations with the European Community to become an associate member, like Turkey, with the hope of joining the Community as soon as possible.

Hungary's problems are now economic, and remain very serious. The Soviet Union has announced that it will no longer sell oil and other raw materials to Eastern Europe at subsidized rates: Hungary and the others must pay the world price, and they must pay in dollars. At the same time, Hungary has to transform its economy from a planned system – inexorably tied to the USSR and the rest of the Eastern bloc – to full participation in the free market. The Democratic Forum won the election on a platform of doing so gradually, rejecting the Polish 'big bang' strategy. This way, the pain will be spread over a longer period – but it will not be diminished.

AUSTRIA

HUNGARY

Ljubljana   SLOVENIA

Trieste

ISTRIAN PENINSULA

Fiume
(Rijeka)

Zagreb

CROATIA

ROMANIA

VOJVODINA

Sava

Danube   Novi Sad

Banja Luka

Zadar

DALMATIA

YUGOSLAVIA

BOSNIA

Split

Sarajevo

HERCEGOVINA

Belgrade

SERBIA

Morava

Adriatic

Sea

Dubrovnik

MONTENEGRO

Kosovo

Priština

ITALY

ALBANIA

Dürres
(Durazzo)

Tirane
(Tirana)

Skopje

MACEDONIA

Vlorë
(Valona)

YUGOSLAVIA
AND ALBANIA

0   50   100   150 km

0   50   100 miles

N

GREECE

Corfu

5 Yugoslavia

The divisions that now afflict Yugoslavia go back to the Middle Ages and beyond. When Theodosius the Great partitioned the Roman empire in the late fourth century, the line ran through the country, and it has been divided between Rome and Constantinople ever since. It was a battle ground between Germans and Slavs, and between Slavs and Turks, for hundreds of years. It was divided and ruled by the Austrians, Hungarians, Italians and Turks.

For four centuries, the frontier between the Habsburg and Ottoman empires separated the Croats from the Serbs, and it continues to be one of the great fault-lines of Europe. The two peoples remain divided, even though their languages are nearly identical, and racially, they are indistinguishable. The Croats are Catholic, use the Roman alphabet and look west and north, to Rome and Vienna, for the sources of their culture and civilization. The Serbs are Orthodox, use the Cyrillic alphabet and look east to Constantinople and Moscow. Twenty-one years of unity in the Kingdom of Yugoslavia followed by nearly 50 years of war and Communism have not lessened the antipathy between the two.

Of the other four republics, Slovenia, to the north of Croatia, is the most completely Western. Macedonia and Montenegro, in the south, are the most backward – and Bulgaria believes that Macedonians are really Bulgars. The remaining republic, Bosnia-Hercegovina, lying to the south of Croatia and Serbia, is half Muslim. There are also two autonomous provinces, both part of Serbia: Vojvodina, in the northwest; and Kosovo, the southern-most province, which is populated by Albanians and is primarily Muslim.

The creation of Yugoslavia in 1918 was something of a miracle and like many miracles, it has not worn well. It has turned out that six republics, three religions, ten minorities and two alphabets do not equal one nation.

The making of Yugoslavia

The Serbs are the most numerous of the peoples of Yugoslavia, and their history is different from that of the others. In the Middle Ages, there was a series of Serbian kingdoms and principalities, culminating in an empire that controlled most of the Balkans. Although it was destroyed by the Turks at the battle of Kosovo in 1389, the Serbs always remembered that once they were an imperial nation. The other components of Yugoslavia have no such independent history to cherish, though Montenegro, in its mountain stronghold, never submitted to Turkey.

The Turks ruled Serbia for over four centuries, with a Muslim upper class and Christian peasants. In 1804 a swineherd called Karadjordje – 'Black George' – Petrović led the Serbs in revolt and established an independent principality based on Belgrade. The Turks reconquered it in 1813, but in 1817, a second revolt led by Miloš Obrenović succeeded in winning a degree of autonomy from Turkey. Obrenović had Karadjordje and most of his family murdered, beginning a blood feud that lasted into the 20th century. The two dynasties alternated on the throne, through a succession of *coups d'état* and murders: when a king was assassinated or deposed, the head of the rival family would be brought back from exile to succeed him.

Serbia won its independence by its own exertions, and its national mission from the mid-19th century onwards was to liberate the other southern Slavs from the Ottomans. This was later expanded to include bringing Croatia and Slovenia into a new Serbian empire, ruled from Belgrade. Other nations had similar ambitions. The Bulgarians, with Russian support, coveted Macedonia, as did Greece. By the Treaty of Berlin in 1878 Austria gained control of Bosnia-Hercegovina from Turkey, and it formally annexed it in 1908. It was the territory that Serbia most ardently coveted, and this dispute provoked the First World War.

Before that catastrophe, Croats and Slovenes, as well as Bosnians and Hercegovinans, had began to debate the advantages of a united South Slav state. Slovenia, the Dalmatian coast and Bosnia-Hercegovina were then ruled by Austria; Croatia and Vojvodina, an area immediately north of Belgrade with a mixed population, were governed by Hungary. Statesmen in Vienna and Budapest began to discuss the notion of extending the empire further south, to include all the Slav lands of the southwest Balkans – including Serbia itself. It was a disastrous fantasy: nationalist fervour was already rising rapidly among Croats, Slovenes and Bosnians, and among the Czechs and Slovaks to the north. The empire was disintegrating, and the idea that it might survive by expansion was completely nonsensical.

The Balkans had a long tradition of secret societies and assassinations. Blood feuds, terrorism and arbitrary executions – frequently backed by kings, princes and governments – were commonplace in Yugoslavia, Albania, Romania and Bulgaria throughout the 19th century and well into the 20th, until they were replaced by Communist state terrorism. In Yugoslavia, Croatian and Serbian secret societies fought a long terrorist war against each other, with disastrous consequences for both countries, and for the world.

In June 1903, King Alexander Obrenović and his wife Draga were assassinated by a group of army officers, who stormed the palace, killed the king and queen and threw their mutilated bodies out of a window; a number of leading political figures were also murdered. The assassins (whose leader was Dragutin Dimitriyevitch known as 'Apis') formed a secret society of terrorists – the Black Hand – whose object was to extend Serbian rule over Bosnia–Hercegovina and Macedonia. The exiled Peter Karadjordjević, who had been in touch with the rebels, then returned to Serbia and was crowned King Peter I. The Black Hand's links with King Peter and the Serbian government, although suspected, have never been discovered.

On 28 June 1914, the Archduke Franz Ferdinand, nephew and heir to the emperor of Austria, was assassinated in Sarajevo, the capital of Bosnia, together with his wife. The assassin was Gavril Princip, a member of the Black Hand. The Austrian government demanded reparations and an act of contrition from Serbia so comprehensive and humiliating that it would have amounted to a surrender of national independence. The Serbs, after a month's frantic hesitation, rejected the ultimatum, and on 28 July, Austria declared war.

In turn, Russia, allied to Serbia, mobilized its army, leading to a declaration of war by Germany, which was obedient to the dictates of the Schlieffen war plan long prepared by its general staff. The Germans then declared war on France, who, allied to Russia, had also begun to mobilize, and the following day (4 August), the German army invaded neutral Belgium, which brought Britain into the conflict. In the ensuing cataclysm, the Austrian, German, Russian and Ottoman empires were destroyed.

Serbia at first held off the Austrians. In September 1915, the Germans and Austrians persuaded Bulgaria to join the Central Powers, and a joint German–Bulgarian offensive across Macedonia forced the Serbian army, with King Peter at its head, to take refuge on the Greek island of Corfu. They suffered frightful losses: Serbia lost a quarter of its adult male population during 1914–18 hostilities, more even than in the Second World War. Then, on 9 October 1915, the Austrians occupied Belgrade.

The British transported the Serbians to the Salonika front, from which eventually they marched home in victory. While still in Greece in 1917, 'Apis', the Black Hand chieftain, and two of his senior allies were court-martialled and shot on the charge of plotting against King Peter's son Alexander; with them died the secrets of Gavril Princip. The court martial and executions were carried out by a rival secret society, the White Hand, whose leader was Peter Zhivkovitch. As a young lieutenant in the palace guard in 1903, he had opened the gates to Apis and the other murderers, who had come in the night to murder King Alexander Obrenović and his wife. Twelve years after the Black Hand executions, when Alexander, by then king, imposed his personal dictatorship on Yugoslavia, he made Zhivkovitch prime minister.

At the end of the war in 1918, Serbia emerged a victor, trebled in size, and set about forming a new kingdom. It inherited the blood feuds among the Serbs, between Serbs and Croats and between Macedonians and Serbs, and these internecine conflicts would dominate Yugoslav politics for a generation.

From kingdom to communism

The Kingdom of Serbs, Croats and Slovenes was proclaimed on December 1918 under King Alexander I Karadjordjević of Serbia. It was never a happy union. One of the reasons why the Croats and Slovenes had agreed to submit to the Serbs was a fear that Italy intended to annex the Dalmation coast and parts of Slovenia. In a series of post-war treaties, Italy and Yugoslavia settled their differences (they were resumed later), and the Yugoslavs were then able to set about the business of squabbling among themselves.

There was a political problem and an economic one, both of which were interrelated and both of which persist. The political question was whether Yugoslavia should be a unitary state or a federation. The economic problem was that Slovenia and Croatia were much more developed than the rest of the country. The kingdom was not the only country to have a rich north and a poor south, but the differences were far greater in Yugoslavia than in Italy or Spain, for instance, and they were compounded by the rival religions, languages and histories.

A constitutional convention in 1921 produced a centralized constitution, and henceforth the government was dominated by Serbs. The main opposition came from Croatia, which constantly demanded a federal constitution. In 1928, during a debate in parliament, a Montenegrin deputy shot the leader of the main Croatian party, Stjepan Radić, and two other Croat deputies. The incident is still remembered in Croatia as an example of Serb treachery.

The murders led King Alexander, in 1929, to abolish the constitution and establish a monarchical dictatorship. Concluding, correctly, that the root of the trouble was Croat dissatisfaction, he changed the country's name to Yugoslavia – 'the land of the South Slavs'. The Croats were not appeased. With his new prime minister, General Zhivkovitch, Alexander suppressed all signs of opposition, a policy followed by their successors throughout the 1930s. Croat and Slovene nationalism was repressed, and democrats were called Communists and thrown in jail. The king issued a new constitution, ostensibly restoring democratic rights, in 1931.

Alexander's foreign policy was based on an alliance with

Czechoslovakia and Romania – the Little Entente – and, separately, with France. The object of these arrangements was to defend the 'successor states' (those created from the debris of the Austro-Hungarian empire) against the 'revisionist states', Hungary and Bulgaria, which had irredentist designs on their neighbours. It was an effective system of alliance as long as Germany remained quiescent, as it did under the Weimar Republic. It failed when Hitler took power in 1933. At the same time, despite the best efforts of his police, the king was faced with two serious domestic threats. Croatian Fascists had set up a secret society, the *Ustache*, with the mission of liberating Croatia from Serbian tyranny and, later, to annex Bosnia and Hercegovina; its intended methods were identical to those of the Black Hand terrorist organization of the previous generation. Equally dangerous, a Bulgarian terrorist group, IMRO, with its headquarters in Sofia, was plotting to restore Macedonia to Bulgaria, which it had twice previously annexed, in 1912 and 1915 (*see* chapter 7).

In 1934, King Alexander set out on a state visit to France, intending to discuss the future of the Little Entente in the light of the new dispensation in Germany. He arrived in Marseille by sea on 9 October, and was met by Louis Barthou, the French foreign minister. As they drove in state through the city in an open carriage, like Franz Ferdinand in Sarajevo, they were both assassinated by a Macedonian terrorist, hired by the Croatian *Ustache*. The scene was recorded on a news-reel, which shows a mounted *garde républicaine*, magnificent in his helmet and breastplate, slashing at the assassin with his sabre.

Alexander's son Peter was only 11 years old, so the dead King's cousin, Prince Paul, became regent. Paul, though a noted Anglophile, considered himself constrained by the circumstances of the time to show much more sympathy for Germany and Italy; in addition, he was half Russian, and detested Communism and feared the Soviet Union.

As the Second World War approached, Yugoslavia, like the other Balkan states, tried to escape the deluge by reaching an accommodation with Hitler. In that endeavour, democracy was a liability, and by the late 1930s, Yugoslavia had become a largely Fascist state. In March 1937, it concluded a friendship treaty with Mussolini. The government did manage one substantial reform: in

1939, it conceded many of Croatia's demands by setting up a new Croatian province with a large measure of autonomy. By then, such reforms were a matter of rearranging the deck chairs on the *Lusitania*. Czechoslovakia and Romania were, in turn, dismembered, Hungary joined the Axis and the Soviet Union was allied to Germany.

In 1940, France was occupied, the British were driven back across the Channel, and Italy invaded Greece. Yugoslavia was completely isolated, except for its friendship with Greece – and that was a trap. When the Greeks drove the Italians back into Albania and occupied the southern half of that country, Hitler decided to go to the rescue, but to get there, he needed to move his troops through Bulgaria and Yugoslavia. Yugoslavia hesitated. Summoning the Yugoslav prime minister to meet him in Salzburg in February 1941, Hitler demanded that Yugoslavia submit. Bulgaria joined the Axis on 1 March. Prince Paul and his government, believing they had no choice, signed a treaty with the Germans on 25 March, in Vienna.

The news provoked a storm of outrage in Belgrade. The next day, Prince Paul was deposed by army officers, the government was arrested and Peter II, now 18 years old, was proclaimed king. Although the new government insisted that it would honour the new treaty with Hitler, this curious gesture was insufficient to protect Yugoslavia. These events were to have a profound effect on the course of the war. Greece had defeated Mussolini and now Yugoslavia had defied Hitler. The *Führer* set aside every other consideration to avenge these affronts. On 6 April, without the formality of a declaration of war, Hitler and his allies invaded Yugoslavia, opening operations with a massive air attack on Belgrade. The German campaign to occupy Yugoslavia and Greece was short, violent and successful, like the conquests of Poland and France in previous years, but the distraction meant that Operation Barbarossa – the attack on the Soviet Union – had to be postponed by six weeks. It is possible that, if Hitler had attacked in May, as he had planned, instead of waiting until 22 June, his *Panzers* might have taken Moscow. As it was, they reached the city's suburbs in November but were stopped by the onset of winter.

The second result of the occupation of Yugoslavia, precipitated by the officers' coup of 26 March, was to tie up many divisions of the German army in the most savage and costly resistance fighting in Europe. In 1943 and 1944, Hitler had over 200,000 troops fighting Tito's Partisans, when they might have been better employed elsewhere.

Within ten days of the first German attack in 1941, the Yugoslav army was overwhelmed, and surrendered on 17 April. King Peter and his government took refuge in London. Yugoslavia was then partitioned: Croatia, together with Bosnia and Hercegovina, became an independent Fascist state under the *Ustache* leader Ante Pavelic; the Germans and Italians divided Slovenia between them; Bulgaria annexed Macedonia for the third time; Hungary took back Vojvodina and parts of Slovenia, which it had lost in 1918; and Italy annexed Dalmatia and Montenegro. Serbia was taken under German 'protection'.

The Fascist Croat 'kingdom' – a relative of the king of Italy was named 'King of Croatia' (though he never visited the place) – was one of the most vicious states in those vicious days. One third of the population was Serb, and Pavelic set about converting them to Catholicism; those who refused were killed. The killers made films of these attempts: congregations of Orthodox Serbs, lined up with their priests, and ordered to covert; they refuse, and the Croat machine-guns mow them down. The demonstration was effective: tens of thousands of Serbs besieged Catholic priests, demanding to be converted to save their lives. In the early days of the Croat kingdom, the Catholic Church there, led by Archbishop Stepinac of Zagreb, welcomed the new dispensation, but as the horrors mounted, Stepinac and most of his bishops offered some criticisms of Pavelic, at least on the matter of forced conversions. The Church never opposed Croat Fascism with the same determination that it later showed in its opposition to Communism.

Pavelic and his minister of the interior, Andriya Artukovitch, set up concentration camps for Serbs, Jews and Croatian democrats. In due course, many Serb and Croat prisoners were sent to slave labour camps in Norway, and the Jews were shipped to Auschwitz. Pavelic recruited Bosnian Muslims to join in the massacre of the Serbs, and the Germans raised a Muslim SS division there, which was inspected by the Grand Mufti of Jerusalem. In the end, the Croat regime was responsible for the deaths of some 700,000 people, out of a population of 6.3 million.

A group of Yugoslav officers, led by Colonel Draza Mihajlović, refused to submit to the Germans. Instead, they took to the hills, calling the resistance group they formed the *Cetniks*, after the ancient Serb warriors who had fought the Turks. In due course, Mihajlović was recognized by King Peter as minister of defence and commander of the resistance army. The British supplied him with arms and munitions and sent a military liaison officer, but because he wanted to avoid provoking German reprisals, which always followed attacks on them, he proved a disappointing leader.

In June 1941, Josip Broz appeared on the stage, using the *nom de guerre* 'Tito'. He had served in the Austrian army in the First World War, had been wounded and captured on the Eastern Front, and had witnessed the Russian Revolution at first hand. He was now secretary-general of the Yugoslav Communist Party, a post he had inherited when the previous occupant and most other party leaders were shot by Stalin. The party inside Yugoslavia was small but enthusiastic, and Tito proclaimed himself commander-in-chief of a new movement: the 'Partisans', named after the Spanish resistance to the Napoleonic invasion. They launched a general insurrection in Serbia in July 1941.

In the beginning, the Partisans were a huge success, liberating most of Serbia and driving the Germans back into the main towns. Tito and his colleagues then set themselves up in liberated territory with all the formality of a provisional government, including 'people's courts' and a party newspaper. From the start they proclaimed that their movement would be not merely a resistance, but a revolution: they intended to conquer the country from the Germans and from the old regime, and establish a Communist government. These policies had two consequences: the resistance provoked savage German reprisals; and the revolution led, by the end of the year, to a civil war between the Partisans and the *Cetniks*.

The Germans reacted violently to the initial Partisan successes. Several armoured and infantry divisions were brought into Yugoslavia to deal with the new enemy, and in November, the Germans counter-attacked – at the same time that, far to the east, the *Wehrmacht's* last attempt to break through Soviet lines in front of Moscow failed. Partisan historians later called the attack the 'First

German Offensive' (there were eventually seven). The liberated territory was quickly reconquered, and Tito and his Partisans hid themselves in the hills. By early December, they had been driven out of Serbia and took refuge in the high mountains of Bosnia, where they joined the guerrillas fighting against Pavelic's *Ustachis*. A second winter offensive, by German and Axis ski-troops, harried the Partisans from their new bases and drove them yet deeper into the mountains. The Germans exacted a terrible revenge upon the civilian population: 300 civilians were killed for every German, hundreds of villages were obliterated, towns were burned, food stores and farms were destroyed. Just as the *Wehrmacht* was faced with a protracted war in the Soviet Union, and not the *Blitzkrieg* that Hitler had promised, it was faced with the dangers and costs of a full-scale guerrilla war in the Balkans.

Meanwhile, the Montenegrins had risen against the Italians and had driven them from the province, until all that was left in Italian hands were three garrison towns, besieged by Montenegrins, Partisans and *Cetniks* together. The Italians then regrouped, sending heavy armoured columns into Montenegro from Albania and Dalmatia, and soon they reoccupied much of the country. Now Montenegro, like Bosnia to the north, was the scene of savage guerrilla fighting. The Italians then reached an understanding with the *Cetniks*, and in the following year, there was active collaboration between the two: the Italians held the towns while the *Cetniks* held the countryside: and both hunted and killed the Partisans.

Tito learned from this experience. For the rest of the war, the Partisans did not try to hold the territory they had liberated. When they were surrounded by the Germans, they would split up into small units, break out and counter-attack elsewhere in the country. Despite its apparent defeats, the Partisan army grew rapidly: at the end of 1941, Tito commanded 80,000 men; by the autumn of 1942, the total had risen to 150,000. In November that year, Tito convened a conference of resistance leaders, which proclaimed itself the Anti-Fascist Council for National Liberation of Yugoslavia (AVNOJ). It had a number of democratic members, but was wholly dominated by the Communists.

Tito proved to be an outstanding guerrilla leader, and soon there were 200,000 German troops and further contingents of Italians,

Bulgarians and pro-Nazi Serbs, Croats and Slovenes fighting him. The strength of the Partisans received a great boost in July 1943, when Italy dropped out of the war. After Tito's guerrillas captured five Italian divisions, with all their weapons and stores, the Germans never succeeded in occupying the whole country.

Meanwhile, the civil war between Tito and Mihajlović continued. They were fighting for the control of Yugoslavia, and in the usual Balkan manner, all other considerations were subordinated to this end. Having lost his Italian ally, Mihajlović threw in his lot with the Germans, hoping that in the end, when Germany itself was defeated, he would be strong enough to seize control of the government. Tito played a much more devious game. He was a devoted Communist and therefore unquestioningly loyal to the Soviet Union, but Stalin did nothing to help him for the first three years of his war. He therefore turned to the British for help, but before he could get it, he needed to persuade them that Mihajlović's *Cetniks* were contributing nothing to the Allied war effort. In due course, he succeeded.

In the early days, Stalin constantly urged Tito not to proclaim a Soviet republic, and to collaborate with the royal government-in-exile and with the British and Americans. He was afraid that, if the Western allies perceived that Tito was intent on founding a Communist state, they would come to doubt the sincerity of Stalin's own democratic utterances and all his promises to liberate Europe. It later emerged that the British, at least, had no illusions about either Tito or Stalin and were perfectly sincere in their professions of indifference as to the post-war constitution of Yugoslavia.

There has been much strenuous disagreement ever since between those who believe that the British were correct in shifting their support from Mihajlović to Tito, and those who think that Churchill was duped and that Mihajlović was in fact a worthy ally. Those who support Tito have had the best of the argument because, whatever his motives, he undoubtedly made an immense contribution to the war effort, while Mihajlović did not.

British support for Mihajlović ended early in 1944. Tito, who had been nearly captured by a German parachute attack on his headquarters, moved to Vis, an island in the Adriatic occupied by the British. He was taken on a visit to British headquarters in Italy that summer, and in August, he met Churchill in Naples.

The accusation against Churchill and his dealing with Tito is the same as that made against Churchill and Roosevelt over Yalta – that they betrayed Eastern Europe to Communism. The answer, in both cases, is that *force majeure* prevailed. The Red Army decided the nature of the governments of Poland, Hungary and Romania, and Tito's quarter of a million Partisans decided the fate of Yugoslavia.

The important distinction between the post-war circumstances of Yugoslavia and those of the other Communist countries of Eastern Europe was that Tito won his revolution by himself. Of course, he would never have survived if the Red Army had not defeated Hitler in the East. In addition, in October 1944, the Red Army liberated Belgrade for him, and it went on to fight the Germans during that last, bitter winter as they retreated through northern Yugoslavia, holding out until Hitler committed suicide in Berlin. But Tito and his Partisans liberated the rest of the country – all of it, in fact, except the northeast corner and the Germans' northern redoubt. The Soviet troops were then withdrawn, leaving Tito undisputed master of the field.

Communist Yugoslavia

The end of the war was marked with typical Balkan savagery. About 250,000 Croats had fled across the border into Austria to escape Tito's avenging sword, but the Western allies refused them refuge and sent them back. Thousands were summarily executed, and in the next few months, there was a general terror throughout Yugoslavia as surviving *Ustachis, Cetniks*, monarchists and democrats were purged. The exact number of those killed is not known, but no doubt it ran into tens of thousands.

Mihajlović, who had tried to continue the fight against the Communists, was arrested, tried for treason, convicted and shot. At his trial, he pronounced his own epitaph: 'Destiny was merciless to me when it threw me into the most difficult whirlwinds. I wanted much, I began much, but the whirlwind, the world whirlwind, carried me and my work away.' Archbishop Stepinac was also tried, and in September 1946, he was sentenced to 16 years' hard labour for collaboration.

Mihajlović's 'world whirlwind' had devastated the country. The government calculated that 1.7 million people had been killed, out of a population of about 16 million, the greatest loss being of young men. Only Poland suffered more proportionately. At the same time, the cities, industries, railways and the rest of the country's infrastructure were severely damaged or destroyed. It was on this scene of desolation that Tito set about imposing Stalinism.

The other countries of Eastern Europe went through a period of transition until 1948, before fully-fledged Soviet Communism was established. Yugoslavia had no respite. It was not needed: the Yugoslav party was quite strong enough to embark upon its socialist revolution immediately. Nor were there any constitutional impediments. When Churchill abandoned Mihajlović in 1943, he obliged King Peter to recognize Tito's National Liberation Front, although a few cabinet posts were given to monarchists. After the Yalta conference, in February 1945, the great powers recognized Tito's government. By the end of the year, the monarchists were gone, the monarchy had been abolished, and an altogether fraudulent election had given Tito absolute control of the country.

Until his break with Stalin in 1948, Tito was the most vehement Stalinist in Eastern Europe. He was one of the great heroes of the war, unlike Rákosi or Gottwald, and his strenuous loyalty to the Soviet Union and loud denunciations of the West played a large role in international affairs. Yugoslavia was one of the few European countries with a completely independent government, and its voice counted. Tito ignored the immense contribution that Britain and the United States had made to his struggle, and started the Cold War immediately, even ahead of Stalin. He supported Communist guerrillas in Greece, who were fighting a civil war, and tried to annex Albania.

The United States Air Force did not adapt quickly enough to the new situation, and its aircraft based in Austria and Italy frequently flew across Yugoslav territory without permission. Tito protested, but the USAF ignored the protests. Then, in 1946, one American plane was forced down inside Yugoslavia and a second was shot down, killing the five-man crew. This time, Tito had gone too far. Stalin told him to back off, and he grudgingly apologized, returned the crew of the first plane and paid compensation for the second.

At the same time, Yugoslavia and Britain were on the brink of war over the ancient Adriatic seaport of Trieste, which had been governed by the Italians since 1918 and which Tito now coveted. The Yugoslavs had already seized all other Italian possessions in the Balkans, as well as the areas that Italy had claimed in Dalmatia, including Fiume (which the Yugoslavs renamed Rijeka) and most of the Istrian peninsula. The British had promised Trieste to Tito during the war, but at its end, they had evicted the Yugoslav troops and occupied it themselves, together with a small area beyond, in what came to be known as 'Zone A'. Yugoslavia held the rest of Istria – 'Zone B' – and as Tito became ever more hostile to the West, Britain and the United States decided to uphold the Italians' renewed claims. The dispute continued until 1954, when both sides recognized the provisional boundaries as permanent. Yugoslavia had also occupied Klagenfurt – about 20 miles inside the Austrian border – in 1945, and had been forced to pull back.

Meanwhile, Tito nationalized all industry, banks and other businesses, began collectivizing the land, and set up a ruthless and efficient secret police. The regime persecuted both Catholic and Orthodox churches, seizing their property and closing monasteries and places of worship. Declaring that 'The most dangerous thing for us now would be to stop half-way,' Tito went on to prepare a 'Five-Year Plan' of massive industrialization. The object was to catch up with British levels of industrial production within ten years. In all things, he was following faithfully in Stalin's footsteps, and like Stalin, he was to discover that the peasantry was bitterly opposed to the state farms.

At this point, Tito was apparently Stalin's favourite satellite leader, and when he visited Moscow, he was showered with honours. At the funeral of the Soviet president, Mikhail Kalinin in 1946, he was invited to review the parade from the top of Lenin's mausoleum, next to Stalin himself.

When Stalin set up a new international Communist organization – the Communist Information Bureau, or Cominform – its headquarters were in Belgrade. When, at its first meeting, the Yugoslavs were instructed to attack the French party for deviation, they did so with such enthusiasm and effectiveness that the French leader, Jacques Duclos, walked out of the session and retreated to the garden, to sit on a bench and sulk.

The break with Stalin

On 28 June 1948, the Communist Party of the Soviet Union and its allies in Eastern Europe abruptly expelled Yugoslavia from the alliance. It was the anniversary of the assassination of the Archduke Franz Ferdinand in Sarajevo and was equally unexpected and sensational.

Stalin was then at the height of his power. The Berlin blockade had begun four days earlier, Czechoslovakia had fallen to Communism in February, and Mao Tse-tung was closing in on Peking. News that one of Stalin's satraps had defied him was as astonishing as the Hitler–Stalin pact of 1939, and threw the chancelleries into confusion. From a distance, it seemed inevitable that Tito must surrender. Stalin certainly thought so: he told Khrushchev, 'I will shake my little finger, and there will be no more Tito.' Things did not turn out like that. The very circumstances that led to the break with Moscow gave Tito the strength to maintain it.

The causes of the dispute between the two governments were much debated in the 1950s, before more serious upheavals threatened the Soviet bloc. The heart of the matter was authority. Stalin was an absolute dictator in the Soviet Union itself and in Eastern Europe. He demanded and got unquestioning and slavish obedience, reinforcing his power from time to time by the use of terror, purging his subordinates and killing them. In 1948, it was time to bring Yugoslavia to heel.

But Tito was not like Gomułka in Poland, Slanský in Czechoslovakia or Rajk in Hungary. His rule in Yugoslavia was as unchallenged as Stalin's own in the USSR, with the further advantage that he ruled his party by true loyalty and affection. He had not murdered his colleagues, like Stalin, and he did not govern them by fear. When the *ukase* came from Moscow and he summoned the party Central Committee, only two of its members voted to obey Stalin, and one of these later recanted when he read the lies that the KGB was publishing about the Yugoslav party. The other dissenter, according to the Yugoslavs, had been a *Ustache* spy during the war – a fact discovered by the MVD, who used the man as its own spy within the Yugoslav government.

The ostensible cause of the dispute was Tito's foreign policy.

He had ambitions for a Yugoslav empire in the Balkans, based on a union with Bulgaria and the annexation of Albania. Although the Bulgarian leader, Georgi Dimitrov, had expressed enthusiasm for the idea, the Soviets forced him to recant, and the Albanians, who also approved, were instructed by Stalin to reassert their independence. Subsequently, Stalin changed his mind and ordered the Yugoslavs and Bulgars to push their federation ahead rapidly, possibly intending to subvert the Yugoslavs with loyal Bulgarian Communists. By then, February 1948, Tito had lost interest and declined the offer.

Another source of dispute was the Soviet determination to exploit the Yugoslav economy, as it was exploiting the other Eastern Europeans. Stalin wanted to set up joint Soviet–Yugoslav companies to develop Yugoslav minerals, and the Yugoslavs resisted: they understood perfectly well that the Soviets intended to take what they wanted and then would decide themselves what, if anything, they would pay. Tito wanted to industrialize his country, on the Soviet model; Stalin wanted to keep Yugoslavia as a supplier of raw materials for Soviet industry, nothing more. Meanwhile, the Soviet army and security services had heavily infiltrated Yugoslav military and police organizations, trying to take control as they had in Hungary, Romania and Poland. Partisans who had fought the Germans for four years did not take kindly to Soviets giving them orders.

In 1937, at the height of the purges, Tito had been summoned to Moscow, and had gone without knowing whether he was to be shot or promoted. He was appointed secretary general of the Yugoslav Communist Party.

In January 1948, he was again summoned to Moscow to discuss Yugoslavia's relations with Albania and Bulgaria. This time he declined. Instead he sent senior members of his Politburo*, who were appalled at the virulence of the attack that Stalin and Molotov launched against them. They were accused of every imaginable sin, most notably of having proposed a federation with Bulgaria without consulting Moscow. It did them no good to show Stalin the telegrams that they had sent to Molotov describing the project.

* See p. 177.

The dispute grew more heated. In March, Soviet military and civilian personnel working in Yugoslavia were abruptly recalled, and Stalin wrote a series of highly abusive letters, denouncing Tito's policies and demanding that he recant. Finally, in June, Tito was invited to attend a meeting of the Cominform in Poland. After careful thought, he again declined: the Yugoslav party refused to attend its own execution.

The Cominform resolution stated:

> Recently, the Yugoslav Communist Party has pursued an incorrect line on the main questions of home and foreign policy, a line which represents a departure from Marxism–Leninism . . . The Information Bureau [Cominform] declares that the leadership of the Yugoslav Communist Party is pursuing an unfriendly policy towards the Soviet Union . . . Instead of accepting [Soviet criticism] in a Bolshevik manner, and mending their ways, the leaders of the Communist Party of Yugoslavia, suffering from boundless ambition, arrogance and conceit, have met this criticism with belligerence and hostility.

The resolution ruled that

> the Central Committee of the Communist Party of Yugoslavia has placed itself and the Yugoslav party outside the family of the fraternal Communist parties, outside the united Communist Front and consequently outside the Information Bureau . . . Such a nationalist line can only lead to Yugoslavia's degeneration into an ordinary bourgeois republic, to the loss of its independence and to its transformation into a colony of the imperialist countries.

The Cominform then called upon 'healthy elements, loyal to Marxism–Leninism' to replace the party's leaders with 'a new internationalist leadership'.

Stalin found that he had been mistaken. He had shaken his finger but nothing had happened. Tito had the almost unanimous support of his Politburo and Central Committee (the two members who disagreed were promptly purged).

Doubters in the party at large were also removed: about 14,000 potential Stalinists were jailed. The most senior defector was the chief of staff, who tried to cross the border into Romania but was shot in the attempt.

Tito then called a party conference and devoted himself to

reaffirming his Communist credentials, to protect himself against the charge of transforming the country into 'an ordinary bourgeois republic'. The party rallied behind him, despite finding it hard to convert overnight from devoted loyalty to Stalin and to the Soviet Motherland – Yugoslav patriotism was much stronger.

Stalin tried economic pressure. All trade between Yugoslavia and other Communist countries was cut off; Soviet aid, such as it was, was ended; and Yugoslavia was left to its own devices. Albania seized the occasion of Tito's excommunication to sever its own ties of dependency with Yugoslavia.

To begin with, Tito continued to pursue a policy of hostility to the West to prove his Communist credentials. The Americans and the British showed understanding: when the time came, they offered to help Yugoslavia without attaching any intolerable strings. The West was perfectly ready to forgive the misapprhensions of the previous three years. There were conditions, of course. In 1949, Yugoslavia ended its support for the Communist guerrillas in Greece and the civil war there soon came to an end. The US returned Yugoslavia's gold reserves, which it had held since before the war. The British signed a trade agreement worth £30 million in December 1948; the first American assistance arrived nine months later; and soon Western military and economic aid was pouring in. It proved particularly valuable during a severe drought in 1950.

Yugoslavia weathered the crisis. By 1950, when it was obvious to the Soviets that the only way to suppress Tito was to invade, it was too late. The Yugoslav army had been rearmed and had regrouped on the eastern frontier, and was ready to fight, and it had sufficiently demonstrated its competence between 1941 and 1945 to give even Stalin pause. Furthermore, Stalin by then had to admit that the Berlin blockade had failed – and the success of the Chinese revolution had established another, yet more formidable rival to his authority in the world Communist movement.

The Yugoslav road to socialism

To begin with, Tito continued to profess unyielding loyalty to the Stalinist model of economic development – Stalin may have disowned the Yugoslav party, but the party would not disown

Stalinism – but by 1950, the failures of this policy were mani-fest. Collectivization of agriculture was abandoned in 1953; and the Yugoslavs invented 'self-management' for industry: factories, though owned by the state, had to manage their own affairs instead of being dependent upon a rigid central plan on the Soviet model. The idea was greatly appealing to socialists throughout the world and still turns up from time to time. However, it proved a failure when applied to the whole Yugoslav economy. One disadvantage was that the party remained in control. Although workers, in theory, managed their own factories, they did so under the direction of party bosses who, in turn, obeyed instructions from Belgrade.

Nevertheless, the ending of detailed central planning and price controls did produce immediate effects: the Yugoslav economy started expanding, and the standard of living improved. It was still an authoritarian state, but from the early 1950s, it was con-spicuously less tyrannous than Hungary, Romania and the other Communist nations. Persecution of the churches was much reduced, and Archbishop Stepinac was released. When one of Tito's leading ministers, Milovan Djilas, broke with him, he was admonished; later, in 1954, as his dissidence persisted, he was jailed; but he was not executed.

Tito proposed an immediate 'withering away of the state', in accordance with Karl Marx's utopian theories. It was quite different from the Leninist concept of the dictatorship of the pro-letariat, let alone Stalin's doctrine of the intensification of the class struggle after the revolution (which required a party dictatorship). In Yugoslavia, state and party were, in theory, separate, and to reflect this, the party was renamed the League of Communists of Yugoslavia. The limits of these policies soon became apparent: Tito insisted on keeping ultimate power for himself. He was particularly concerned to suppress any sign of nationalistic enthusiasm in the various republics. Whenever Croats or Slovenes began to challenge the central authority, Tito at once stepped in to reaffirm Belgrade's pre-eminence.

In foreign affairs, Tito rapidly discovered the joys of non-alignment. He made common cause with leaders of former colonies, notably Nehru, Nasser and Sukarno, and together they proclaimed the 'Third World', as opposed to the 'First (Capitalist)

World' and the 'Second (Communist) World'. It was a confusing concept, especially when China insisted on joining, but it gave Tito a far greater authority abroad than his own country's rather meagre importance would otherwise have allowed. He travelled the world in a series of resplendent uniforms, and was received everywhere as a hero.

Relations with the Soviet Union started to improve as soon as Stalin died. In the summer of 1953, the two countries agreed to exchange ambassadors again. Tito's apotheosis came in May 1955, when Nikita Khrushchev travelled to Belgrade, like the emperor Henry IV to Canossa, to confess that the breach between Yugoslavia and the Soviet Union had been an error. It was all most gratifying.

Despite the fact that Tito still refused to rejoin the Soviet bloc – Yugoslavia would sign neither the Warsaw Pact nor the Comecon – Khrushchev consulted him on major questions, as one of the world's elder statesmen. Although Tito gave his approval to the invasion of Hungary in 1956, he later concluded that it had been a mistake, and relations cooled again. He also opposed the invasion of Czechoslovakia in 1968, having enthusiastically welcomed Dubček's 'Communism with a human face', seeing it as a latter-day Titoism. He remained a Communist, but insisted on following the 'Yugoslav Way', and, in matters of foreign policy, he resembled Romania's Ceauşescu, though his regime was far less authoritarian.

By the 1970s, the 'Yugoslav Way' was becoming much less appealing. The country was no longer developing economically. Like other Eastern European countries, it suffered increasingly from the depressing contrast with Western prosperity, particularly during the recession following the oil crisis. Furthermore, its intellectuals were demanding greater liberty: it was all very well praising Dubček, but why was there still less freedom in Yugoslavia than Dubček had allowed in Czechoslovakia? At the same time, the deterioration in East–West relations, as well as the fissiparous tendencies of the Third World, reduced Yugoslavia's role. The new leaders of Asian and African countries paid much less attention to the ageing Marshall than had Nehru and Nasser. Their role model was Castro, not Tito.

Tito died in May 1980, at the age of 88. He left a precarious constitution behind him, with a weak central government directed by a rotating presidency: each of the country's six constituent republics would nominate a president for a one-year term once every six years. The party remained the glue that was to hold the federation together, and as the 1980s wore on, it proved insufficient.

One problem Tito did not solve was the question of the minorities, cut off from their compatriots by the frontiers of 1919. Their rights and privileges are all supposedly protected by the constitution. This theoretically admirable state of affairs has been most severely tested in Kosovo, the autonomous province of Serbia that lies immediately north and east of Albania and which is the poorest region of Yugoslavia. Ninety per cent of its population of 1.7 million are Albanians (also known as the Shqiptars) and speak that language, and most of them are Muslim. According to Serbian propaganda, there were as many Serbs as Albanians in Kosovo a generation ago, but the majority of Serbs were driven out by Albanian terrorism. None of this is true: Kosovo has been solidly Albanian for centuries, and those of its Serbian minority who left did so to find greener pastures in the north. In all the redrawing of maps that followed the breakup of the Ottoman empire in the 19th century and during the Balkan wars (1912–18), Albania's neighbours were always too powerful to permit ethnographically just frontiers. During the Italian occupation in World War II, Kosovo was annexed to Albania, but in 1944, Enver Hoxha (*see* Chapter 6) dutifully returned the province to his patron, Tito. He had no choice.

In 1981, there were pogroms against the Serb minority in Kosovo, many of whom were murdered (50 by official count), and there were the usual Balkan reports of frightful atrocities perpetrated by the Albanians. As for the Albanians, they claimed that they were the victims of extreme discrimination in their own homeland. The whole situation closely parallels that in Nagorno-Karabakh, in Azerbaijan in the Soviet Union, a region chiefly populated by Armenians and claimed by both republics.

No one in his right mind would wish to be united with modern Albania as long as its reclusive tyranny endures. The Kosovo Albanians who have been demanding independence for the past decade claim that they want to create a new Yugoslav republic, like Slovenia. When President Alia of Albania goes the way of Ceauşescu of Romania, their demands will doubtless become the more insistent, and might well then swerve towards secession from Yugoslavia and union with Albania. The parallel, this time, would be with Soviet Moldavia.

The Serbs utterly reject the idea, declaring that Kosovo has forever been part of Serbia (in 1389, the Turks defeated the Serbs in a famous battle there, a Balkan Flodden). They take the same position that the Azeris take over Nagorno-Karabakh, with the same violent consequences. In 1989, Serbia sent large numbers of troops to patrol Kosovo and support the local regime, which was appointed by the Serbian government in Belgrade.

Other national antagonisms persist. Serbs have not forgotten that the Croats and Slovenes joined the Germans during World War II. The Croats, conversely, resent domination from Belgrade, as do the Slovenes. Other distinctions and disagreements go back to the Austro-Hungarian period and beyond.

Yugoslavia likes to think that it could be a Balkan Communist Switzerland, with its many nationalities cohabiting peacefully together. It is nothing of the sort. Its survival so far has been a miracle, and from 1948 until recent times, its unity has owed a great deal to its nationalities' deep hostility to the USSR: however much Slovenes and Macedonians disliked Belgrade, they much preferred it to Moscow. Now that this threat has been lifted, they are free to quarrel among themselves, and they are increasingly availing themselves of that dispensation.

Yugoslavia's economic situation deteriorated steadily during the 1980s, and the collective government set up after Tito's death quite lacked the authority to deal with the underlying economic and political problems. By 1988, the signs of dissolution had become evident. Serbs began to demand that their numbers and historic role as leaders of Yugoslavia be recognized. The Serbian party leader, Slobodan Milosevic, put himself at the head of a xenophobic Serb movement, and won a degree of popularity that no Yugoslav leader had enjoyed since Tito. As a result, of course, he was widely distrusted in the other regions.

Milosevic demanded that Kosovo and Vojvodina, the other autonomous province, in the northeast, should both lose their autonomy and be completely reintegrated into Serbia. Early in

October 1988, he organized a mass demonstration of 100,000 Serbs in Vojvodina, which deteriorated into violence and led to the resignation of the entire local government. On 9 October, he instigated similar riots in Montenegro, Yugoslavia's smallest republic, demanding the local government's resignation. Montenegrins are Serbs in language, though they have a separate history, and they share Serbians' feelings about Kosovo. On that occasion, the authorities suppressed the rioters.

On 20 October 1988, at a meeting of the party Politburo, Milosevic repeated his demands that Kosovo and Vojvodina be incorporated into Serbia and that Serbia's role in the federation be strengthened. The Politburo ruled against him and voted to uphold the loose system bequeathed by Tito. The Serbian leader would not accept the verdict and, in November, succeeded in forcing the resignations of party leaders in Kosovo, whom he accused of abetting the 'persecution' of the Serbian minority. The following week, he called for an enormous demonstration in Belgrade against the alleged Albanian atrocities in Kosovo; at least 600,000 people answered the call. Then, on 11 January 1989, a further series of demonstrations in Montenegro stirred up by Milosevic's supporters forced the resignation of the entire government and party leadership there. Milosevic now controlled Kosovo, Vojvodina and Montenegro, as well as Serbia itself. Meanwhile, Albanians were demonstrating in Pristina, the capital of Kosovo, demanding the reinstatement of the dismissed officials.

Yugoslavia's economic crisis continued to worsen, as in the rest of Eastern Europe. Inflation reached an annual rate of 250 per cent by the end of 1988, accelerating briefly to 10,000 per cent per annum a year later. The 'self-management' of industrial enterprises introduced by Tito has proved a disaster. Large numbers of these enterprises are bankrupt but cannot be closed. The six republics compete against each other: Serbia initiated an economic boycott of Slovenia in 1989, and all the republics consider themselves both economically independent and the victims of the machinations of the others. There is far less cooperation between them than there is between unrelated independent states elsewhere in the world, let alone between the 12 members of the European Community. In the autumn of 1988, the federal government, headed by an economist, Branko Mikulic, proposed stringent reform measures, in consultation with the IMF. The reforms were rejected by parliament (which refused to pass the budget), and the government resigned on 30 December. This is a Western phenomenon and it was the first time such a thing had happened in a Communist country.

It failed to resolve Yugoslavia's problems. A new government appeared, in March 1989, led by Ante Markovic, a former bank manager and prime minister of Croatia. Proposing even stiffer economic reforms, he used the government's constitutional weakness to his advantage, by persuading parliament (then controlled by the party bosses) that, because of the crisis, they should give him emergency powers. He promptly tied the Yugoslav *dinar* to the German *Mark*, and announced that the Yugoslav currency would become fully convertible from 1 January 1990; at the same time, he permitted unlimited foreign ownership of Yugoslav companies. He then set about using the economic reforms to provoke the country and party into agreeing to political reforms along the lines of those of the rest of Eastern Europe. He is now the only Yugoslav politician with a national reputation, and the only person who can effectively challenge Milosevic.

The winds of change

The conflict between the various republics was steadily increasing. In December 1989, the Communist parties of Croatia and the Communist party in Slovenia both voted to hold free elections in 1990, abandoning the Communists' 'leading role'. Having observed events in the rest of Eastern Europe (their conferences occurred during the Romanian revolution), they had concluded that their only salvation lay in adopting a market economy – and applying to join the European Community.

Kosovo had suffered severely from the country's economic recession and from the heavy hand of Slobodan Milosevic, and the situation there grew steadily worse, building up to full-scale rebellion in January 1990. In 1989, over 20 people were killed in disturbances in the province, most of them Albanians, and in the last week of January 1990, another 20 were killed.

On 20 January 1990, a national party convention broke up in disorder when the Slovene delegates walked out, leaving the national party hopelessly split. The Slovenes, supported by the Croatians – and by the other two republics, Macedonia and Bosnia-Hercegovina, though with less vehemence – had demanded that the constitution be amended to guarantee freedom of the press and other human rights; and that the party commit itself to the dismantling of Communism. They had been defeated by the block vote of Serbians and Montenegrins. The conference did, however, vote to abandon the party's 'leading role'.

The party was disintegrating, an event that left the prime minister, Ante Markovic, unmoved. 'Yugoslavia will function with or without the Communist party,' he said. It was not at all clear that he was right. On 8 April 1990, in free elections in Slovenia, a large majority went to an anti-Communist coalition; the Communist party won only about 20 per cent of the vote, although a reform Communist, Milan Kukan, was elected the republic's president. The following month, an anti-Communist alliance, headed by a former general, Franjo Tudjman, won a sweeping victory in free elections in Croatia. The new governments in both republics insisted that they would only remain in the federation on their own terms, which amounted to a dismantling of virtually all the powers of the central government. Even that was not enough for many Croats and Slovenes, who demanded complete independence; other Slovenes wanted a federation with Austria; and many more wanted to abandon the sinking Yugoslav ship and join the European Community. Tudjman proposed a series of constitutional changes that would affirm Croatia's 'sovereignty'. If Belgrade objected, he would take Croatia out of the federation – an event that would inevitably lead to Slovenia's secession, too.

6 Albania

At the end of 1989, Albania was a last fossilized remnant of Stalinism in the Balkans, whose government desperately insisted that it would never bow to the hurricane sweeping away the rest of Communist Europe. In the spring of 1990, the government promised reform, and in the summer the first public signs of dissidence appeared in the capital, Tirana. Albanians scaled the walls of foreign embassies demanding asylum and the right to emigrate, like the East Germans a year before.

When the winds of change from Eastern Europe blow away the regime, the outside world will at last discover how much of the old, tribal structure has survived, whether Albania is still Muslim, and how the Albanians have preserved their own identity despite nearly 50 years' teaching of Marxism, Leninism, Stalinism and the *Thoughts of Chairman Mao*.

There is no doubt they have preserved it. Their history is one of stubborn independence over the millennia. The Communist regime, set up by Enver Hoxha in 1944, survived so long because it defied all foreign influences: Italian, American, Yugoslav, Soviet and, finally, even the Chinese. From 1970, it reduced the country to a degree of self-imposed isolation for which there is hardly any modern parallel – perhaps Burma is the only other recent case of a country secluding itself in righteous poverty at the behest of a dogmatic tyranny. Albania is one of the crossroads of Europe, but it has locked itself away in its mountains, refusing to entertain even the most cursory diplomatic relations with most other nations. Xenophobia is a national characteristic, carried to an extreme by the Communists, and quite sufficient to preserve Albania's traditional identity despite all the regime's efforts to create a socialist utopia.

The Albanians are descendants of the prehistoric inhabitants of the Balkans – the Illyrians and Thracians who shared the peninsula with the Greeks before Agamemnon sailed for Troy. They were conquered by the Romans because their port Dyrrhachium (modern Durrës; Durazzo in Italian) controlled the entrance to the Adriatic (there are no Italian ports across the Straits of Otranto). One of the main roads of the empire – the Via Egnatia – ran from Dyrrhachium eastwards to Byzantium.

The Illyrians were notable warriors – the emperors Aurelian, Probus, Diocletian and Constantine were all Illyrians – and unlike the Gauls, the Spaniards and all the tribes of Italy, they retained their own language. The Albanians resisted the Slav invasions, which overwhelmed all the rest of the Balkans except Greece itself, and they were the last to be conquered by the Turks: in the 15th century the national hero, George Kastriota, known as Skanderbeg, defended Albania against no less formidable enemies than the sultans Murad and Mohammed the Conqueror.

Ten years after Skanderbeg's death in 1468, the Turks finally conquered Albania. In the four centuries during which they ruled the country, most of the inhabitants were converted to Islam, and many of them served in the armies of the sultan as their ancestors had served Rome. A number of grand viziers were Albanians, as was Mehemet Ali who made himself Khedive of Egypt in the 19th century. Kemal Atatürk, the founder of modern Turkey, may also have been part Albanian.

Albania, along with the rest of the Balkans, revolted against the Turks in the 19th century but remained in the ramshackle Ottoman empire into the 20th century, largely because the major powers could not determine what to do with it. The Greeks, Italians, Serbs and Austrians all coveted it, especially the ports of Durrës and Vlorë (Valona). Finally the Albanians took the matter into their own hands: in 1912, during the general upheaval which finally drove the Turks out of the Balkans, they asserted their independence.

The powers imposed a monarch upon the new nation, a German prince called William of Wied: he arrived in March 1914 and was driven out again in November, leaving Albania independent but ungoverned. The powers also settled the frontier question. They were determined that Serbia should be kept away from the Adriatic but, as a consolation, allowed it to keep Kosovo, a province with a large Albanian majority. The Greeks were forbidden to occupy southern Albania, which had a Greek population and which they called 'Northern Epirus', and the frontier between Albania and Macedonia left many Albanians on the wrong side of the line, subject to Greeks, Bulgars or Serbs according to the varying fortunes of the Balkan wars. Like so many other decisions concerning Balkan frontiers, these are all still the subject of heated debate.

Albania had no effective central government during the First World War. The Serbian army, defeated by the Austrians and Bulgarians, retreated across Albania to Corfu. One of the secret wartime treaties provided that Greece, Italy and Serbia would partition Albania, and by the end of the war, it was occupied by competing Italian, Serb, Greek, Austrian and French armies. Diplomatic efforts removed all but the Italians. The Albanians once again rose in revolt against their oppressors, in 1920 driving out the Italians, who vowed to return. The Albanians then set about establishing a state of their own, for the first time in their long history.

A national assembly was convened in 1920. Among its leaders was Fan Noli, who had studied at Harvard and had appointed himself the Albanian Orthodox bishop of Boston, and who, on his return to Albania, had become bishop of Durrës. Another was Ahmet Bey Zogu of Mati, a Muslim, who was one of the country's principal tribal leaders. These two competed for power for most of the 1920s, until in 1928 Ahmet Bey proclaimed himself King Zog. The name means 'Bird', and his official title translates as 'Bird I, King of the Sons of the Eagle'. Skanderbeg's crest was the eagle, and modern Albanians chose it as their national symbol.

Albanian politics were violent and unpredictable, which was only to be expected in a country which included the blood feud among its most cherished traditions. On one occasion, during a visit to Vienna, Zog and his guards fought a gun battle with an assassin on the steps of the opera house. It was a Balkan habit: assassination was just as common in Yugoslavia, Romania and Bulgaria. Meanwhile, the country moved slowly towards the 20th century. Its government remained corrupt and its population illiterate, with an annual *per capita* income in 1927 of $40.07 – half that of the other impoverished Balkan countries. There

were no railways, few roads, no university and few other signs
of modernity.

The Italians continued to be closely interested in Albanian
affairs. Mussolini sent officers for the Albanian army and advisers
for the Albanian government. Zog alternated between cooperation
with the Italians, accepting their bribes, and opposition to them. It
was a difficult balancing act: Greece and Yugoslavia still aspired to
partition Albania between them, and Zog understood perfectly the
dangers of relying on Mussolini to protect him.

The end was inevitable. In April 1939, as Hitler led Europe into
war, Mussolini occupied Albania and Zog fled the country. Victor
Emmanuel III was proclaimed king of Albania, which became
a province of Italy, as preparations began for Mussolini's next
imperial adventure: the invasion of Greece.

That enterprise began in October 1940 and proved a disaster.
The Greeks soundly defeated the Italians and, in their turn, invaded
Albania, occupying the south of the country. As spring approached,
they prepared to resume their offensive and conquer the rest. Hitler,
who was preparing for the invasion of the Soviet Union, was
enraged at his ally's defeat. Mussolini had not informed him of
his intentions and was suitably humiliated by his failure. Hitler
decided to rescue him, out of Fascist solidarity. The Yugoslav
government was induced to sign a treaty of alliance, which would
have permitted German troops to cross the country on their way
to Greece, but a *coup d'état* in Belgrade, on 26 March 1941, put a
stop to that. The Germans occupied Yugoslavia and partitioned it
with their allies, and then they invaded and occupied Greece. Italy's
rule was restored in Albania, and it added Kosovo, a province of
Yugoslavia populated by Albanians, to its new possessions.

Tito sent emissaries into Albania to form a Communist party
there. A number of factions were brought together and held a
founding conference at which the party was established, in November 1941. The new party was about 100 strong, and its first
secretary was Enver Hoxha, who had studied in France and
worked in Belgium. The party immediately set about recruiting
partisan groups and preparing for an insurrection against the
Italians. Soon there were strikes, riots and attacks on the occupying
forces. The party followed the Yugoslav lead in forming an alliance
with non-Communist resistance groups, establishing the National

Liberation Movement (LNC). Many Albanians refused to join this Communist-front organization, and a rival resistance movement, known as the *Balli Kombetar* (BK), was set up. Soon there was a civil war between the LNC and the BK, like the one in Yugoslavia between Tito's Partisans and Mihajlović's *Cetniks*.

The partisan movement in Albania was an extension of the war in Yugoslavia, but less violent. After Italy dropped out of the war in 1943, the Germans occupied Albania. They showed more finesse there than they had in Yugoslavia, setting up a regency council to govern the country while restricting their occupation to the coastal regions and the main roads through Albania into Greece. In early 1944, the LNC was decisively defeated: Hoxha's forces were completely encircled by the Germans, and he had to be rescued by a guerrilla contingent led by Mehmet Shehu, the most effective Albanian guerrilla leader. The LNC was kept going by Tito and by arms deliveries from the British, who supported the LNC against the BK as they supported Tito against the *Cetniks*. The two situations were not the same, something that the British did not appreciate: the BK did not collaborate with the Italians and Germans as the *Cetniks* did in Yugoslavia. It is at least possible that, if the British had supported the BK, it might have won its civil war. On the other hand, Tito's 150,000 Partisans would most probably have decided the issue in Hoxha's favour, whatever the British did.

By the middle of 1944, as the Germans started to withdraw from the Balkans, a full-scale civil war flared up between the LNC and the anti-Communists, dominated by the guerrilla troops of King Zog. The Communists won, with the help of Tito's Partisans, and Hoxha occupied the capital Tiranë (Tirana) and the other cities in August and September 1944, and proclaimed the republic.

Communist Albania

The Albanian Communist Party won control of the country thanks to Tito, much as the Romanian, Hungarian and Polish parties were installed in office by Stalin. They were all faced with the same problem: how to create the instruments of government out of tiny political parties with little popular support. The Albanian party had about 2000 members in 1944 and solved its problem in the same way that the Hungarians, Poles and others did: by coercing other parties into a coalition government dominated by the party, and then progressively purging all opposition while using the threat of foreign intervention – Yugoslav in the case of Albania, Soviet elswhere – to guarantee their position.

Unlike the other Eastern Communist states, the Albanians were not united behind a strong leader supported by Moscow. The Kremlin was remote, no loyal band of Albanian exiles in Moscow took control after the liberation, the Red Army never reached Albania and the influence of Tito's Yugoslavia was overwhelming. The divisions in the party leadership were partly personal and partly a question of which leaders were most loyal to Tito. The ostensible division was between 'workers' and 'intellectuals'. Enver Hoxha was an 'intellectual': he had studied in Montpellier University in France and had retained an affection for things French, admired General de Gaulle and had restored good relations with Italy. He was therefore accused by his proletarian rivals of having Western sympathies. The proletarians – whose leader was the minister of the interior Koci Xoxe (or Kochi Dzodze) – were supported by the Yugoslavs. Xoxe set about eliminating the 'intellectuals' from the party, directing a purge of Fascists, royalists, democrats and tribal dissidents, and he also battled with his rivals in the party. For the three years 1945–48, there was a bitter feud between the two factions.

Tito intended to annex Albania and make it the seventh republic in the Yugoslav federation. This was the fate that Albanian nationalists had been fighting against for 50 years, made no more palatable by the disguise of proletarian internationalism. Yugoslav military and civilian experts flooded the country, taking positions of responsibility at every level and behaving exactly like the Soviets in Romania and Poland; and in 1947, the Albanians agreed that two Yugoslav divisions should be stationed in the country. Stalin watched these developments with interest.

The fate of Albania was one of the issues that came between the Soviet Union and Yugoslavia. Stalin objected to other Communist countries having satellites; that was the Soviet Union's prerogative. When the Cominform was set up in 1947, Albania was not invited to participate because it would have voted for Yugoslavia in any dispute – and Stalin already anticipated having serious trouble with Tito. In January 1948, a Yugoslav delegation was summoned to Moscow to discuss the Albanian problem. It was led by Milovan Djilas, and in his book *Conversations with Stalin* (1962), he offers an account of the dictator's methods.

> I had not even finished when, to my surprise, Stalin said, 'We have no special interest in Albania. We agree to Yugoslavia swallowing Albania!' At this, he gathered together the fingers of his right hand, and bringing them to his mouth, he made a motion as if to swallow them.
>
> I was astonished, almost struck dumb by Stalin's manner of expressing himself and by the gesture of swallowing, but I do not know whether this was visible on my face, because I tried to make a joke of it and to regard this as Stalin's customary drastic and picturesque manner of expression. Again I explained: 'It is not a matter of swallowing, but of unification!'
>
> At this Molotov interjected: 'But that is swallowing!'
>
> And Stalin added, again with that gesture of his: 'Yes, yes. Swallowing! But we agree with you: you ought to swallow Albania – the sooner the better.'

Reflecting on the matter the next day, Djilas concluded that Stalin was perhaps setting a trap for the Yugoslavs. They would swallow Albania, and the USSR would then come to the rescue of the unhappy victim. Two months later, Stalin launched his offensive against Tito in a series of letters accusing him and his party of every imaginable Leninist deviation, and in June, Yugoslavia was expelled from the Cominform.

This was the occasion Hoxha had been looking for. Within 72 hours, he had broken with Yugoslavia, sending all the Yugoslav military and civilian advisers packing, and joined vehemently in the Soviet denunciations of the errant comrades. It was a disaster for Koci Xoxe, Albania's leading Titoist. At first, he tried to defend himself by denouncing Tito and purging alleged Titoists from the party, but with the Soviet Union now wholly committed to Hoxha, his cause was lost. Tito could not save him: his own survival was problematic, and he dared not offer Stalin an excuse to invade Yugoslavia by intervening directly in Albania's affairs. In September 1948, Xoxe was forced out of the post of minister of the interior, and was succeeded by Mehmet Shehu. The following spring, Xoxe was purged with a number of other senior party leaders, and in May, they were tried in secret. Xoxe was shot; the others were sentenced to long terms of imprisonment.

Hoxha was then able to complete the establishment of his own personal dictatorship, which lasted until his death in 1985, and which was modelled closely on Stalin's practices. The purge of his enemies continued and, over the years, was periodically renewed. Economic and social policy followed the Soviet line. All religions were persecuted: the clergy were harassed, imprisoned or executed, and in 1967, every mosque and church in the country was closed and Albania proclaimed itself the world's first officially atheist state. Land was collectivized, private property abolished and every punitive measure a paranoid and nervous leadership could devise was inflicted upon the population to ensure its quiescence. In the general elections of 1950, there was a turnout of 99.43 per cent, and the National Front (the Communists and their allies) received 99.18 per cent of the vote – a remarkable achievement. More remarkable still, the party was able to increase its percentage of the vote in subsequent elections.

Some of Hoxa's paranoia was justified. In 1947, the British tried to start a guerrilla war in Albania, using surviving royalists in King Zog's native Mati in eastern Albania. A number of exiles were trained in guerrilla tactics by British specialists and parachuted into the Mati, where they were ill received. The peasants had not yet felt the full effects of Communism (the land was not collectivized until later) and saw no need to resume the civil war so soon. In 1948 and 1949, after Tito's break with Stalin, the newly created US Central Intelligence Agency joined the British and greatly increased the scope of the operation, in an attempt to start a real conflagration that would lead to Hoxa's over-throw. Its more ambitious agents also hoped to provoke uprisings against the Soviet Union throughout Eastern Europe. There was still residual guerrilla activity against the Communists in Poland, Romania, the Ukraine and the Baltic countries, and optimists thought a victory in Albania might encourage them to greater efforts.

The CIA set up a 'Committee of Free Albanians', recruited

fighters in the refugee camps of Europe and trained them in special facilities in Cyprus. Commanded by officers from ex-King Zog's personal guard, about 300 men were parachuted into Albania, or landed by sea, between 1950 and 1953. The Albanian security police were waiting for them, and all but a handful were captured. Most were killed on the spot; a few were put on trial and then shot. Credit for the Albanian success goes in part to Kim Philby, at that time the top Soviet agent in the British Secret Intelligence Service (SIS). He had been one of the people in charge of the operation in its early days, in the late 1940s, and then had moved to Washington to become the SIS's liaison with the CIA.

Communist Albania's foreign policy since 1948 has been one of increasingly intransigent independence. Immediately after the war – well before the SIS–CIA fiasco – Albania, like Yugoslavia, followed a bitterly anti-Western policy. The American and British governments had never recognized Albanian independence during the war. Afterwards, though perfectly ready to establish normal relations, their military missions in Tirana (their only representatives in the country) were treated with such suspicion that they were withdrawn in 1946. Neither country has had any diplomatic relations with Albania since then.

There also remains a long-standing diplomatic dispute between Britain and Albania. On 22 October 1946, two British destroyers sailing through the Strait of Corfu were seriously damaged by Albanian mines, and 40 sailors were killed. (Corfu is a Greek island in the Adriatic, opposite the Greek–Albanian frontier.) The British demanded an apology and compensation and when the Albanians refused to give either, took the matter to the newly established International Court of Justice in The Hague. It was the International Court's first case, and it ruled that Albania had indeed set the mines and should pay Britain £830,000 in damages. Britain was then in possession of Italy's gold reserves, a portion of which had been set aside to pay war reparations to Albania. This portion, now worth $40 million, is still in London and the dispute is still unresolved.

During the dangerous years after Tito's quarrel with Stalin, Albania had every reason to fear that Yugoslavia, Greece and/or the Western powers would decide to liberate the country from its Communist government. Albania shared no land frontier with any of its allies, was isolated on the Adriatic and offered the Soviets no sufficient strategic advantage to guarantee that they would defend it against a sudden attack, although they did establish a naval base at Vlorë which offered Hoxha some measure of protection. The guerrilla incursions supported by the British and Americans and the more effective operations launched from Yugoslavia, combined with the regime's unpopularity, all contributed to the government's nervousness. Hoxha and Shehu prepared against the coming invasion by building pill-boxes across the country – 100,000 in all – to serve as defence points against their enemies.

In the event, the Western powers, though ready enough to try to incite a domestic revolt, proved altogether unwilling to become embroiled directly in a new Balkan conflict. By the mid-1950s the danger was past, and Hoxha could at last indulge his paranoia to the full.

Isolation

In 1948, Albania had broken with Yugoslavia, the country that had created the Albanian party and brought it to power. When Khrushchev restored good relations with Tito in 1955, Hoxha feared for his own safety, but the 1956 Soviet invasion of Hungary again alienated Yugoslavia from the USSR and thus guaranteed continued Soviet protection of Albania.

In the following years, however, Khrushchev pursued a policy of *détente* with the West (despite the interruption of the Cuban missile crisis), and Albania felt threatened once more. In 1961, on the occasion of the rift between the Soviet Union and China, Hoxha broke with the USSR and closed the Soviet base at Vlorë; then, in 1968, he withdrew from the Warsaw Pact after the invasion of Czechoslovakia, which he opposed for the same reason Nicolae Ceauşescu did. The Brezhnev Doctrine was anathema to independent Communist states. Albania remained staunchly Stalinist: there is still a large statue of Stalin in the centre of Tirana, and towns, villages and factories bear his name.

Albania, looking to China for protection, became that country's most dedicated supporter, to the extent that it launched its own 'cultural revolution' in 1966 (and 'abolished' religion the following year). Its first doubts about Chinese orthodoxy occurred when President Nixon visited Chairman Mao in 1972. For the Albanians, it was a marvel and a scandal that the prophet of global revolution should cordially receive the world's leading capitalist. Perhaps even Mao was sliding into revisionism? Albania was also the only European country that refused to take part in the 1975 Helsinki conference, where agreements were reached on cooperation in security, economics, science, technology and human rights. The following year, after the death of Mao and the overthrow of the Gang of Four, Albania ended its alliance with China. Hoxha denounced Deng Xiao-ping with the same fervour that he denounced Soviet and Yugoslav leaders (he was particularly outraged when Tito visited Peking). Albania preserved diplomatic relations with China, however, and there is still a Chinese ambassador in Tirana.

In the mid-1970s, the Albanians' isolation had become institutional and habitual, but by then, the rest of the world, including their traditional enemies, had lost interest in them and they were forgotten in their mountains. In 1961, when Hoxa had defied the USSR, Khrushchev evidently decided that it was not worth worrying about Albania's defection; unlike Hungary five years earlier, others would not follow the Albanians' example, and besides the Soviets were preoccupied with their quarrel with China.

As Albania retreated into total isolation, it renounced economic development along with foreign entanglements. It might have been possible for Stalin to practise 'socialism in one country' in the vast Soviet Union, but it was wholly impractical in Albania. The best the government could manage was mere survival, making no economic progress but keeping the population as ignorant as possible of the conditions beyond their borders. Foreign travel was, of course, wholly forbidden, and foreign visitors were hardly ever permitted to enter the country. To complete the deception, the government regularly published statistics demonstrating its remarkable economic progress and the success of its industrialization policies – statistics that were as impressive and as reliable as those put out by Ceaușescu's Romania. Hoxha's political doctrines, coupled with its inhabitants' inherited xenophobia, sustained Albania's isolation for 45 years. Rejecting peaceful co-existence, *détente* and the idea of a 'peaceful transition to socialism', he believed in the inevitability of revolution, insisting that only through armed struggle could the oppressed masses gain political power and establish a stable people's democracy. Vietnam proved the point in 1975, and the overthrow of Allende's government in Chile two years earlier showed, according to the Albanians, the impossibility of achieving socialism peacefully.

Hoxha's most loyal colleague was Mehmet Shehu. A veteran of the Spanish Civil War and the partisan campaign, and the regime's main hardliner, he had become prime minister in 1954, and was also minister of defence. Hoxha would make speeches denouncing the republic's enemies; Shehu would have them killed. The two men ruled Albania together from 1948 until December 1981, when suddenly, the government announced that Shehu had been discovered to be a Western spy and *agent provocateur* and had been tried and executed. There were also reports that he had been summarily shot by his colleagues during a Politburo meeting. Presumably he had been intriguing for power against Hoxha who was then nearing the end of his life.

Signs of dissent

Hoxha died in 1985 and was replaced by Ramiz Alia. Hoxha's widow survived to guard the flame of the dead leader's ideological purity, and Albania's domestic and foreign policies continued unchanged until the revolution of 1989 swept away the Communist governments of Eastern Europe. It was soon apparent that the revolution had not run out of steam, that it was spreading to Yugoslavia and even to the Soviet Union itself. Albania had long denounced all those countries as 'revisionist', but it was a quite different matter that they should all suddenly become capitalist. There was no place for Albania in Gorbachev's 'Common European House'. Journalists began to speculate how long the Albanian regime would last, and Alia took to issuing statements proclaiming the permanency of his regime, sounding for all the world like Nicolae Ceauşescu in November 1989. It is notable that those of Alia's statements that were published in the West concentrated on patriotic themes, rather than the virtues of the Albanian road to socialism.

The Albanian people have never bothered anyone. Neither have they ever allowed anyone else to dictate to them. Our people have chosen their own way of development and preservation of their national identity, and no one else can decide what should be done, what changes are required by time, what processes to follow for the socialist development of the country . . .

When national identity, freedom and independence are at stake, everyone who calls himself Albanian, wherever he is, will stand up ready to make any sacrifice and even to lay down his life for the homeland.

The people of Albania are masters of their own destiny, determined to march forward on the socialist road, to preserve their freedom and independence.

For 45 years, Albanians have been attacked, insulted, criticized and pressured to abandon the road of our revolution, freedom, independence and social justice. We have always withstood these attacks, and our people will continue to do so.

Let the enemies of Albania bark as much as they can – the Albanian caravan will always continue to march forward.

That statement, and others like it, made clear that the Albanian leaders were seriously concerned that they might go the way of Ceauşescu. They fell back on appeals to the nation's traditional paranoia, particularly towards Yugoslavia, which was attacked vehemently for oppressing the Albanian minority in Kosovo.

There were reports of student demonstrations in Shkodër (Scutari) in the north of the country, which had in the past been the centre of Roman Catholicism in Albania, and there were also signs of disaffection among Greeks in the south. Demographic pressure was bearing down heavily upon the government: Albania has the highest birth rate in Europe, and has to find jobs for 70,000 young people every year (full employment is guaranteed under the constitution). At the same time, the decline in world commodity prices has severely affected Albania's main exports: chrome, copper and nickel.

In the autumn of 1989, as the regimes in the rest of Eastern Europe collapsed one after another, Alia began proposing what he described as 'democratization', and he travelled the country, exhorting meetings of students and party workers to prepare for change. At a party conference in May 1990, he announced various reforms, among which were permission for Albanians to travel abroad, the loosening of restrictions on religious observance, and the introduction of some aspects of a market economy, including liberating at least some prices from central control. However, the essential elements of Albanian socialism would be maintained.

In addition, Alia declared his government's desire to improve relations with the United States and the Soviet Union (diplomatic relations had already been established with France, West Germany, Italy and Greece). For the first time in 44 years, American and Albanian diplomats met at the United Nations in New York. Alia also announced that Albania would now consent to take part in the European Security Conference that had been set up at the Helsinki Conference which Albania had boycotted 15 years earlier.

None of this amounted to a revolution, or even the beginnings of a revolution – but it should not be forgotten that the revolutions in East Germany, Czechoslovakia and Romania in 1989 had begun without warning, and then had swept away everything and everyone that opposed them.

7 Bulgaria

The Communist Party of Bulgaria was the only one in Eastern Europe that managed to reform itself and keep control of the country. On 10 November 1989, the day after the opening of the Berlin Wall, the party's Central Committee abruptly dismissed the country's president, Todor Zhivkov. The party then went on to purge other conservatives, change its name to the 'Socialist Party', give up its constitutional 'leading role' and hold free elections – which it won.

This was the course that Mikhail Gorbachev had recommended to all the Eastern Communist parties. None of the others carried it off – and only Hungary tried – and it is far from clear whether Gorbachev will manage the trick himself. The Bulgarian party's success was the more remarkable because there had been no discernible dissident movement before the *coup de théâtre* of 10 November. On the contrary, the party's history had been, in its early years, one of extreme violence and terrorism, followed by the usual paranoid purges and, under Zhivkov, a prolonged period of stagnation. In many ways, Bulgaria's revolution was the most surprising of a suprising year.

Bulgaria has been a nation – that is, a people speaking a distinctive language living in a settled area – for 14 centuries; but in modern times, before the revolution of 1989, it was an independent state for no more than a single lifetime – from 1878 to 1944. Bulgaria suffers as much as any other country, and more than most, from the weight of its history. It is littered with the ruins of past civilizations; it was itself a flourishing kingdom in the Middle Ages; and it was oppressed by the Turks for five centuries. In the short period between the departure of the Turks and the arrival of the Soviet Communists, independent Bulgaria was repeatedly thwarted in its efforts to establish what it considered to be its historic frontiers. Its government was always authoritarian and usually corrupt, disturbed regularly by *coups d'état*, terrorism, wars foreign and domestic, and assassinations. Marx, Lenin and their disciples claimed that Communism would supercede history, and the Communists suppressed Balkan nationalism everywhere. Now that their system has collapsed, and Bulgarians, Romanians and the rest are again masters of their own destiny, we will see how many of the old quarrels will re-emerge.

The Bulgarians are a Slav nation, closely related in language to the Russians. The Slavs flooded into the Balkans in the sixth century AD, overwhelming all the indigenous inhabitants but the Greeks, the Romanians and the Albanians. In the seventh century, a series of Asiatic nomads – Magyars, Avars, Huns and Bulgars – conquered the Slavs, and set up kingdoms in central and southeast Europe. Only the Magyars – like the English at the same time, far to the west – imposed their language and culture on the native people. The Bulgars, a Turkic tribe from Central Asia, made a kingdom in the Balkans, as the Franks made a kingdom in Gaul, but were then absorbed into the local population, leaving nothing behind but their name.

The first Bulgarian kingdom was established in 679, and its borders fluctuated over the years according to the success or failure of its warriors and diplomats. In 811, the Bulgarians defeated the Byzantine emperor Nicopheros I and killed him, but modern Bulgarians look back to the kingdom of Simeon I (893–927), which included what are now Bulgaria, Macedonia, Albania and much of northern Greece, as the beginnings of their nation and the delimitation of its historic frontiers. These were much reduced in Simeon's successors' wars with the Byzantines, but the kingdom recovered later in the 10th century. Its ruler then was Tsar Samuel, and for a while he governed much of the same territory as Simeon, from his capital in Macedonia. However, he had the misfortune to confront one of the greatest of Byzantine emperors, Basil II, who was to become known as Bulgaroctonos – 'Slayer of Bulgars'. Basil defeated Samuel's army in 1014, capturing about 15,000 soldiers. These were divided into groups of 100 men: 99 in each group were blinded; the 100th lost one eye and was given the task of leading the others back to Tsar Samuel, who is reported to have dropped dead of shock at the sight.

In later centuries, as the Byzantine empire decayed, the Bulgarians re-established their independence. The second kingdom lasted from 1185 to 1393, when the Turks crossed the straits and conquered Bulgaria, later extending their rule to the gates of Vienna. They remained for 500 years.

During that long period, the Bulgarian peasantry lived in serfdom, undisturbed on their lands, subject to Turkish overlords. They were impoverished and persecuted, and their culture and civilization were almost completely suppressed. The Turks did not distinguish between their various Christian subjects: they were all considered to be 'Rumelians', a word derived from 'Rome'. That the Bulgarian language survived, and some sense of nationality, was thanks to the Orthodox Church. This was not intentional: the Church was completely dominated by the Greek Patriarchate in Constantinople, which was in turn wholly subservient to the sultan, but the lower clergy were Bulgarian and preserved the essentials of their culture.

The Ottoman empire decayed progressively throughout the 18th and 19th centuries: the Russians and Austrians advanced from the north, the Greeks and the Serbs won their independence, and by the middle of the 19th century, the Bulgarians, too, began to stir under the long oppression. The future of Turkey in Europe became a matter of deep and exaggerated concern to the European powers: it was known as the 'Eastern Question'.

In 1870, the Turks permitted the Bulgarians to set up their own church, partly independent of Constantinople. A plebiscite was held in Macedonia and the people voted for the Bulgarian exarch (head of the independent Orthodox church). Bulgarians have claimed ever since that this vote proves that Macedonians are really Bulgarian. Then, in 1875, an uprising in Bosnia spread to Bulgaria, and the Turks suppressed it in their usual manner: about 12,000 people were massacred and their villages burned.

Western Europe, particularly Britain, was outraged. William Gladstone, the former Liberal prime minister, emerged from a rather unconvincing retirement in 1876 to denounce the 'Bulgarian horrors' and he campaigned across Scotland on the slogan that Turkey should clear out of Europe 'bag and baggage'. (An enterprising manufacturer then invented the Gladstone bag.) Disraeli, who was the Conservative prime minister, naturally took the opposite position.

The future of the Balkans thus came to depend on British domestic politics, with the Liberals supporting Russia and the Conservatives supporting Turkey. Britain and France had been Turkey's allies for 50 years, on the grounds that the decaying '*Porte*', as it was known – or the 'Sick Man of Europe' – was in every way preferable to the Russians. The greatest danger was that Russia might acquire Constantinople and so penetrate the Mediterranean.

The crisis led all the Balkan powers to advance their claims. Serbia and Montenegro attacked Turkey, and were defeated. Russia then came to the rescue, keeping Austria neutral by supporting its claim to Bosnia and Hercegovina. Russian armies swept across the Danube, defeating the Turks in December 1877. Constantinople lay open before them.

The Russian tsar Alexander II hesitated at the last moment – one of the great missed opportunities of history – and his dithering gave Disraeli time to send a fleet to Constantinople. The British, or at least the Conservatives among them, entered one of their phases of bellicosity. This was the occasion of the celebrated music-hall song:

> *We don't want to fight, but by Jingo, if we do,*
> *We've got the ships, we've got the men,*
> *We've got the money, too.*
> *We've fought the Bear before,*
> *And while Britons shall be true,*
> *The Russians will not have Constantinople.*

The war fever in London and St Petersburg lasted through the winter of 1877/78. The Russians imposed their terms on the Turks, in the Treaty of San Stefano. They recovered southern Bessarabia which they had been forced to cede to Romania after the Crimean war; in compensation, Romania was promised the Dobrudja, on its frontier with Bulgaria, and would become fully independant. Bulgaria, too, recovered its independence, and was also given most of Macedonia and short stretches of the Aegean coast. Turkey was allowed to keep Albania and the rest of Macedonia (now northern Greece and Salonika). These arrangements remained in force for a few months only, and Bulgaria never actually occupied Macedonia.

For the next 70 years, its national ambition was to recover the lands promised at San Stefano. It fought four wars on the issue, losing the last three.

The British government was unalterably opposed to San Stefano, and was joined by Serbia and Austria, which felt left out of the arrangements. Bismarck, the German chancellor, offered his services as an 'honest broker' and in June 1878, the powers gathered in Berlin for a congress to settle the matter. The tsar was persuaded to abandon Bulgaria. Instead, a small Bulgarian principality was created between Sofia and the Black Sea, which would theoretically still be subject to the Turkish sultan, and southern Bulgaria became another semi-independent principality called 'Eastern Rumelia'. The Austrians were bought off with Bosnia and Hercegovina, which they administered for the next 30 years under theoretical Turkish suzerainty. Serbia and Romania became formally independent (they had already enjoyed *de facto* independence for 50 years), and Turkey recovered Macedonia. Disraeli, who had represented Britain at the Congress, returned home in triumph, proclaiming that he had won 'peace with honour – and Cyprus', although it has never been clear why he wanted the island.

Germany, Austria and Britain were satisfied by these arrangements. Russia had little to show for fighting a major war, in which it claimed to have lost 200,000 men in the typical Russian manner: through disease, incompetence and a complete disregard for the lives of its soldiers. As a result, it was more hostile to Britain than ever, and more inclined to listen to Bismarck's blandishments. Serbia, Bulgaria and Turkey bitterly resented the new treaty. Serbia's quarrel with Austria became the lodestone of its politics for the next generation, leading eventually to the First World War. Bulgaria and Turkey, betrayed by their allies, came to look to the Central Powers for support in future conflicts. The Congress of Berlin is one of many examples of a peace treaty planting the seeds for the next war.

Independent Bulgaria

On 29 April 1879, Prince Alexander of Battenberg (whose elder brother was later to become a British admiral and First Sea Lord, and change his name to Mountbatten) was elected prince of Bulgaria and set up his court in Sofia. He confronted a difficulty that later Balkan governments would also face: the Russians – who in Bulgaria filled the senior ranks of the army – controlled the country, and showed no sign of giving it up.

In 1885, during another period of Turkish weakness, Eastern Rumelia abruptly overthrew its government and joined Bulgaria. The tsar, like Stalin with Tito 70 years later, was vexed at this gesture of independence, and abruptly withdrew the Russian military contingents. There followed Bulgaria's first war with Serbia, which was settled at a conference in March 1886. All this occurred while Bismarck's 'Three Emperors' League' held sway, and the Kaiser and the Austrian emperor supported the tsar in his displeasure. Prince Alexander was therefore alone and friendless when, five months after the settlement, the Russians arranged a military *coup d'état* against him. The officers of his guard seized his palace on the night of 20/21 August and forced him to sign an act of abdication on a page torn from the palace visitors' book. Then they shipped him off to Russia. Stalin and his successors would follow the tsar's example in this respect, too.

A new prince was chosen: Ferdinand of Coburg, an Austrian officer. The Russians disliked the choice, but since they no longer had any direct military power in Bulgaria, they could not veto it. From then on, distance led to enchantment: the Bulgarian people remained staunch Russophiles until after 1944, when direct experience caused them to think again. Their successive kings and governments were, by contrast, steadfastly pro-German.

Meanwhile, the continuing deterioration of the Ottoman empire nourished competing Serbian, Greek and Bulgarian irredentist claims on Macedonia. It was a province some of whose people were undoubtedly Serbs, and some others undoubtedly Greek or Albanian, but the majority had much more in common with Bulgaria, both linguistically and culturally: they spoke Bulgarian; and they were members of the Bulgarian Orthodox Church. There was no reason why they should not be united with Bulgaria – except that everyone else opposed it. Another point of contention was Salonika, the major port of the northern Aegean. It remained Turkish (Atatürk was born there in 1881), and Greece, Serbia and Bulgaria all coveted it. The Congress of Berlin had not solved the Eastern Question.

Bulgarian politics, like those of the rest of the Balkans, continued the traditional mixture of comic opera and terrorism. In the 1890s, the Internal Macedonian Revolutionary Organization (IMRO) was formed, a terrorist group whose intention was to unite the province with Bulgaria, and which was alternately protected and suppressed by the government in Sofia. It staged a revolt in Macedonia in 1903, protesting against Turkish misgovernment, after which the powers once again tried to impose reforms on Turkey.

There was a revolution in Turkey in 1908, during which the sultan Abdul Hamid II was deposed by the Young Turks. Bulgaria took the occasion to proclaim its full independence, Prince Ferdinand elevating himself to tsar, and Austria annexed Bosnia-Hercegovina. This precipitated the 'Bosnia crisis', the first of a series that would culminate in 1914. Serbia, supported by Russia, denounced the Austrians, who were in turn supported by Germany.

In 1912, Bulgaria, Serbia, Montenegro and Greece formed the Balkan League, whose object was to partition Turkey's remaining territories in Europe. A dispute over the future of Albania, which was then in a state of revolt, developed into the First Balkan War, in which the four allies defeated the Turks, at last driving them out of Europe, except for a foothold around Constantinople. In the Treaty of London, signed on 30 May 1913, Bulgaria recovered its San Stefano frontiers, Greece annexed southern Macedonia and Salonika, Serbia got northern Macedonia, and Albania proclaimed its independence.

The victors fell out at once. Romania intervened, claiming a further slice of the Dobrudja from Bulgaria. Both Greece and Serbia demanded that the brand-new frontiers in Macedonia be adjusted in their favour, and formed a new, anti-Bulgarian alliance. Instead of trying diplomacy, Bulgaria attacked Serbia and Greece simultaneously on 30 June – exactly one month after the Treaty of London had been signed. It was soundly defeated. In the Treaty of Bucharest, signed on 30 July, Macedonia was divided between Serbia and Greece, Romania took the southern Dobrudja, and even Turkey, which had joined the war at the last moment, recovered some of the territory it had lost only two months before. Bulgaria was left with only a short stretch of the Aegean coast, east of Salonika, as its share of the final dismemberment of Turkey in Europe.

These distant events still cast a shadow upon Balkan politics. The enmity between Bulgaria and its neighbours continued unabated until subsumed by the Soviet imperium and the Cold War. Bulgarians and Greeks have been fighting each other since the Middle Ages: Basil II has not been forgotten, and the two nations have fought three wars this century, and hesitated on the brink of further ones. The persistent hostility between Bulgarians and Turks was demonstrated in 1950 and in 1989, when Bulgaria expelled several hundred thousand Turks. As for Macedonia, Bulgaria continued to assert its claims well into the 1950s, and the progressive disintegration of Yugoslavia could very easily revive that ancient dispute.

When the First World War broke out, the Central Powers offered to restore Bulgaria to its San Stefano frontiers. The Triple Entente, disregarding Serbian susceptibilities, also offered Macedonia to Bulgaria: Serbia would be compensated with Austrian territories. Tsar Ferdinand hesitated between the two offers for a year and then chose the Central Powers, joining with Austria and Turkey and declaring war on the Allies. It proved a mistake. The Allies won. At the end of the war, Bulgaria lost its toehold on the Aegean to Greece and further portions of Macedonia.

Ferdinand lost his throne. He retired to Germany, perhaps consoled by the fact that, unlike the ancient Habsburg, Romanov, Hohenzollern and Ottoman dynasties, the parvenu Coburgs retained their throne: Ferdinand was succeeded by his son, Tsar Boris, who proceeded to repeat his father's mistakes.

The politics of terrorism, *coup d'état*, assassinations, government corruption and international intrigue, typical of the whole of the Balkans between the wars, were all more extreme in Bulgaria. Most of its population were peasants, who owned their own land (the Turkish landlords having been dispossessed) but lived in great poverty – agricultural production was only half the European average. There was also a considerable class of under-employed intellectuals and professionals in the cities – the ideal breeding ground for revolutionary politics – but no proletariat to speak of. A social democratic party, founded in 1891, advocated modernization and industrialization as a necessary first step towards socialism, on sound Marxist principles. In 1919, after the Russian Revolution, the party's radical wing broke away (like so many of their comrades elsewhere in Europe) and founded the Bulgarian Communist Party. Its principal leader was Georgi Dimitrov.

The Agrarian Union, under the leadership of Alexander Stambolinski, formed the first post-war government, the royal government and army having been discredited by their defeat. Stambolinski's peasant radicals set about reforming the country according to their own ideas, and as a result, there was a state of near civil war in the country, with peasants fighting townspeople, a radical insurrection, and various right-wing factions competing in murder. The new government repressed its enemies vigorously.

Stambolinski established a 'Green International', an alliance of the peasant parties of Europe. However, when he advocated reconciliation with Yugoslavia, he was overthrown for his pains, in a *coup d'état* on 9 June 1923. He was captured and beheaded six days later. That put the peasants in their place, and henceforth they supplied the backbone of the revolutionary movement, while the intellectuals took care of its theoretical side.

The civil war continued. The Communists launched a campaign of revolutionary terrorism, quite against Lenin's teachings. Their most notable achievement was the planting of a bomb in Sofia cathedral in April 1925, during the funeral service of a general whom they had murdered the previous day. The bomb killed 125 people, and led to a ferocious 'white terror' in which the army ruthlessly suppressed the Communists. For over 20 years, the party denied responsibility for the bombing; then, when it was safely in power, Dimitrov at last admitted that it had been the work of the 'ultra-left' and that it had been an error.

Right-wing terrorism was an equal danger. IMRO split in two, and its factions fought a war of assassination and massacre that dominated the country's politics until 1934. At the same time, it continued its campaign to subvert Macedonia by generalized terrorism. IMRO terrorists also carried out missions in Yugoslavia and Greece, finally collaborating with Croatian *Ustachis* in the murder of King Alexander of Yugoslavia in Marseille in 1934.

Bulgaria suffered from other tribulations, apart from the constant level of extreme violence. The government was notoriously corrupt: in the late 1920s, it was calculated that half the ministers in all the governments since 1878 had been indicted for corruption. A secret military faction – the *Zevno* (the 'Link') – was formed to purge the country of corruption, and they took power in a coup in 1934. They began reforming the government and, in the wake of Alexander of Yugoslavia's assassination, finally suppressed IMRO, but they were not notably successful otherwise. In one respect, Bulgaria was luckier than other Balkan countries: its Fascist parties were never very strong. In 1935, Tsar Boris deposed the military government and set up his own dictatorship, like King Carol of Romania, King Alexander and then Prince Paul in Yugoslavia, and King Zog of Albania.

The Depression devastated the Balkan peasant economies, and strengthened the appeal of extremists of all persuasions. The Communists won a local election in Sofia in 1932 (but were not allowed to take their seats), and the following year, Dimitrov became an international hero for defying Hermann Goering, then Hitler's minister of the interior, during the *Reichstag* trial in Leipzig. He and two other Bulgarians had been caught in Berlin by the *Gestapo*, and were charged with complicity in the alleged plot to set fire to the *Reichstag*. Stalin made Dimitrov a Soviet citizen and persuaded Hitler to release him. Dimitrov moved to Moscow to head the Comintern, announcing the new 'united front' strategy in 1935, and then played a leading role in organizing the Internation Brigades in Spain. His prominence may have saved his life during the purges.

The Bulgarian Communist Party was considerably stronger than the others in Eastern Europe because of the country's tradition of peasant radicalism. When Stalin permitted the formation of 'popular fronts', the party did remarkably well in parliamentary elections, though only as junior partner to traditional left-wing parties. However, Tsar Boris's government ensured that it retained control of parliament, whatever the vote. When Hitler and Stalin signed their alliance in 1939, Bulgaria was one of the few countries that welcomed it wholeheartedly: the king and government supported the Germans; the peasantry remembered the Russians with affection; and of course, the Communist party was loyal to Dimitrov and the Comintern.

In 1941, Tsar Boris was faced with the choice that his father had confronted in 1915: should he join the Axis or the Allies, or try to stay neutral? This time, the Allies consisted of Britain and its dominions alone; Hitler had already disposed of France and most of the rest of Europe. The choice seemed obvious; and Hitler's ultimate victory appeared to be a sure thing. Besides, Bulgaria had already recovered the southern Dobrudja from Romania, in 1940, and a year later was offered the possibility of recovering Macedonia and as much of Greece as it wanted. Boris did not hesitate: he signed the Axis treaty on 1 March 1941, and allowed Hitler to send his armies through Bulgaria to attack Yugoslavia and Greece a month later. The following December, at Hitler's behest, he declared war on the United States and Britain – but at all times refused to declare war on the USSR. The Soviets were too popular.

As a result, Bulgaria's role in World War II consisted of occupying parts of Greece and Yugoslavia, and supporting Germany in every way save militarily. In 1942 and 1943, the Bulgarian government accepted German proposals to deport the country's Jews 'to the East', and about 14,000 were sent, mostly from Macedonia. Then the opposition parties protested so strongly that the government reversed itself, and refused any further deportations. The 50,000 remaining Jews in Bulgaria survived.

Tsar Boris died in August 1943. Since his heir, Simeon II, was only six years old, a regency was set up. By then the collapse of Italy, followed by the Allied invasion, had allowed the American and British air forces to attack Bulgaria; and Sofia was heavily bombed.

Over the following year, Bulgaria, like Romania and Hungary, tried to escape its alliance with Hitler. To begin with, it hoped to hold on to its Macedonian conquests; later, its only concern was to time its defection from the Axis so that it could avoid German occupation. Various approaches were made to the British and Americans, who told the Bulgarians that they must return all the Greek and Yugoslav territories that they occupied and declare war on Germany.

After the collapse of Romania in August 1944, the Red Army reached the Danube. The Bulgarian regents then installed a pro-Western government, which prepared to accept the Allies' terms, realizing that there was no longer any possibility of retaining the conquered territories. The regime, which had managed to preserve its independence from Hitler, though allied to him, still hoped to escape falling into Stalin's clutches. It was too late. Stalin could see perfectly well what the Bulgarians were planning, and on 5

September 1944, the Soviet Union declared war on Bulgaria. Bulgaria surrendered three days later, and Soviet troops marched on Sofia.

There had been a certain amount of small-scale partisan activity in Bulgaria during the war, directed against government troops because there had been no Germans to fight. The Communist underground had been harried by the police: among those who had been arrested and tortured was Traicho Kostov, the party's 'internal' leader, who had been lucky not to be executed. The Communists were allied to various democratic parties in a 'Fatherland Front', and when the Red Army crossed the border, the Front staged a coup and seized power. The Communists took the ministries of the interior and justice, the two positions that they used throughout Eastern Europe to establish their hegemony.

Bulgaria now declared war on Germany and, in alliance with Tito, drove the *Wehrmacht* out of the Balkans. At the same time, the Bulgarians reluctantly pulled out of Macedonia and Greece. The Soviets allowed them to keep the southern Dobrudja, which they had taken from Romania: after all, Romania had been an enthusiastic ally of Hitler and had marched its armies as far as Stalingrad, while the Bulgarians had stayed at home.

Communist Bulgaria

The Communists took power in Bulgaria immediately and ruthlessly. Although it had only 8000 members, the party was powerful and determined enough to do without 'slicing salamis', as in Hungary, or slowly building up its position, as in Romania and Poland. It relied on the presence of the Red Army to intimidate its opponents, who were already demoralized by the political and military fiasco of the war.

In the best Bulgarian tradition, the party instituted an immediate mass terror. There are no reliable figures of the numbers killed in the first purge in 1944 and 1945: according to the regime's own account, about 2000 people were tried in the people's courts and then executed; but the final total may have been between 15,000 and 20,000. In 1990, the new government admitted that, between 1944 and 1950, there had been at least 85 concentration camps in Bulgaria, closely modelled on Stalin's *gulag*, and survivors and their families were at last able to tell the stories of their sufferings.

The dead included the three regents who had ruled the country after the death of Tsar Boris, dozens of ministers of various governments, senior military officers, party politicians and civil servants. In addition, more people were executed for 'war crimes' in Bulgaria than anywhere else in Europe except Yugoslavia, even though there had hardly been any real war crimes committed there. The Communists took power by force and established themselves by terror, and so continued in office for 45 years.

The Fatherland Front, which took power in 1944, was ostensibly a coalition of all democratic parties, but the Communists dominated it completely. They also controlled the countryside through the Front's local committees, which were directed by Tsola Dragoicheva. A formidable woman, she had remained in Bulgaria during the war and had taken part in the resistance; then she had been arrested and interned in a concentration camp for several years. Now, in addition to organizing the local committees, she showed her metal by drawing up 'black lists' of enemies to be tried by the people's courts. She was violent, ruthless and cold-blooded – a Bulgarian Ana Pauker (*see* p. 217) who suffered the same fate: she was a close associate of Traicho Kostov, and when he was purged in 1949, she fell into disgrace, though she was not herself tried.

In the summer of 1946, the army was purged: 2000 officers were dismissed and arrested, and many of them were shot. The new regime also, at last, wiped out the remnants of IMRO, which had contributed so much to the country's sufferings for the previous half century.

Representatives of the legitimate democratic parties had withdrawn from the Front in August 1945, in protest at government terrorism. Three months later the Front held elections that were so blatantly corrupt that the opposition parties refused to participate. The British and Americans demanded that the Bulgarians abide by the terms of the Yalta agreement, which provided for free elections in liberated Europe, and refused to recognize the new government until proper elections were held. Stalin resented this outside interference: had not Churchill agreed, a year earlier, that Bulgaria was within the Soviet sphere of influence? Stalin evidently interpreted Yalta differently from the Western allies. In any event, wishing to mollify the Americans for the moment, he instructed Dimitrov to offer government positions to the leaders of the two main opposition parties: the Agrarian Union and the Socialists.

The opposition insisted on occupying important posts, not mere token ministries, even when Andrei Vyshinsky, Stalin's executioner in the Balkans, made them a final offer – take it or leave it. It would have made no difference: Stalin was determined to keep control of Bulgaria, and in the Communist party he had an instrument ready at hand. In September 1946, the Front organised a plebiscite on the monarchy and, of course, won an overwhelming victory. Young Tsar Simeon was packed off into exile and a republic was proclaimed. New elections were held in October. They were rigged, of course, but despite intimidation, treachery and ballot stuffing, the opposition won about 30 per cent of the vote.

The leader of the Agrarian Union, Georgi Dimitrov (who had the same name but nothing else in common with the Communist leader), had received death threats and so had taken refuge with the American mission, which got him out of the country. His successor, Nikola Petkov, with astonishing courage defied the Communist Dimitrov on the floor of parliament. Dimitrov threatened him with the fate of Draža Mihajlović (who had recently been shot in Yugoslavia), but Petkov refused to be intimated. Accused of being an agent of foreign powers (i.e. the Americans) he replied that since Dimitrov had been a Soviet citizen until two days before he became prime minister, he obviously was an agent of a foreign power – the USSR. Petkov was spared until the peace treaty between the Allies and the defeated Axis countries was signed in Paris in February 1947; then, on 5 June, the day after the treaty was ratified by the US Senate, he was arrested by security police on the floor of parliament, amid scenes of great confusion – a dramatic gesture of the Communists' contempt for the legislature. In September, he was tried, convicted and hanged for plotting to overthrow the government. A week later, the United States recognized the Bulgarian government. The Agrarian Union was then dissolved: it was later reconstituted as a wholly-owned subsidiary of the Communist Party. The following July, the Socialist members of parliament, in another extraordinary act of personal bravery, voted against the new constitution that the Communists had introduced. They were promptly arrested. Their party leader, Kosta Lulchev, who was old and sick, was sentenced to 15 years' imprisonment, the equivalent of a death sentence. Then the Socialist Party, too, was dissolved.

As soon as it had eliminated all political and military opposition, the government attacked religion. The Protestant churches were merged, and in 1949, 15 of their leaders were tried, convicted of espionage and jailed. The Roman Catholic Church in Bulgaria was abolished, and in 1952, 40 prominent Catholics were put on trial: four of them, including a bishop, were executed. The heirarchy of the Bulgarian Orthodox Church was purged, the exarch was forced to resign, one of the archbishops was murdered on the steps of his cathedral, and suitably accommodating successors were found. Then, in 1950, in an abrupt reversal, the government convened a national congress of the Orthodox Church, which elected a patriarch for the first time since the 14th century, and thus the Bulgarian Church became completely independent of the Ecumenical Patriarch of Constantinople. At the same time, it gave up its claims to direct the Macedonian church, thus at last abandoning its irredentist claim to the province.

The Bulgarian horrors were not limited to the regime's opponents. There was the usual conflict between members of the 'internal' party, who had stayed inside the country between the wars and during World War II, and the 'external' wing, led by Dimitrov, who had spent those years in Moscow. During that period, the internal comrades had been frequently arrested and tortured, and some had been executed; the external comrades, far from those dangers, faced the greater peril of Stalin's paranoia – many Bulgarian leaders, like those of the Poles, Hungarians and the rest, did not survive the purges.

Dimitrov and his chief deputy, Vasil Kolarov, another external comrade who had become Bulgaria's first president, were by now old and ill. Their obvious heir was Traicho Kostov, the most prominent member of the internal party. He had survived prolonged torture at the expert hands of the Bulgarian police, and after the war, he was one of those who directed the 'red terror', and was later in charge of economic policy. He opposed the excessive Soviet demands on Bulgaria, and tried to protect the country against the pillaging that took place in Romania and elsewhere. In March 1949, he was purged.

Dimitrov died in Moscow in July 1949. There were rumours that he had been quietly liquidated because Stalin had come to distrust him and he was too well known to be purged, tried and murdered like other East European leaders. However, Yugoslavs who saw him in his last years reported that he seemed a sick man. His body was embalmed, like Lenin's, and installed in an extravagant mausoleum in the centre of Sofia.

The purge of the internal party continued. Kostov was tried in December. He had, of course, confessed to the usual list of improbable crimes, but at his trial, which was held in public in the presence of a number of foreign observers and the world's press, he loudly announced that he was innocent of all charges – a gesture that was extremely unusual in the long and gruesome annals of Stalinist show trials. But it was to no avail: he was hanged.

Bulgaria set about closing itself off to all Western influences. The United States, accused of complicity in the Kostov spy case, broke diplomatic relations in 1950, blaming the Soviet Union for 'striving to deprive Bulgaria of all contacts with the outside world and to keep its people at the mercy of their present rulers'. (Relations were not resumed until 1960.) Also in 1950, Bulgaria expelled about 150,000 of its Turkish citizens, in an act of blatant racism. It also permitted its 50,000 or so Jews to emigrate to Israel in the 1950s; only a handful now remain.

From 1944, Bulgaria was the USSR's most loyal ally, following every twist of Soviet policy with instant obedience. There was only one, covert, moment of dissidence: in the spring of 1948, as Stalin's campaign against Tito was building up, Dimitrov passed through Belgrade by train. Since Bulgaria had joined in the secret denunciations of Yugoslav heresy, he was not invited to stay, but as a protocol gesture, Milovan Djilas, one of the four leading members of the Yugoslav government, went to meet his train. In the privacy of his railway carriage, in a hurried whisper, Dimitrov advised Djilas to hold firm against Stalin at all costs. Whatever his public position, Dimitrov privately supported Tito. Doubtless he spoke from long experience, knowing that if the Yugoslav party were to bow down before Stalin and depose Tito, Djilas and the rest, they would all be shot.

After Dimitrov's death in 1949, he was briefly succeeded by Vasil Kolarov, who died the following year. Then Dimitrov's brother-in-law Vulko Chervenkov became general secretary of the party and prime minister. A thorough-going Stalinist, utterly loyal to the Soviet Union, he imposed the same bleak dictatorship upon Bulgaria that Rákosi had installed in Hungary, Bierut in Poland and Gheorghiu-Dej in Romania. When Stalin died in March 1953, the Bulgarians, with their customary loyalty, were the first to initiate a 'new course' – first modifying and then abandoning Stalinism. Chervenkov was obliged to give up the party secretaryship to Todor Zhivkov in 1954, and after Khrushchev's speech denouncing Stalin in February 1956, he was also forced to resign as prime minister, accused of 'encouraging the harmful cult of the personality'.

Chervenkov was succeeded as prime minister by Anton Yugov, who had been the first Communist minister of the interior, in 1944–46, and had directed the murderous purge of the former regime. He had also been purged along with Kostov seven years earlier, and had been lucky to escape alive. Kostov was now posthumously rehabilitated. For the next few years, Zhivkov manoeuvred against the remaining Stalinists: Chervenkov and Yugov were finally purged together in 1962.

Bulgaria's traditional hostility towards Greece persisted after the war. The Bulgarians helped the Greek Communists during the Greek civil war, and tried to recover eastern Thrace, the strip of territory along the Aegean that had been repeatedly swapped between the two countries. The Soviet Union, hoping to get an outlet on the Mediterranean, supported Bulgaria, but the Americans stood firm and eventually Bulgaria recognized the existing frontier. In 1955, Bulgarian anti-aircraft guns shot down a civilian Israeli airliner flying from London to Tel Aviv. Fifty-eight people were killed, and Bulgarian relations with the outside world deteriorated still further.

The Zhivkov years

After Albania's Enver Hoxha, Todor Zhivkov was the longest-lasting of all European Communist party leaders. He ruled in the modern Soviet manner, as *primus inter pares* rather than as absolute dictator. He was as dull, grey and predictable as Honecker in East Germany or Husák in Czechoslovakia, never permitting Bulgaria to deviate in the slightest from the Soviet line in foreign or domestic affairs. In 1967, he broke diplomatic relations with Israel, and the following year, he sent a Bulgarian contingent to join in the invasion of Czechoslovakia. He followed the precepts of Soviet economic policy year after year, ignoring the evidence that the system was failing and the economy steadily deteriorating.

In the first few years of Communist domination, in Bulgaria as elsewhere, there were plenty of people who gained from the new dispensation, when the former ruling classes were swept away and new officials took their places. However, very soon the only people who continued to benefit from the peoples' republic were party bureaucrats. After a brief improvement in the standard of living immediately after the Communist coup, based on the fact that Bulgaria had suffered very little in the war, the people began to pay the price of industrialization, collectivization and the nationalization of all businesses and property. Living standards recovered somewhat during the 1950s, thanks to the 'new course', but the gap between Bulgaria and Western Europe has grown inexorably over the years. The main Communist success was probably in education: illiteracy has practically vanished and there is now a well-educated and ambitious professional class.

In domestic affairs, the most remarkable incident was an attempted coup against Zhivkov in 1965, a few months after Khrushchev had been purged in the Soviet Union. The regime admitted that an attempt had been made to remove Zhivkov, saying that it had been carried out by 'Maoists' displeased at his loyal support of the Soviets in the dispute with China. The alternative and more probable explanation was that the unsuccessful coup was the work of military officers and Bulgarian nationalists, trying to take advantage of Soviet disarray to escape from Moscow's iron grip.

The Turkish question

Despite all the movements of population of the 20th century – and the forcible expulsion of some 150,000 of them in 1950 – there remains a considerable Turkish community in Bulgaria, at least several hundred thousand strong and perhaps as many as 1.5 million. It is impossible to be more precise. Bulgaria under Zhivkov denied that there were any Turks at all and, in 1984, set out to prove the point by ordering all citizens to adopt Bulgarian names; this was accompanied by various other punitive measures. It was flatly contrary to Communist doctrine, not to mention the UN Declaration on Human Rights and the Helsinki Final Act, but was standard Balkan practice. The new decrees were enforced at gunpoint, and by some reports, hundreds of people were killed.

In May 1989, Turkish Bulgarians demonstrated against their oppression in various parts of the country. It was the first sign of public dissidence in over 40 years, and the demonstrations were firmly repressed. That summer, about 320,000 Bulgarian Turks fled the country and settled in Turkey, which welcomed them as a matter of principle while finding considerable difficulty in absorbing them. About 50,000 of the refugees returned home, after discovering that Turkey's economic problems were worse than Bulgarian persecution.

The quiet revolution

The first signs of change occurred in 1987, in the wake of Gorbachev's first reforms in Moscow. Zhivkov, then 77 years old, contemplated similar reforms himself, announcing in July that they would be introduced at the next party conference. He abandoned the idea at the last moment. It was Zhivkov's last chance. In the event, he resisted change like the leaders of East Germany, Czechoslovakia and Romania until they were all overwhelmed. Like them, he may have realized that any loosening of his own control would reveal the secrets of his regime – the killings, the concentration camps, the corruption, the oppression of the Turks – and that he would be held responsible. His only hope was to hold firm. It did not work.

Even Bulgaria was subject to the winds of change blowing through Eastern Europe. In January 1989, a Committee on Human Rights was formed in Sofia. Then an ecology movement called 'Eco-Glasnost' was founded, and on 26 October 1989, its members tried to collect signatures in Sofia to protest against pollution and government economic policies; the police beat them up. On 3 November, to coincide with an international conference on the environment in Sofia, there was a demonstration of about 5000 Eco-Glasnost supporters in the capital. This, too, was broken up, presumably on Zhivkov's orders – an event that deeply embarrassed those, including foreign minister Petar Mladenov, who had invited the ecologists from other countries to Sofia. The event proved to be a catalyst for change, though much less dramatic than the demonstrations in Leipzig, Prague and Timisoara that started the revolutions in East Germany, Czechoslovakia and Romania.

Mladenov and other party reformers could see the writing on the wall. On 10 November 1989, the day after the opening of the Berlin Wall but before the collapse of the governments in Prague and Bucharest, the Bulgarian Communist Party started to reform itself. Zhivkov was abruptly dismissed as president and party general secretary and replaced by a team of reform Communists headed by Mladenov, who became party leader and president, and an economist, Andrei Lukhanov. The minister of defence, General Dobri Dzhurov, reportedly played a key role in ensuring that Zhivkov would go quietly into the night. It is also suspected that Gorbachev played a part in these changes: Mladenov had visited Moscow shortly before the party coup against Zhivkov.

The Bulgarians immediately plunged happily into their own brands of *perestroika* and *glasnost*. It was the most peaceful of reform movements, at least to begin with. The party purged the old guard, and soon charged Zhivkov with corruption. The opposition emerged rapidly, forming an umbrella organization – the Union of Democratic Forces – under which sheltered new parties, soon numbering 13. They demanded that the Communist party renounce its 'leading role' in society, and call free elections in 1990. The party reformers resisted the more extreme demands, but with moderation. This was not Czechoslovakia under Miloš Jakeš, let alone Romania under Ceauşescu. The Bulgarians wanted to proceed at their own pace, or at Mikhail Gorbachev's, and no faster.

The pressures that had brought down the Communists to the north continued to mount, however, and the Bulgarian party could not hold out for long. On 17 November, the penal code was reformed, deleting the article that had been used to suppress political dissent, and about 200 political prisoners were released. Limits on foreign travel were ended, and partial freedom of the press was restored. On 15 January 1990, parliament abolished the party's 'leading role' and opened round-table talks with the opposition. These led to an agreement to hold free elections in June 1990, but the opposition parties refused to join a coalition.

At that stage, the government did not repeal the first article in the constitution that said that Bulgaria is a socialist state headed by the working class – the party may have been in retreat, but it was not yet routed.

Members of parliament who had fawned over Zhivkov for years now denounced him as the man responsible for all the crimes and follies of the Communist regime. It was notable that nobody yet dared criticize the Bulgarian Stalin, Georgi Dimitrov, who, with colleagues such as Traicho Kostov and Anton Yugov, had directed the 'red terror' between 1944 and his death in 1949, and was therefore chiefly responsible for thousands of deaths.

On 30 January, a Communist party conference was held which voted a reform programme – but one that did not go as far as those of the Hungarian and East German parties. The hardliners who remained in the party – and a third of its 900,000 members were pensioners – resisted the most radical measures. Mladenov and his supporters succeeded in keeping control of party and government, promising sweeping reforms, but still trying to preserve the essentials of socialism. In particular, Mladenov specifically rejected capitalism as a solution to Bulgaria's economic problems.

Mladenov was by now only president, the conference having elected a new party leader, Alexander Lilov, who had been expelled from the Central Committee in 1983 after quarrelling with Zhivkov. On 1 February, the government resigned. Andrei Lukhanov, Mladenov's chief supporter, became prime minister and nominated a new cabinet drawn exclusively from the Communist party: the Agrarian Union, which had been an acquiescent member of the government for over 40 years, ever since its leaders had been murdered by Dimitrov, refused to join it in a coalition.

In April, the Communist party changed its name, becoming the 'Socialist Party', and Mladenov was elected to the newly created position of executive president. In the same wave of reform, press censorship was abolished, the secret police were instructed to stop spying on the public and on opposition figures, and the first revelations of past misdeeds were made. The fact that a modified reign of terror had been in force from 1944 was at last admitted, and so was the existence of the concentration camps which were allegedly all closed in 1962: the 80-year-old former director of the camps was arrested and charged with working prisoners to death.

It should be noted that all crimes and omissions were still blamed only on Zhivkov and his associates. The government flatly denied that the Bulgarian secret services had had anything to do with the murder of the exiled writer Georgi Markov in London in 1978 (he was jabbed in the leg with a poisoned umbrella). That case would have to wait for a new government and a proper investigation.

The anti-Turkish hostility whipped up by the Zhivkov regime was not artificial: it survived the change in government. One of the first big opposition rallies held in Sofia after Zhivkov's fall was addressed by a series of dissidents, one of whom called for a repeal of all anti-Turkish legislation; he was roundly booed by the crowd and denounced as a traitor. Early in 1990, after the new government lifted all restrictions on the Turks' freedom of worship and permitted them to use their own names – birth certificates carrying Turkish names were issued for the first time in ten years – there were anti-Turkish demonstrations all over the country, with the crowds denouncing the government. It was a striking sign of the longevity of the old quarrels. The Bulgars had not forgotten or forgiven the long centuries of Turkish rule or the 'Bulgarian horrors' of the 1870s.

In Bulgaria, as elsewhere, Communism had pushed the economy to the point of collapse by 1989. The country had overseas debts of over $10 billion, and agriculture was chronically depressed: this exceedingly rich country now has to import food. Bulgaria also suffers from an ecological disaster as bad as anywhere else in Europe: two steel mills near Sofia pollute the atmosphere with a pall of heavy, choking yellow smog and dump over 20,000 tons of grime on to the city centre every year; a copper refinery in the mountains has polluted local towns and their water supply with arsenic, lead and other contaminants; and 60 per cent of farmland has been 'damaged', according to the government, by the overzealous use of pesticides and fertilizers.

Like all the other countries of Eastern Europe, Bulgaria produces goods that cannot be sold on the open market anywhere in the world – and now even Soviet importers refuse to take its products. What is more, the USSR insists that, from 1991, it must be paid in hard currency for the raw materials on which the Bulgarian economy depends. Pay is low – a wage of $270 a month is considered high – and the shops are empty. The government itself reported that

Bulgaria is facing 'an increasing budget deficit, considerable foreign debt and a structure of economy favouring production of capital and industrial goods and underestimating consumer goods'. Inflation is over 10 per cent a year, and rising.

The party remained in control. In East Germany, Czechoslovakia and Hungary, the Communist parties had disintegrated; in Poland, the party first agreed to share power with Solidarity, and then disintegrated. The new 'Socialists' tried to keep ahead of the Bulgarians' revolutionary impulses, like Gorbachev in the Soviet Union. The opposition Union of Democratic Forces, led by Professor Zhelio Zhelev, feared that the Communists under their new name could still dominate the country, even with free elections.

In June, 1990, the Socialist Party of Bulgaria, the ex-Communists, won the first free elections in the country's history. The Union of Democratic Forces, which had argued that the elections were too soon after the overthrow of the Zhivkov regime to be either fair or democratic, came a respectable second, doing particularly well in the cities: it carried Sofia. The Socialists relied on the remaining Communist machinery in the countryside to bring in the majority, and at least some of them continued to stir up anti-Turkish feeling. Afterwards, the Socialists proposed a coalition but the opposition refused. Students started a series of demonstrations against the government, demanding that former Communists should leave office and Zhivkov should be put on trial. They scored a major success in July when president Mladenov suddenly resigned. The students had found a television tape of him saying that tanks should be brought in to break up an anti-government demonstration in December 1989.

Compared to Romania, the difference was striking. Groups of Communist dissidents had seized power in both countries, but the non-Communist opposition was much stronger in Bulgaria, and the government there allowed it great freedom of expression. The summer demonstrations that provoked Mladenov's resignation were not violent, nor did the government violently suppress them – just the opposite of the situation in Romania. Above all, the new government in Sofia appreciated that the country would need all possible help from the West to escape from its economic difficulties, and realised that the essential condition for help was that Bulgaria must establish a real democracy. The Bulgarian Socialists have perhaps two years to achieve what Mikhail Gorbachev has so far failed to accomplish in the Soviet Union – a peaceful transition from a totalitarian economy to a free one. If they fail, the examples of Hungary, Poland, Czechoslovakia and East Germany demonstrate clearly enough what will happen to them.

8 Romania

Nicolae Ceauşescu wept as the soldiers tied his hands behind his back. His wife, Elena, protested that she had been a mother to them, that they could not do this. The Ceauşescus were not blindfolded nor were there any of the traditional macabre formalities of a military execution. The firing squad simply opened up on them, and the scene was recorded for posterity on video, to be shown on television. Thus Romania marked Christmas Day, 1989.

The revolution had broken out three days earlier as crowds stormed the party headquarters in Bucharest and Ceauşescu fled for his life. It was the most sudden and by far the most violent event in that year of revolutions. The other fallen leaders of Communist Europe, contemplating the photograph of Ceauşescu lying in a pool of blood by a barracks wall, a comrade and colleague they had known for years, must have paused in horror, realizing how near they had come to sharing his fate. If Honecker or Zhivkov or Husák had tried to resist, had ordered their secret police to fire on the demonstrators demanding their dismissal, they, too, would have ended, alone and frightened, before the vengeful guns of their countrymen.

The Romanian revolution did not end with the death of Ceauşescu. There is little hope of an orderly evolution into parliamentary democracy, and it will be years before the country's economy and environment recover from the catstrophe of Communist rule. None the less, the Ceauşescus' execution was the abrupt end of an experiment begun in August 1944. Communism in Romania was killed, along with its last, monstrous tyrant.

The kingdom of Romania

The Romanians, after the Greeks and Albanians, are the oldest nation in the Balkans, and like them, they stubbornly maintained their language and religion through centuries of foreign domination: Turkish, Russian and Hungarian. The two original Romanian principalities – Moldavia and Wallachia – were sometimes semi-independent, sometimes directly administered by the Turks and, for a period, were even governed by Greek merchants from Constantinople.*

In the 19th century, as the Ottoman empire disintegrated, the two principalities finally attained their independence, and in 1859, they elected Prince Alexander of Cruza as their ruler, under whom they were united as Romania in 1861. Five years later, he was deposed, and Prince Charles of Hohenzollern-Sigmaringen, related to the Prussian dynasty, was elected in his place. Following the Russo-Turkish war, the great powers recognized Romania's independence, and in 1881 Prince Charles became King Carol I. This period of Romanian history became known as the 'Old Kingdom' or the 'Regat'.

Romania was backward, impoverished, and ambitious. Half the Romanians lived outside the new kingdom's frontiers – in Transylvania, which was part of Austria-Hungary, and in Bessarabia (now called Moldavia), which was part of Russia. The kingdom's ambition was to reunite these severed brethren into a Greater Romania. Romanian is a Latin language, and Bucharest boastfully described itself as the 'Paris of the Balkans'. At the same time, the Romanian intelligentsia assiduously cultivated the French language and culture to distinguish themselves from the Germans, Slavs and Hungarians who surrounded them.

In the Second Balkan War of 1913 (*see* Chapter 7), Romania extended its territory southwards into the Dodrudja, at the expense of Bulgaria. At the outbreak of World War I, after long hesitation, Romania chose the cause of the allies, who promised it Transylvania, the Banat and Bukovina, all territories of the Dual Monarchy. In 1916, Romania invaded Austria – and was

* The principalites' most famous ruler, in the 15th century, was Vladul Tepes Cvlad (the Impaler), also known as Vladul Dracul ('Vlad the Devil').

soundly beaten. The Germans occupied Bucharest, the Bulgarians recovered the Dobrudja, and Romania sued for peace.

Then the Russian empire fell apart. In 1917, Bessarabia declared its independence, and, the following year, joined Romania with the Germans' blessing, despite the protests of the allies. The Romanians were clearly going to do well out of the war, whoever won. When the tide turned and the allies, invading from Salonika, defeated the Bulgarians and Turks and then marched across the Danube into Romania, the Romanians again declared war on Austria and Germany, liberated the national territory and invaded Transylvania. Greater Romania was thus created in a blaze of glory. In 1919, the Romanians had the added pleasure of invading Hungary and overthrowing the soviet set up there by Béla Kun.

Greater Romania survived for 20 years. It had to maintain itself against the implacable irredentist claims of Hungary and the Soviet Union, an effort that inexorably dragged it into the Second World War as Hitler's ally and led afterwards to 45 years of Communist enslavement. It was a heavy price for glory.

Carol's kingdom

Romania before the Communist conquest in 1944 was a comic opera country, the victim of endless jokes, scorned and mistreated by the rest of Europe. Diplomats joked that 'Romania is not a nationality, it is a profession.' Harold Nicolson, writing of the negotiations leading to the Treaty of Versailles of 1919, describes the ceaseless importunings of the queen of Romania, pestering Woodrow Wilson and Lloyd George for yet another swathe of Hungary.

In 1926, the heir to the throne, Prince Carol – whose dissipations, extravagances and unreliability had made him the most unsavoury member of all European royalty – was persuaded to renounce his claim to the throne and leave the country with his celebrated mistress, Magda Lupescu. When King Ferdinand died in July 1927, Carol's infant son Michael was proclaimed king, and a council of regents was set up. Carol (and Madame Lupescu) returned home in 1930, and within six months he had organized a *coup d'état*, deposed his son and established himself as King Carol II. In due course, he set up a monarchical dictatorship, like those in Bulgaria and Yugoslavia.

Carol ruled in an uneasy alliance with the army and conservative political parties, constantly threatened by the Fascist Iron Guard, which had been founded in the 1920s as the 'Legion of the Archangel Michael'. In addition to the usual Fascist paraphernalia of coloured shirts, salutes and leader worship, it had a unique line in theatrical necrophilia: the dead bodies of the Guards' heroes were carried around like talismans. Romanian politics between the wars was notably violent, and several party leaders (including prime ministers) were assassinated, as well as the head of the Iron Guard, Corneliu Zelea Codreanu, and 13 of his lieutenants, who were shot in prison on Carol's orders in 1938. The king thought he had Hitler's tacit approval for this Romanian version of the Röhm purge, but he was mistaken – Hitler took violent exception to the murder of the Iron Guard's *Führer*, and he put Codreanu's successor, Horia Sima, under his protection, as a possible alternative to the king.

After eliminating Codreanu, Carol established a thoroughgoing dictatorship, with General Ion Antonescu as minister of defence; his other ministers were all convinced Fascists. It was enough to stifle internal dissent, but not enough to protect the kingdom from its enemies.

By then, Romania's diplomatic position was unravelling. It had been a founder member of the Little Entente, an alliance with Czechoslovakia and Yugoslavia against Hungarian and German irredentism. Romania was also allied with France and Poland, and was a member of the Balkan Pact, together with Yugoslavia, Greece and Turkey, which was chiefly aimed against Bulgaria. All these alliances looked splendid enough on paper, but it was always obvious that the small countries of eastern and southeastern Europe could never, collectively or individually survive the hostility of Germany and the Soviet Union without determined allies in the West.

Czechoslovakia was the first victim, in 1938: at Munich, Britain and France abandoned it to its fate. Romania and Yugoslavia could do nothing to protect their ally, and the Little Entente collapsed. In September 1939, it was Poland's turn. Romania proclaimed its neutrality and watched horrified on the sidelines, like the rest of Europe, as the Nazis swallowed country after country.

King Carol and his government put their faith in German promises and accepted German hegemony – Romania, they said, was a 'neutral ally' of the Axis. They were unaware that the Hitler–Stalin

Pact of August 1939 had settled the question. One of its secret protocols stated: 'As for the south east of Europe from the Soviet side, the interest of the USSR in Bessarabia is stressed. The German side declares the complete lack of political interest in these regions.'

On 24 June 1940, three weeks after Dunkirk and two days after the French surrender, the Soviet foreign minister V. M. Molotov summoned the Romanian ambassador in Moscow and presented an ultimatum: the Romanians had 24 hours to surrender Bessarabia and northern Bukovina. To demonstrate what he meant, Molotov scrawled a line on a map in thick pencil, carelessly including several areas that had never been part of Russia. In panic, the Romanians appealed for help to Berlin, but were advised to accept the Soviet *diktat*. Bessarabia and northern Bukovina (and those additional areas of Moldavia behind the Molotov line) were evacuated within a week.

A month later, on 23 August, Bulgaria seized the southern Dodrudja, with Hitler's consent, and then Hungary gave the *coup de grace*: it demanded the return of Transylvania. Hungary was Hitler's ally, but he needed Romania, too, for the invasion of the Soviet Union, and he therefore told his foreign minister, Ribbentrop, to mediate between the two countries. On 30 August 1940, in the 'Vienna Award', the Romanian government was informed that it must surrender northern Transylvania to Hungary. This was far less than the Hungarians wanted, but Hitler instructed them to accept. Thus was Greater Romania dismembered, 20 years after its creation.

In September, Antonescu deposed King Carol, who fled the country with Madame Lupescu, leaving behind his son, King Michael, then aged 17. Ruling in Michael's name, Antonescu became dictator, like Mussolini in Italy, and took to calling himself the '*Conducator*', the Romanian equivalent of '*Duce*'. Horia Sima became his deputy, and the government was filled with other members of the Iron Guard.

War and revolution

Antonescu believed that Germany was destined to rule Europe and that the smaller nations would have to adapt themselves to this situation. In the autumn of 1940, the Germans occupied Romania, and set about expanding and training the army for the war to come. For this, Hitler needed peace and quiet, and when the Iron Guard attempted a revolution in January 1941, murdering its political opponents and massacring Jews, the Germans joined Antonescu in suppressing it. Sima was once again shipped off to Germany.

When Antonescu was informed that Hilter intended to attack the Soviet Union, he agreed at once to join in the invasion. German and Romanian troops crossed the frontier together, on 22 June 1941, and within a few weeks, Antonescu had liberated Bessarabia and restored it to Romania.

Antonescu had defeated one of Romania's hereditary enemies and restored part of its lost territories. It was a great victory, a consolation for all the humiliations of the previous two years. Then Hitler demanded that Antonescu lead his armies across the river Dniester into the Soviet Union itself, and the dictator weakly acceded. The Romanians were given the southern Ukraine to administer. They called it Transnistria – 'the land across the Dniester' – and governed it from Odessa. However, the new empire was never formally annexed.

Antonescu was by then a thorough Fascist dictator, and as such, he set about persecuting the Jews. There were 757,000 Jews in Greater Romania, of whom 150,000 in northern Transylvania were transferred to Hungary in 1940 and subsequently murdered. Carol and, later, the *Conducator*, enforced anti-Semitic legislation as stringent as the Nazis' Nuremberg Laws, and after the invasion of the Soviet Union, Antonescu began deporting Bessarabian Jews to Transnistria. The Romanians of Bessarabia enthusiastically supported the policy, following a tradition of virulent anti-Semitism going back to tsarist times. About 200,000 Jews were deported, and most died, large numbers being murdered by Romanian *Einsatzgruppen* (murder squads). In 1942, Antonescu agreed to deport all surviving Romanian Jews to Poland, but then changed his mind, perhaps influenced by allied protests. As a result, about 300,000 Romanian Jews survived the war.

Antonescu's folly in invading the Soviet Union at Hitler's behest was compounded the following year when he was persuaded to send Romania's armies east in the great advance on Stalingrad. The Romanian divisions guarded the left flank of the German front, and when the Red Army counter-attacked and broke through the

German rear, cutting off von Paulus in Stalingrad, they chose to strike through the Romanian army. The Romanians lost heavily in the battle as well as in the retreat across the Ukraine in 1943, and it became obvious to King Michael, and even to Antonescu, that the war was lost. They both separately contacted the allies to sound them out about the possibility of an armistice.

The allies did not trust Antonescu, but serious negotiations were started in Cairo with representatives of the opposition parties, who kept the king informed. They were told that Romania would have to surrender to all four allies simultaneously, and it could not look to the West to protect it from the Soviet Union. Stalin's terms were that Bessarabia would be returned to the USSR, and Romania must immediately declare war on Germany. In a public press conference in Moscow, in April 1944, Molotov stated:

> The Soviet government declares that it does not pursue the aim of acquiring any part of Romanian territory [except Bukovina and Bessarabia] or of changing the existing social order in Romania. It equally declares that the entry into Romania of Soviet troops is solely the consequence of military necessities and of the continuation of resistance by the enemy forces.

It was a promise as formal and reliable as Hitler's assertion in 1938 that he had no further territorial ambitions in Europe.

The Soviet Union also promised to restore Romania's pre-war western frontier. By surrendering ahead of Hungary, Romania ensured that it would recover Transylvania, as some compensation for again losing Bessarabia and Bukovina. It did not, however, recover the southern Dobrudja; Stalin allowed the Bulgarians to keep it.

The Red Army reached the Carpathians in August 1944 as, in the west, the Americans were advancing on Paris and the British on Brussels. King Michael and his advisers decided that the time had come for Romania to abandon the disastrous alliance with Germany and come to terms with the allies, before the Soviets crossed into Romania itself. On 23 August, the king summoned Antonescu to the palace and proposed that Romania should immediately conclude an armistice. The dictator temporized, and told the king that he would inform the German ambassador. Michael was ready for this eventuality. He summoned his bodyguard, who arrested Antonescu and incarcerated him in King Carol's stamp room.

The king then formed a new government, which immediately sent a telegram to the allies, informing them that Romania accepted the armistice on the terms agreed. Michael broadcast to the nation that evening, and there were huge demonstrations in his support. The German ambassador committed suicide. There was no time for the Germans to occupy the country and reverse Michael's coup (as they had done in Italy in 1943 and were to do in Hungary in October 1944). The Red Army poured across Romania into Hungary and Bulgaria. The Romanian army, hastily reorganized, was sent to fight the Germans. It lost a further 170,000 troops in the remainder of the war.

In October 1944, Winston Churchill visited Stalin in Moscow. One of the matters they discussed was the future of the Balkans. The discussion was one of the most blatant examples of *realpolitik* on record – and the record is Churchill's own:

> The moment was apt for business, so I said, 'Let us settle about our affairs in the Balkans. Your armies are in Romania and Bulgaria. We have interests, missions and agents there. Don't let us get at cross-purposes in small ways. So far as Britain and Russia are concerned, how would it do for you to have 90 per cent predominance in Romania, for us to have 90 per cent predominance in Greece, and go 50–50 about Yugoslavia?' While this was being translated, I wrote out on a half sheet of paper:
>
> Romania
> | | |
> |---|---:|
> | Russia | 90% |
> | The others | 10% |
>
> Greece
> | | |
> |---|---:|
> | Great Britain (in accord with USA) | 90% |
> | Russia | 10% |
>
> | | |
> |---|---:|
> | Yugoslavia | 50–50% |
> | Hungary | 50–50% |
>
> Bulgaria
> | | |
> |---|---:|
> | Russia | 75% |
> | The others | 25% |
>
> I pushed this across to Stalin, who had by then heard the translation. There was a slight pause. Then he took his blue pencil and made a large tick upon it, and passed it back to us. It was all settled in no more time than it takes to set down.

Of course we had long and anxiously considered our point, and were only dealing with immediate, war-time arrangements. All larger questions were reserved on both sides for what we then hoped would be a peace table when the war was won. After this, there was a long silence. The pencilled paper lay in the centre of the table. At length I said, 'Might it not be thought rather cynical if it seemed we have disposed of these issues, so fateful to millions of people, in such an off-hand manner? Let us burn the paper.' 'No, you keep it,' said Stalin.

[From Churchill's war memoirs].

There was no resistance movement of any consequence in Romania. The Romanian Communist Party, which is thought to have had about 1000 members in 1944, had played no part in the war. A number of Communists including Gheorghe Gheorghiu-Dej, were in prison. Another group, including Lucretiu Patrascanu, were living semi-clandestinely in Bucharest; and a third and more important group, led by Ana Pauker, Vasile Luca and Teohari Georgescu, were in Moscow. One of the Moscow group, Emil Bodnaras – a former army officer who had been converted to Communism – was flown into Romania during the summer of 1944, and took part in Antonescu's arrest. On this very slight basis, the Communist party was later to claim credit for the overthrow of the dictatorship. In 1944 and 1945, no such claim was made. In July 1945, King Michael was awarded the Soviet Order of Victory, a ruby-studded diadem of great value reserved for those who had contributed most to the allied cause. Stalin had one, too.

The division between the 'internal' party and those in Moscow was common to all Communist parties in occupied Europe. In Romania, as elsewhere, the Soviet Union supported the Muscovites, and dissension was exacerbated by the fact that the Muscovites' leaders were not ethnic Romanians: Ana Pauker, née Rabinovici, was a rabbi's daughter from Bessarabia; Vasile Luca (real name László Lucas) was a Hungarian from Transylvania; and Emil Bodnaras was a Ukrainian from Bukovina. Pauker, the most dedicated Stalinist of them all, was for several years the dominant personality in the party. As soon as she arrived in Bucharest, in the wake of the Red Army, she set about recruiting new members, caring nothing about their antecedents. As a result, many former

members of the Iron Guard and supporters of King Carol joined
the Communist party.

King Michael had appointed Lucretiu Patrascanu minister of
justice after the 1944 coup, but the Communists soon demanded
greater authority. Real power in the country was exercised by the
Red Army, which appointed local authorities in all areas it occupied
and set about briskly Communizing the country. In February
1945, following Communist demonstrations in Bucharest that were
suppressed by the police, Andrei Vyshinsky, the Soviet deputy
commissar for foreign affairs, was sent to pacify the Romanians.
He did so by surrounding the royal palace with Soviet tanks and
demanding that the king appoint a pro-Soviet government. This
episode occurred three weeks after the Yalta conference at which
the Soviet Union had agreed to permit the countries of Eastern
Europe to decide their own destinies.

The king was forced to comply. The new prime minister was
Petru Groza, leader of the fellow-travelling 'Ploughmen's Front'.
Gheorghe Gheorghiu-Dej became minister of communications, and
one of the Muscovites, Teohari Georgescu, was given the all-
important post of minister of the interior. The cabinet was pad-
ded out with other fellow-travellers and dissident members of
democratic parties, as well as two notorious Fascists: Gheorghiu
Tatarescu as foreign minister and Father Burducea as minister of
religious affairs. Thus Romania began the period of the 'duality
of power'. All the countries of Eastern Europe except Yugoslavia
and Albania passed through this phase, and all ended as 'people's
democracies'.

King Michael resisted as best he could. In August 1945, alleging
that the government was clearly not representative, he ordered
Groza to resign, and when he refused, the king in turn refused
to sign decrees and laws, in theory bringing the government to
a halt. In practice, of course, the Communists continued to rule
as they pleased. The Soviet Union systematically pillaged the
country, a favourite device being the institution of 'Sovroms' –
joint Soviet–Romanian companies that took over major industries
and managed them to the great benefit of the Soviet Union.

There were huge pro-democracy demonstrations in November
1945, on the occasion of the king's 24th birthday. At the end
of the year, under pressure from the United States and Britain,

Stalin instructed Groza to appoint some non-Communist ministers, and King Michael resumed his duties. The United States and Britain then recognized the Romanian government. In November 1946, following elections that were conspicuously fraudulent, the government reported that the National Democratic Front, wholly controlled by the Communist party, had won 89 per cent of the vote.

The Communists then proceeded to suppress all opposition. Democratic leaders were arrested and charged with treason. They were tried before a judge who had commanded Antonescu's prisons and concentration camps during the war, and were all convicted. By the end of 1947, the foreign service, the civil service, police, army and every other state organ had been purged of all non-Communists. Tatarescu was removed as foreign minister, and replaced by Ana Pauker. Vasile Luca became minister of finance and Emil Bodnaras minister of war. That left King Michael. He was forced to abdicate on 30 December 1947, and flew into exile.

Communist Romania

The Communist assumption of power was completed in 1948. The party, greatly expanded by the efforts of Ana Pauker, now controlled every aspect of national life, and celebrated its victory in the traditional way by purging one of its leaders. The designated victim was Lucretiu Patrascanu, minister of justice, who was suddenly denounced as a Menshevik and a friend of war criminals and capitalists. He was arrested in February 1948, bitterly denounced by all his best friends in the party, and expelled from it. (He was tried and executed in 1954, in a general tidying up when Gheorghiu-Dej was consolidating his dictatorship.) The Romanian party prided itself on having discovered and purged a 'Titoist' even before that doctrine was revealed to be rank heresy.

For the next four years, the government pushed industrialization and the collectivization of agriculture. In January 1950, there were 50 state farms; by the end of the year, there were 1029. As a result of the collectivization, Romania, which possesses some of the richest agricultural land in Europe, was reduced to starvation. In a report to the party in 1961, Gheorghiu-Dej admitted that the militia and army had been needed to impose collectivization, and that more than 80,000 peasants had been sent to trial for opposing it. He blamed Pauker. All opposition was ruthlessly suppressed. Hundreds of thousands of Romanians were incarcerated in concentration camps, and 180,000 were drafted into forced labour to build various Stalinist projects, including a Danube–Black sea canal which was abandoned before completion some years later. The historian Ghita Ionescu claims that 60,000 people were executed during this period.

The Romanian Orthodox Church sold out to the new regime. A Communist priest was appointed patriarch, and he purged the Church of all opposition. The Jewish community, too, was reduced to obedience. Over the next 40 years, Jews were sometimes persecuted, sometimes permitted to emigrate. Most eventually went to Israel, among them Ana Pauker's father and brother.

The Muscovites kept the upper hand, although Gheorghiu-Dej (he had added the suffix 'Dej' after a period of exile in a town of that name) was titular general secretary of the party. It proved a temporary ascendancy. Gheorghiu-Dej assiduously cultivated his own contacts with Stalin, pointing out that Pauker was Jewish and therefore probably unreliable – like Slanský in Czechoslovakia – and Luca was equally suspect, being Hungarian. Gheorghiu-Dej, a former railway worker, proved to be one of the most subtle politicians in Eastern Europe, successfully outmanoeuvring the formidable Pauker (who had had her husband shot as a Trotskyite in the 1930s) and the other Muscovites, and winning complete control of the party in 1951. He purged his rivals the following year, obviously with Stalin's concurrence. Pauker, Luca and Georgescu were expelled, Pauker being accused of having 'lived on the slope of the aristocracy and tore herself from the masses' – the implication being that she was an intellectual, not a worker. In due course, Luca was tried and given a life sentence; Pauker was allowed to retire in disgrace. It was the only case in Eastern Europe, apart from Yugoslavia and Albania, where the 'internal' party defeated the 'Muscovites'. Subsequent events showed Stalin's wisdom in insisting on loyalty among the satellite leadership, when Gheorghiu-Dej established his independence from Moscow.

Gheorghiu-Dej made himself prime minister, as well as first secretary of the party. He had attained some degree of popularity by purging the most detested Stalinists from the government, and he continued to blame them for the food shortages and other economic problems facing the country. After Stalin died, and it became possible to reconsider the economic regime imposed by the Soviet Union, Gheorghiu-Dej admitted that the rate of industrialization had been excessive, and that the slogan 'Complete the Five-Year Plan in Four Years!' had been an error. He did not spell out the details. Romania had pursued a grotesque investment policy. In this poor, agricultural country, 50 per cent of the budget had been devoted to investment. 42 per cent of the investment went to heavy industry, 9 per cent to consumer industries and 10 per cent to agriculture, the rest to other essential services. By contrast, Czechoslovakia devoted 27 per cent of its budget to investment, East Germany 13 per cent.

In October 1956, in the wake of the upheavals in Poland and Hungary, there were demonstrations in Bucharest and unrest among Hungarians in Transylvania, and it seemed for a moment that Romania might be engulfed in an uprising of its own. However, there were no reformists in the party – no Romanian Gomułka or Nagy – to lead the charge against Gheorghiu-Dej. Furthermore, there were still large numbers of Soviet troops in the country, and they were soon heavily reinforced in a great show of strength as the Red Army passed through Romania on the way to Budapest. Gheorghiu-Dej took further precautions: there were many arrests and he ordered that the minimum wage be raised. After the Hungarian uprising had been crushed, he reduced some of the pressure in Romania and closed the concentration camps.

These were tactical gestures. In fact, Gheorghiu-Dej remained resolutely Stalinist in his conception of state power and of his own role. Other Communist parties might reform themselves, adopt a collective leadership or even reconsider the fundamental principles of Leninism. The Romanian party, from first to last, remained loyal to its Stalinist roots.

In the early 1950s, Romania set up an autonomous district in Transylvania for the Szeklers, one of the two Hungarian minority groups, and prided itself on its generosity. It also devoted itself to Communizing the German, Tartar and Turkish minorities, but persecuted the Serbs living in the Banat, who were suspected of Titoism. Later, all minorities were persecuted together. In 1959, Gheorghiu-Dej ordered the merging of the Romanian and

Hungarian universities in Cluj, the capital of Transylvania. It was the first step in the long process of oppression of the Romanian Hungarians that has been one of the worst legacies of Communism. Later, in 1968, the Szekler autonomous district was abolished by Ceauşescu.

The Romanian Communist Party, having enthusiastically supported the Soviet invasion of Hungary in 1956, then proceeded to affirm its own independence from Moscow. In the late 1950s, Gheorghiu-Dej mounted various campaigns against 'Titoists' and 'cosmoplitans', by whom he actually meant those who would be more obedient to Moscow than he was. The last Soviet troops were withdrawn from Romania in 1958, 14 years after they arrived. It was a less generous move than it seemed: they could always return, over the long common border between the two countries, or from Hungary to the west. None the less, Gheorghiu-Dej was slowly developing a relatively independent economic and foreign policy. He opposed Khrushchev's proposal to institute supra-national planning in Comecon, allocating each member particular tasks, to avoid duplication; under his blueprint, Romania's role would have been limited to providing raw materials for other countries' industries. The Romanian party firmly declared that it would make its own decisions. It then plunged into industrialization again, and forced through the complete collectivization of agriculture – despite all the criticisms that had been levelled against Ana Pauker for following those same policies ten years earlier.

By this time, the Communist bloc was split down the middle. The third congress of the Romanian Workers' Party (i.e. the Communist party), in June 1960, occurred during the Sino–Soviet split, and in the shadow of that great dispute, Romania was able to develop its own interests and policies. Soviet bookshops were closed, the compulsory study of Russian in Romanian schools was ended, and street names that had been changed to honour Soviet comrades and Soviet triumphs were restored to their Romanian originals. In foreign affairs, Romania remained neutral between the Soviet and Chinese parties, and restored relations with Albania (which had followed China in breaking with Moscow). Finally, in April 1964, the party issued a formal declaration of independence proclaiming its inalienable right to national and party autonomy.

It was a remarkable achievement. Tito had been expelled from the Soviet bloc for making the same claims, Poland had been threatened and Hungary invaded. Romania got away with its act of defiance. China and Albania had also escaped Moscow's power, but China was too big to be coerced, and Albania was protected by its insignificance, as well as by the fact that it had no common frontier with the USSR. None of these considerations applied to Romania, and it is a tribute to Gheorghiu-Dej's political skills that he avoided bringing retribution down upon his head. He was protected, to some extent, by China: Khrushchev and his successors wanted to rally Western parties to their side in the great dispute, and there would have been little hope of that if they had invaded Romania. The Soviets also doubtless took into consideration the inescapable fact that Gheorghiu-Dej was no heretic; on the contrary, he was a most doctrinaire Communist. His only sin was to proclaim his independence from Moscow.

Gheorghiu-Dej died suddenly in March 1965. He was succeeded by Nicolae Ceauşescu, an *apparatchik* who had risen through the party ranks since the war without ever distinguishing himself, but also without making any mistakes. The comrades who voted him into office could hardly have known that this drab little man was the 'Greatest Genius of the Romanian Nation', 'Father of His People' – 'Big Brother' incarnate. They also probably did not realize that Ceauşescu had been the party's principal leader since the early 1940s, the mastermind of the glorious revolution of 1944 and the guiding spirit of party and nation ever since. They soon learned.

When Ceauşescu made himself president in 1967, he proceeded to blacken and then obliterate the memory of Gheorghiu-Dej and every other party leader. A party commission was established which concluded that Patrascanu had been unjustly tried, convicted and executed. He was posthumously rehabilitated – and Gheorghiu-Dej was blamed for the crime. However, Ana Pauker, who had died in 1961, remained a non-person.

Ceauşescu pursued his predecessor's independent policy, even while denouncing Gheorghiu-Dej himself. He refused to follow the Soviet example and break diplomatic relations with Israel after the Six Day War in 1967, and in 1968, he first opposed the invasion of Czechoslovakia and then openly condemned it. Romania soon became the Warsaw Pact member most favoured by the West. Bucharest was useful for various diplomatic initiatives, including Kissinger's approaches to China in the early 1970s, and Romania was rewarded with trade and credits. Ceauşescu, that megalomaniac Stalinist, was received with all honours in Washington by a series of American presidents, by the Queen of England and by an array of Western presidents. It was all very gratifying.

The Ceauşescu dictatorship

Ceauşescu – who ruled with the aid of his wife Elena, their children, their brothers, and various other relatives – was the focus of a grotesque cult of the personality, exceeded only in North Korea. Ceauşescu himself favoured grandiloquent titles such as 'Great Genius of the Carpathians', and on his 70th birthday in 1988, the party proclaimed:

> The entire Romanian people . . . pays these days a deep homage, expressing its deep gratitude to Comrade Nicolae Ceauşescu, General Secretary of the Party, President of the Republic – the most beloved son of the people, outstanding revolutionary militant, hero among the nation's heroes, architect of modern, socialist Romania, of a society that fulfills, at a higher historical stage of the new system, the ideals of the forerunners, the maker of the Romanians' new destiny of national freedom and dignity, prestigious statesman of the contemporary world who, serving with abnegation and inexhaustible resourcefulness the country's supreme interests, has definitively guided the country on the road of the most fertile advancement; with his revolutionary thinking and action, with his inestimable contribution to the creative enrichment of world revolutionary theory and practice, through his vast work placed in the service of peace, international understanding and collaboration, for the defence of people's and nations' sacred right to free and dignified existence, for the building of a better and more just world, he raised the country's prestige to levels unattained so far.

The party did not, however, forget Mrs Ceauşescu. The proclamation continued:

> On this occasion of great national celebration, our entire people expresses its deepest esteem and respect for Academician Elena

Ceauşescu, DSc, luminous example of a revolutionary and politician, of a remarkable scientist of world repute, who makes an
inestimable contribution to the activity devoted to the elabo-
ration and implementation of the plans and programmes for
the country's socio-economic progress, to the development of
science, education and culture in our homeland, striving also
for the attainment of the lofty ideals of peace, collaboration and
friendship among all the world's people.

Unlike Stalin and Mao, Ceauşescu was personally corrupt. He
embezzled enormous sums, and ruled like any Third World despot,
with a court, palaces and all the tacky trappings of an instant bil-
lionaire. He decided to leave his mark on Bucharest by demolishing
a number of important 19th-century buildings to make way for new
avenues, notably the Victory of Socialism Boulevard, which leads
to a palace he built for himself in the centre of the city. This was
called the 'House of the Republic', stands 300 feet (100 metres)
tall and cost billions of dollars. The only thing comparable in
modern Europe were the megalomaniac plans for Berlin that
Albert Speer drew up for Hitler – including a gigantic avenue
and an immense palace. Most of Speer's buildings were never
begun, but Ceauşescu's reign lasted twice as long as Hitler's and
his palace was almost complete at the time of the revolution. The
new government is now faced with the puzzle of what to do with
it. In all, a third of the city centre was to be razed for his projects
– and most of the demolition work had been carried out before the
revolution.

Romania came to resemble George Orwell's vision of a Communist dictatorship in *1984*: a miserable tyranny where the people
starved in the cold and their every act was monitored by the
Thought Police. It was a reminder of what the economic conditions
in Europe had been like in the late 1940s, when everything was
rationed. There was not enough power to heat buildings during
the winter, or even to light them adequately at night: heating
was permitted no more than four hours a day, and this was often
reduced to two hours, and no room in a house was allowed more
than one 60-watt light bulb. Speaking to foreigners was illegal;
all typewriters and personal computers were registered with the
police. Ceauşescu wanted to raise the population from 22 million
to 30 million by the year 2000, every woman was expected to bear

five children: abortion and other forms of birth control were illegal; and all women had to submit to a gynaecological examination every three months to confirm that they were obeying the law. All these controls were enforced by the secret police – the *Securitate* – the most vicious in Europe since the heyday of the *Gestapo* and the NKVD.

Ceauşescu's economic policies were a national disaster, particularly when he decided, in 1980, to pay off the entire foreign debt – about $11 billion. For the next eight years, Romania exported food, oil and anything else that could be sold for hard currency; at the same time, it drastically reduced its imports, even those that were essential to the national economy. Factories were neither modernized nor properly maintained, and productivity therefore steadily declined.

Romanian hospitals were unable to import medical supplies, and Romanian industry produced none. The government's ban on contraception and its attempt to increase the birth rate succeeded at first but after a year or two of a baby boom, the rate dropped again, as people rediscovered older methods of birth control and the number of illegal and self-induced abortions rose dramatically. There was a medical crisis, and the lack of supplies compounded it. There were great numbers of orphans in state hospitals, many of them sick and undernourished. Romanian doctors continued the practice of giving blood transfusions as the quickest way of restoring badly undernourished babies to health. The blood supply had become contaminated with the AIDS virus and there was no equipment to test blood. There were quite inadequate supplies of needles and sterilization equipment, so the same needles were used repeatedly. As a result, there was an epidemic of AIDS in Romanian paediatric hospitals, but the regime, under Elena Ceauşescu's urging, refused to recognize that the disease existed in socialist Romania. Of all the horrors discovered after the Christmas revolution, the hundreds of babies dying of AIDS was the most painful.

Elena Ceauşescu's malign influence also cast its pall over science education. She herself had studied chemistry briefly, and was awarded many distinctions on the strength of that slight experience. As a result, she concluded that no one else needed a longer period of education in that discipline, and the study of chemistry in Romania was therefore interrupted for two decades.

Romania's irredenta

Romania has had territorial disputes with all its neighbours throughout its modern history. These disagreements lay dormant throughout the years of Soviet hegemony, but have now revived.

The most difficult concerns Transylvania, the wild country west of the Carpathian mountains, whose history goes back to ancient times, when it was part of the kingdom of Dacia. It was conquered by the Emperor Trajan in AD 106, but was abandoned by the Emperor Aurelian in 270. However, the occupation had been long enough for the Dacians to adopt Latin, and the Romanians claim to be their descendants. The Hungarians, whose ancestors conquered Transylvania in the ninth century, claim that there were then no Daco-Romans left and that the Romanians are descendants of another Latin-speaking tribe, known as the Vlachs, who insinuated themselves among the Hungarian Transylvanians during the years of Turkish domination. This matter of remote philological and archaeological dispute is current enough to get people killed in the late 20th century. In the spring of 1990 readers of the correspondence columns of the *New York Times* must have been much astonished to find a Hungarian passionately asserting his nation's claim to Transylvania, by using the argument that there are no Romanian place names older than the 12th century.

In any event, the region remained an unquestioned part of Hungary until it was ceded to Romania in 1920. By then, its population had become hopelessly mixed. Many cities had two or three names: Brasov was also Kronstadt; Timisoara was also Temesvar; and the principal city of Transylvania was Cluj to the Romanians, Klausenburg to the Germans and Kilozsvár to the Hungarians. The inhabitants of central Transylvania were predominantly Magyars or Szeklers (related to the Magyars); western Transylvanians were chiefly Romanians. In the eastern Banat, on the frontier between Romania, Hungary and Yugoslavia, Romanians, Hungarians and Serbians were totally intermingled. There were also hundreds of thousands of Germans, Jews and gypsies throughout Transylvania, and the whole area, until 1918, had been administered by Hungary as an integral part of the Austro-Hungarian empire.

Transylvania changed hands twice during World War II but has been Romanian since 1944, and in the decades that followed the Hungarian minority steadily lost all its privileges, including universities, schools, newspapers and the possibility of working in the Hungarian language.

In the mid-1980s, there were between 2 and 3 million Hungarians in Romania: no more precise figure is available because the results of every census taken during the past 50 years has been completely unreliable, like the rest of Ceauşescu's economic statistics. Relations between Romanians and Hungarians had been steadily deteriorating under Ceauşescu, until, in about 1985, he decided to solve the 'Hungarian question' once and for all by forcing the complete assimilation of the Hungarian population. Since most of them lived in the small towns and villages of the Carpathians and in Transylvania, Ceauşescu ordered that every village in the country – starting with the Hungarian villages – should be razed, to be replaced by 'agro-industrial complexes' The razing of the villages was just getting under way in 1989.

About 50,000 refugees from Romania escaped to Hungary between 1981 and 1989. Most of them were Hungarians, but some were Romanians, fleeing the economic calamity that Ceauşescu's policies had caused. The Romanian-Hungarian border came to resemble the Iron Curtain of 30 years before, with people to the east desperate to escape the horrors of their native country to reach the comparative freedom and affluence of Hungary. For the first time in the history of European Communism, great numbers of people tried to get into a Communist country – and were welcomed.

Romania's other irredentist problem is Bessarabia. The province was annexed from Turkey by the Russian empire in 1812, the year that Napoleon marched on Moscow. Despite the usual Russian persecution, and the imposition of the Cyrillic alphabet, the Bessarabian people retained their language and their connections with the Romanian principalities across the river Prut. Bessarabia had a population of about 3 million in 1917, half of them Romanians, and between the two world wars, it was more easily assimilated into Greater Romania than was Transylvania. The Soviet Union, however, never recognized the annexation. Stalin always intended to recover the lost province when the opportunity offered itself – as it did in 1940. Romania recovered it when Hitler invaded the Soviet Union in 1941 but lost it again in 1944 when the Red Army invaded Romania.

The Bessarabian question, in theory at least, could be more easily solved than the problem of Transylvania. Southern Bessarabia, which has been added to the Ukrainian Republic, has a population that was chiefly Ukrainian, the Jews who lived there having been murdered by the Germans or emigrated to Israel, and the other minorities having also departed. The majority of the population of the Soviet Socialist Republic of Moldavia, which comprises the rest of Soviet Bessarabia, are now Romanians and have already shown signs of wanting to follow the example of the Lithuanians and secede from the Soviet Union. In January 1989, there was a vast demonstration in the republic's capital Kishinev (known to Romanians as Chisinau) to demand that the Roman alphabet be restored and that Romanian be declared the official language. The local authorities promptly complied. The Moldavians did not then demand independence, let alone federation with Romania – no one would voluntarily submit to Ceauşescu. Living conditions in Romania were clearly inferior to those of the Soviet Union (an unusual distinction), but the pull of language and tradition, resentment at centuries of Russian oppression, and hopes for better things may very well revive demands for reunification, as they did in Germany.

Northern Bukovina, also annexed from Austria-Hungary in 1920 and taken by Stalin during the war, is now chiefly populated by Ukrainians and it is unlikely that Romania will revive its claims there. The eastern Banat, whose capital is Timisoara, was part of Hungary until 1918 and still has a mixed population. It, too, may become a source of tension.

Revolution

There were periodic protests against Ceauşescu, including riots in Brasov in November 1987, as well as isolated demonstrations against the 'agro-industrial complexes'. In March 1989, a group of six distinguished Romanians (all former Communist officials) sent a letter of protest to Ceauşescu and published it abroad. They accused him of violating human rights (including those guaranteed by the Helsinki Final Act, which he had himself signed), the bloody suppression of the Brasov demonstrations, ignoring the constitutional rights of citizens, mismanaging the economy and alienating Romania's allies. The signatories included: Constantin Parvulescu, then aged 94, one of the party's founders; Gheorghe Apostol, aged 77, a former member of the Politburo; Silviu Brucan, a former ambassador to the United States; and Corneliu Manescu, a former foreign minister and president of the United Nations General Assembly. They were all put under house arrest, and Brucan's son was arrested and charged with espionage.

Romanian television, limited to two hours of broadcasts a day, concentrated on the doings of the 'Hero of the Nation's Heroes' and his wife; and the press and radio were wholly devoted to the regime. But despite the *Securitate*'s efforts to keep them out, people could listen to the Voice of America and the BBC and to Hungarian, Yugoslav, Bulgarian and even Soviet radio (broadcasting in Romanian, from Moldavia) to discover what was happening in the rest of Eastern Europe.

On 24 November 1989, while Communist governments were collapsing in East Germany, Czechoslovakia and Bulgaria, Ceauşescu held the 14th party congress, which devoted itself to praising him, his wife, his son, his brothers and all his other relatives – and reaffirmed the immovable correctness of the party line. The congress was conspicuously ignored by foreign Communist parties. At its conclusion, everyone stood for the 'Internationale'. Alan Riding of the *New York Times*, observing from the gallery, noted that Ceauşescu appeared to be the only person singing the words, and he did so with gusto, waving his arms in time to the music. Everyone else stood silent.

On 14 December 1989 in Timisoara, the *Securitate* tried to arrest the Protestant Hungarian pastor László Tokes. His neighbours and parishioners intervened, forming a human chain around his house to keep the secret police away. The disturbance rapidly turned into a riot, and continued for days. Romanians in Timisoara came to the aid of the Hungarians, and the local party, rather than indulging in the usual coercion, tried to persuade people to go home.

On Sunday 17 December, Ceauşescu summoned party leaders across the country on the government's closed-circuit television network. He denounced the 'hooligans' in Timisoara, and ordered the army and police to suppress demonstrations by shooting to kill.

His orders were carried out in Timisoara: at the large demonstration against the regime that afternoon, police and troops fired on the crowds. According to one report, a group of soldiers who refused to shoot demonstrators were themselves shot by *Securitate* agents. Pastor Tokes was finally arrested.

There was great confusion about how many people were killed in the Timisoara massacre. Protestors came up with the figure of 4700 and this was broadcast by foreign radio stations. However, much later, it was established that the number was actually less than 100.

The demonstrations and killings in Timisoara continued during the following week – a ceasless confrontation between citizens, troops and police. Ceauşescu, after giving the shoot-to-kill order, departed on a three-day visit to Iran. In the films of his meetings with Iranian leaders, he seemed distracted. He returned to Romania on Wednesday, 20 December, just as the army pulled out of Timisoara. Evidently, the troops had had enough. Ceauşescu broadcast to the nation, denouncing hooligans, Fascists, foreign agents and *agents provocateurs* in Timisoara and ordering the army to reoccupy the town. In addition, he praised the army for shooting the rioters, a statement that led many soldiers to revolt two days later: they felt disgraced by the suggestion that they had shot fellow-citizens.

Those whom the gods will destroy, they first make mad: on Thursday, 21 December, Ceauşescu summoned a mass rally in Bucharest to demonstrate his power and popularity. It was broadcast live, Ceauşescu on his balcony denouncing hooligans and Fascists, with his wife stony-faced beside him. Then came one of the great moments of the television age: students at the back of the crowd started booing, and the whole crowd joined them, chanting, 'Ceauşescu assassin!' The president stopped in mid-speech, looked amazed, indecisive, gestured with his arms for the protests to stop. Technicians cut off the sound, and for a few moments, viewers could watch as Ceauşescu stared, baffled, at the scene before him. Then, as tens of thousands of Romanians shouted their defiance, the screen went blank. The *Securitate* tried to arrest the protestors, and started shooting: hundreds of people were killed that night. Ceauşescu ordered his minister of defence, General Vasile Milea, to have his troops fire on the crowds. Milea refused, and committed suicide. When the news of his death was broadcast, it was universally assumed that he had been shot on Ceauşescu's orders, and the event encouraged the army to join the demonstrators.*

The 22nd December was to become the Romanian 14 July. Huge crowds gathered in the centre of Bucharest that morning. The army did not interfere, the police hesitated and the crowd stormed the Central Committee building just before noon, as the Parisians had stormed the Bastille 200 years earlier. It was a spontaneous uprising.

Ceauşescu and his wife escaped by helicopter from the roof; they had no plan and no destination, until the helicopter put them down near Tirgoviste, 100 kilometres from Bucharest. Commandeering a car, they drove to one of their country houses, where they hastily packed some of their possessions into suitcases before driving on. Then they were recognized and took refuge in a collective farm where, for a few hours, they were held in a grain silo. Then they were driven back towards Bucharest, but were intercepted by an army patrol, arrested and taken to an army base. Ceauşescu was kept in an armoured car, which drove around the base for three days, to prevent any rescue attempt by the *Securitate*.

In the evening, the *Securitate* launched a counter-attack on the army and demonstrators, and there was heavy fighting in Bucharest and other cities. For three days, there was civil war and the outcome appeared uncertain: the *Securitate* was much better equipped and trained than the army, and according to the fevered rumours of the time (later shown to be unfounded), the secret police had a network of tunnels, arsenals and command posts under the streets of Bucharest. Other rumours put the dead at tens of thousands, and it was alleged that Ceauşescu had established a special corps of Arab terrorists in the *Securitate*. In Timisoara, 23 bodies were dug up in a paupers' graveyard, and were exhibited as the *Securitate*'s victims. Many of them had been cut open, and for a few days the world believed that this was evidence of further atrocities, until the local hospital established that the bodies were in fact those of

* Milea's alleged murder was one of the charges brought against Ceauşescu during his trial. The fallen dictator maintained that Milea was a traitor who 'did not urge his unit to do their patriotic duty'. A month later, during the trial of Ceauşescu's senior collaborators, the details of the suicide were published.

paupers who had died of natural causes in the hospital, and on which autopsies had been performed.

One of the main scenes of the fighting in Bucharest was around the television station. As Ceauşescu escaped from the Central Committee building, a group of rebels seized the main television studios. Corneliu Manescu, one of the six signers of the letter of protest to Ceauşescu in March, appeared on television to announce the revolution, and called on the army to defend it. It was the key event. It informed everyone, not only in the capital but all over Romania, that the Ceauşescus had been overthrown. The National Salvation Council (*see below*) was proclaimed on television, and its members – including Manescu and former ambassador Silviu Brucan – called on the army and people to defend the television station against counter-attack by the *Securitate*. For several days, the building was under siege as *Securitate* agents tried desperately to take it. This was the first revolution broadcast live on television, and its defenders were determined to win.

There was also heavy fighting in the centre of the city, most of it occasioned by *Securitate* snipers firing from buildings. The army's tanks and artillery then destroyed the buildings; in this way, the university library was destroyed and the royal palace badly damaged. It was all very dramatic, but later, when calm was restored, it became clear that the *Securitate* had never been a real threat after the first 24 hours of revolt – above all, because the Ceauşescus had by then been arrested. No senior members of the regime took the lead in fighting against the revolution: junior officers resisted spontaneously, unthinkingly, until they were overwhelmed.

On the day Ceauşescu was overthrown, a committee calling themselves the National Salvation Council and consisting of dissidents, former officials and student demonstrators had proclaimed itself the new government. Its leader was Ion Iliescu, formerly a senior member of the government, who had fallen into disgrace in the 1970s for criticizing Ceauşescu. On Monday, Christmas Day, the Council struck at the head of the old regime: it ordered that the Ceauşescus be tried and executed. The trial, which was later broadcast, was a travesty of justice. No evidence of Ceauşescu's or his wife's guilt was offered, nor were there any coherent charges against them: they were accused of 'genocide', killing 60,000 people during the revolution, undermining state power, destroying the country's economic and spiritual values, and embezzling $1 billion and hiding it in foreign banks. The trial lasted two hours, and the Ceauşescus were then marched outside and shot.

The film – and especially a close-up of Ceauşescu's body lying in a pool of blood – was shown repeatedly on television, and within a few days, the *Securitate* abandoned the struggle. The real number of those killed in the fighting was not easily or quickly established. Three weeks later, the figure was reduced to 10,000, and at the trial of some of Ceauşescu's senior ministers in January, an overall figure of 689 dead for the whole country was offered, including 90 in Timisoara. The army had suffered 196 men killed and 450 wounded.

There were many rumours that the National Salvation Council had been formed six months earlier, in secret, and had plotted Ceauşescu's downfall. It was also suggested that Ion Iliescu, who had studied with Mikhail Gorbachev in Moscow in the 1950s, had been in touch with the Soviets in advance. Silviu Brucan said in a television interview that he had approached the Soviet government during a visit to Moscow in November 1989, and had won its reluctant agreement to the overthrow of Ceauşescu. Certainly the new leadership emerged with astonishing speed, and the Soviet Union recognized the new regime immediately.

The new regime issued a series of decrees repealing Ceauşescu's repressive laws, abolished the death penalty, stopped the export of agricultural produce (to put food in the shops) and ended restrictions on the use of electricity (consumption promptly rose 40 per cent).

The majority of the Council was composed of former Communists and associates of Ceauşescu's, and on 7 Janaury, there was the first student demonstration in Bucharest protesting against the Council's composition and policies. Five days later, the Council called a day of national mourning for those killed in the revolution. In Bucharest, the event turned into a wild demonstration against the Council, because of the dubious antecedents of many of its members.

With the mob baying for blood, three leading members of the Council announced, on the spot, that the Communist party was outlawed, and called a referendum to determine whether to restore

the death penalty for former officials. The next day, the Council
countermanded the decree, ruling instead that there would be a
referendum on the question of outlawing the Communist party,
as well as the death penalty. A week later, both referendums
were cancelled. The new government was evidently off to a shaky
start.

The Council was not only indecisive and afraid of the mob: it
had no legitimacy. In all the other changes in Eastern Europe,
from Poland to Bulgaria, the old leaders had resigned and handed
over to the new. In Romania, there was a complete revolution: all
the organs of the state were dissolved, the Communist party ceased
to exist and, in the short run, the only institution capable of filling
the vacuum was the army.

Romania faced a bleak and difficult future as it re-established
a democratic system (its last free elections were in 1928), and
started to restore its economy from the ravages of the Ceauşescu
years. Trouble between Romanians and Hungarians was a continuing danger.

The new government promised the Hungarians a restoration of
all their lost rights, but hostility between the two communities,
based on decades of painful experience, continued to trouble the
country. There is no obvious territorial solution to the Transylvania
dispute because the bulk of the 2.5 million Hungarians who live
in Romania are isolated from Hungary itself: if the frontier were
moved eastwards, to incorporate them into Hungary, an even
greater number of Romanians would be forced into Hungary,
reversing the present balance without solving it.

In addition, although Romania was unlikely to provoke the Soviet
Union by advancing an irredentist claim on Moldavia and the
Bukovina, the Moldavians themselves might well provoke the
crisis: in the spring of 1990, the barriers were at last lowered,
and Romanians and Moldavians could cross the frontier freely,
in both directions, to see for themselves the conditions in each
country. It is also entirely possible that Fascism may reappear
in Romania. The Iron Guard has revived from its ashes: pam-
phlets signed by the 'Legion of the Archangel Michael', praising
the Guard and advocating Fascist policies such as persecuting
Hungarians and Jews, appeared within a month of the revolution.

The National Salvation Council continued to come under cease-less attack by students and others, who accused its members of being Communists in disguise, and on 1 February 1990, it agreed to form a coalition government with opposition groups, to be known as the Provisional Council for National Unity. Elections were set for 20 May.

The Council soon showed that it had the support of a large majority of the population, however vociferous the opposition from students and others. It employed the Communist technique of rounding up workers in their factories, taking them by bus into the centre of Bucharest and having them demonstrate loudly in support of government ministers who appeared on balconies. In late February, the Council's headquarters was invaded and its files ransacked by a group of opposition supporters: they were arrested and tried immediately, and given short prison terms.

There were other serious problems. On 19 March, in Tirgu Mures, in Transylvania, a Romanian mob killed six Hungarians, and about 300 people were wounded in fighting that lasted until the army intervened to separate the two communities. The Hungarian government accused the Romanians of continuing to mistreat the Hungarian minority, and Romania claimed that the rioting had been started by Hungarians crossing the border. The Iron Guard was allegedly involved in the fighting.

Other voices from the past made themselves heard. King Michael, who had been living in exile in Geneva, tried to return on a visit in April. The government at first gave him a visa, but withdrew it at the last moment. Surviving leaders of the Peasants' and National Liberal parties successfully returned from exile and offered themselves as candidates in the elections, but it soon became apparent that none of them enjoyed any serious support. In the May elections, Iliescu won 85 per cent of the presidential vote, and the Council won 65 per cent in the parliamentary elections. The largest opposition party turned out to be a Hungarian party.

Foreign observers admitted that the elections had been fair, in the sense that the voting had been honest. They claimed, however, that, in the fevered atmosphere immediately after the revolution, the National Salvation Council had enjoyed most undemocratic advantages. The election had been held too soon, the campaign had been too short and other parties had had no time to make themselves known. In any event, Iliescu won his majority and now had the right to grapple with the Ceauşescu legacy.

In education, Romania had 71 students in universities for every 10,000 citizens, the lowest proportion in Europe (except, presumably, Albania). It had fewer radio and television sets *per capita* than Burkina Faso, Kenya and Zaïre. The National Commission on Statistics reported that 42 per cent of the country's scientific research equipment was worn out, as were 39 per cent of its industrial equipment and 37 per cent of its buses and trains. The Ceauşescu regime had invested every available resource on a few gigantic industrial plants, and did so with monstrous inefficiency: one aluminium factory used more electricity than all 23 million Romanian citizens; there was three times as much oil refining capacity as Romania needed; and many factories operated at less than 50 per cent capacity. An optimistic Romanian official claimed that the country's technology was ten years behind the rest of Europe; others put it at 20 or 30 years behind. In the 1970s, Romania had developed a computer industry, in partnership with European firms; that industry, cut off from the world in the 1980s, was now worthless. Bucharest was filled with partly completed building projects bequeathed by Ceauşescu. Apart from the 'House of the Republic', there were apartment buildings for the élite, a National Science Institute and other grandiose edifices.

Agricultural production dropped steadily during the Ceauşescu years, and at the end, the government was inflating the statistics of agricultural yields by up to 600 per cent. One of the new government's first moves was to liberate agricultural prices, as the only means of increasing production. It also promised to end collectivization, though there would still be limits on the size of private farms. Peasants all over the country started reclaiming their land, taken from them or their families 30 or 40 years before. The government also decreed that private companies with up to 20 employees would be permitted. This was a first breach with Communist doctrine, though it did not restore the free market. More extensive reforms were promised after the elections.

Romania seems destined to suffer many dreary years of economic difficulty and political uncertainty before it can recover from the legacy of Communism. The rest of Eastern Europe, of course, faces severe difficulties, but most of the other countries have the political, moral and intellectual resources to surmount their problems. Romania has yet to find them. There was in Romania none of the tradition of dissent that provided the essential cadres for the new governments in Poland, Czechoslovakia and Hungary. The country, paradoxically, had rejected Communism but embraced former Communists, who now head every government ministry. It remains to be seen whether Iliescu and the rest of them are capable of repudiating not merely Ceauşescu and his megalomaniac excesses, but the doctrines and practices of the past 50 years – and, indeed, habits that go back much further than that.

This is not just a matter of economic backwardness: the new regime conducts itself very much in the manner of the old. Public opinion is ruthlessly manipulated. The press, radio and television are all strictly controlled and fed with lies and provocations about the opposition. Iliescu denounced the students demonstrating against him as gypsies (*golani*) and called on loyal workers to destroy them – just as Ceauşescu had denounced those same students as 'hooligans' and summoned workers from suburban factories to defend him. Opposition parties are harassed, their offices sacked and their leaders attacked, with the active connivance of the police; they are described as Fascists who intend to restore all the alleged evils of capitalism.

The students, proudly calling themselves *golani*, staged a protracted occupation in University Square in the centre of Bucharest. On 10 June 1990, Iliescu sent the *Securitate*, miraculously reborn, to break up the demonstration. Students were savagely beaten, and the event soon turned into a full-scale riot, with cars burned in the streets, and public buildings (including the television studios) briefly occupied. Iliescu then called on Ceauşescu's most loyal supporters – the miners – to come to the rescue. They were fetched by train from mining towns and instituted a reign of terror in Bucharest for three days. Their targets were students, intellectuals and foreigners, and at least half a dozen people were killed.

The government puts all the blame for Romania's continuing miseries on Ceauşescu, and the opposition blames Iliescu for suppressing democracy only six months after the revolution. But, as Western reporters uncover further details of cruelty and backwardness, it has become obvious that Romania still suffers from practices and attitudes far older than Communism, and it has a long way to go before it can be welcomed into the European family. It was, perhaps, a direct order of Elena Ceauşescu that concealed the AIDS epidemic among the infants in state hospitals, but it was a national scandal, far surpassing the Ceauşescus or Iliescu, that up to 100,000 Romanian orphans were kept in conditions of unremitting squalor – worse than in the most primitive asylums of Africa – in orphanages all over the country, and were often left to die of neglect. African children may die of famine or disease, but they are not abandoned callously by their parents, the state and those appointed to care for them.

This cruelty to children, like Iliescu's reversion to totalitarian methods six months after the revolution, was a throwback to the old Balkans, preserved through the Communist years. This, together with a complete lack of democratic instincts, will not be ended merely by changing the man on the balcony.

9   The Baltic Republics

The first crack in the splendid facade of the Soviet Union appeared in March 1988 when fighting broke out between Armenians and Azerbaijanis. In the next two years, there was fighting in Georgia and Central Asia, and independence movements sprang up in almost every corner of the union – including the Russian Republic itself. The crisis in the USSR continues.

Of the three Baltic republics, Lithuania proclaimed its independence on 11 March 1990, and its example was soon followed by Estonia and Latvia. The republics consider themselves part of Europe, not the Soviet Union. They are as much Stalin's victims as Poland because they, too, recovered their independence in the wake of the First World War and lost it again at the onset of the Second. In 1990, they demanded their right to freedom, and if they failed to win it immediately, they could legitimately hope that the further dissolution of the USSR would reward them in the near future.

It was a quiet revolution. There was no need for the long political struggle that led to the revolutions of Poland and Hungary, or for the mass demonstrations in East Germany and Czechoslovakia, or for the violence of Romania. Instead, parties supporting independence won large majorities in elections in all three republics in February and March 1990 and the new parliaments then voted to defy Moscow.

It was a brave act: the Red Army was still in full occupation of the three countries, and tanks drove past the parliament in Vilnius in a crude show of force on the day Lithuania voted for independence. There was never any doubt that the Soviet Union could crush the rebels if ever it decided to do so. But in times of revolution, victory goes to the brave. Gorbachev might insist that independence be postponed, but it seemed quite possible that his other problems would prove so intractable that he would not oppose the independence movements any further. The postponement would not be very long.

The destiny of Estonia, Latvia and Lithuania through the centuries has been to be crushed between the upper and nether millstones of Russia and Germany. The Baltic states have been independent infrequently, and only for brief intervals. They were absorbed into the Russian empire in the 18th century, and the last time they recovered their independence, it was only by accident of war. When the Germans conquered them in their advance on Petrograd in 1917 and 1918, the revolution and ensuing civil war distracted the Russians, and Lenin recognized their independence in 1920 and 1921. This freedom lasted just two decades and was always precarious. On the one hand, Stalin was determined to recover all the lost territories of the tsars; and on the other, the three republics, isolated from all possible help on the far shore of the Baltic, stood in the way of Hitler's ambitions.

Lithuania was the first victim. In 1923, the German port of Memel, on the extreme eastern tip of East Prussia, was seized by Lithuania, which renamed it Klaipeda. In March 1939, Hitler demanded it back. The Lithuanians had no choice, and lost their principal port.

Then, in August 1939, Germany and the Soviet Union signed a treaty of friendship and non-aggression. They also signed a 'Secret Additional Protocol':

> While signing the Non-Aggression Treaty between Germany and the Union of Soviet Socialist Republics, the undersigned representatives of both parties strictly confidentially discussed the question on the delineation of the spheres of mutual interest in Eastern Europe. The results of the discussion were as follows:
>
> 1. In the case of the territorial–political restructuring of the regions, included in the Baltic republics (Finland, Estonia, Latvia and Lithuania), the northern border of Lithuania shall be simultaneously the boundary between the spheres of interest of Germany and the USSR. Accordingly, the interest of Lithuania with respect to the Vilna region is recognized by both parties.

2. In case of the territorial–political restructuring of the regions comprising part of the Polish state, the boundary between the spheres of interest of Germany and the USSR shall pass along the rivers Narew, Vistula and San.

The question as to whether it is in mutual interest to preserve the independent Polish state and what the boundaries of this state should be, can be ultimately solved only in the course of further political development.

In any case, both governments are going to approach this question on the basis of friendly mutual accord.

3. As for the southeast of Europe from the Soviet side, the interest of the USSR towards Bessarabia* is stressed. The German side declares the complete lack of political interest in these regions.

4. This Protocol should be kept top secret by both sides.

On behalf of the USSR	On behalf of the German
goverment	government
[signed] V. Molotov	[signed] J. von Ribbentrop

Moscow, 23 August 1939

This translation, together with other related documents, was put out by the Novostni press agency in Moscow in 1990. A year earlier, the Soviet government had still been vigorously denying the existence of the protocol.

What the protocol meant was, *first*: the Soviet Union intended to annex Finland, Estonia and Latvia, and Germany intended to annex Lithuania; Vilnius (Vilna in Russian, Wilno in Polish), which was in the part of Poland allocated to the Soviet Union, was to go to Lithuania – and thus to Germany. *Second*: Germany and the USSR intended to partition Poland along the line of the three named rivers, and to decide later whether any independent Polish state should be preserved – all 'on the basis of friendly mutual accord'. *Third*: The USSR intended to annex Bessarabia, which was part of Romania (*see* Chapter 8).

Hitler invaded Poland on 1 September and Stalin occupied eastern Poland 16 days later. On 28 September, when the occupation of Poland was complete, Ribbentrop returned to Moscow to continue his discussions with Molotov. A second 'Secret Additional Protocol' to the August treaty was then concluded:

* For details see pp. 213 and 228.

The Secret Additional Protocol signed on 23 August 1939, is to be changed in Point 1 so as to include the territory of the Lithuanian state into the sphere of interest of the USSR, for, on the other side, the Lublin Province and parts of the Warsaw Province are included into the sphere of interest of Germany (see the map to the Treaty of Friendship and Boundary between the USSR and Germany signed today). As soon as the USSR government takes special measures on the Lithuanian territory to safeguard its interests, to achieve a natural and simple establishment of the boundary, the existing German–Lithuanian boundary shall be changed so that the Lithuanian territory to the southwest of the line shown on the map is passed over to Germany.

It is further stated that the existing economic agreements between Germany and Lithuania shall not be violated by the above mentioned undertakings of the Soviet Union.

This meant that a large part of Poland, occupied by the Soviet Union, was to be handed over to Germany (the new line was now to be the frontier between Poland and the USSR), and in exchange, Hitler allowed Stalin to take Lithuania (with some minor border adjustments). He could afford to be generous: he intended to make war upon the USSR in due course.

Stalin did not immediately 'take special measures . . . to safeguard [the Soviet Union's] interests'. On 28 September 1939, the day that Ribbentrop arrived back in Moscow, Estonia was forced to sign a non-aggression treaty with the USSR, providing for the stationing of 25,000 Soviet troops there. Then, on 5 October, Latvia was forced to submit to a similar treaty, and five days later, it was Lithuania's turn. Molotov did not, of course, inform the Estonians, Latvians or the Lithuanians that their fate had already been settled, by agreement with Hitler. The new treaty with Lithuania stated:

> The realization of the present treaty should in no way violate the sovereign rights of the parties, in particular, their state structure, economic and social system, military measures, and, in general, the principle of non-interference in internal affairs.

It provided that Vilnius should be handed over to Lithuania, and permitted the USSR to station 20,000 troops in Lithuania, as a measure of joint security.

Finland

On 30 November 1939, the USSR attacked Finland, which defended itself valiantly until 12 March 1940, when an armistice was concluded, in which Finland lost territory to the Soviet Union but retained its independence. On 14 December 1939, in a last spasm of indignation, the League of Nations expelled the Soviet Union because of its invasion of Finland. The League then went out of business.

The Red Army's poor performance during the 'Winter War' much encouraged Hitler, who took it as proof of the Soviets' military incompetence. In 1941, after it joined Germany in the invasion of the USSR, Finland was occupied by Germany and used as a base of operations against Leningrad. It managed to extricate itself from the war in time to avoid the fate of Hungary and Romania, by signing a peace treaty with the USSR on 19 September 1944, and declaring war on Germany. It was forced to cede its easternmost province of Karelia (14,000 square miles) to the USSR and to pay large reparations.

The first Soviet conquest

At midnight on 14 June 1940, the day that the *Wehrmacht* entered Paris, Molotov, then both prime minister and foreign minister of the USSR, presented an ultimatum to the prime minister and foreign minister of Lithuania, whom he had summoned to Moscow. He demanded that the Red Army be permitted to occupy the country by 10 a.m. the following morning, and that a government acceptable to the USSR be formed immediately. Molotov informed the Lithuanian ministers, 'Whether you agree or not is irrelevant, because the Red Army is going in tomorrow anyway.' The president, Smetona, and some of his ministers managed to flee the country as the Soviets marched in. The next day, 16 June, Molotov presented similar ultimata to Estonia and Latvia. They, too, were occupied by Soviet troops.

June 1940 was a busy month for Mr Molotov. On the 24th, a week after he had dealt with Estonia and Latvia, he presented an ultimatum to Romania, demanding that it give up Bessarabia and northern Bukovina. The partition of Eastern Europe – between Hitler and Stalin – was complete.

Stalin sent his most trusted hatchetmen into the Baltic states, to complete arrangements for their annexation. Andrei Zhdanov went to Tallinn, the capital of Estonia; Andrei Vyshinsky to the Latvian capital of Riga; and V. K. Dekanozov to Kaunas, then the capital of Lithuania. They brought new governments with them, and ensured that all prominent citizens who had failed to escape were deported eastwards. Most of them died in the camps, but a few survived to return after the thaw of the mid-1950s, including the Lithuanian foreign minister, Jonas Urbsys, who had been given Molotov's ultimatum in June 1940. He lived long enough to see the Lithuanian declaration of independence in 1990.

All political parties and independent organizations were dissolved and replaced by 'workers councils'. These bodies then prepared lists of candidates in 'people's fronts' for the elections which were held a month after the occupations, on 14 and 15 July 1940, and resulted in splendid victories for the fronts: their percentage of the votes ranged from 92.8 per cent in Estonia to 99.19 per cent in Lithuania. The new assemblies immediately applied to join the USSR, and were admitted in August. The flavour of the times is suggested by the proclamation of the Lithuanian 'People's *Sejm*':

> The criminal Smetona regime, indifferent to the real interests of the people, has led the country into an impasse in the fields of both domestic and foreign policy. The vital interests of the Lithuanian people have been sacrificed to the mercenary interests of a handful of exploiters and rich people. The only thing left to working people in the towns and in the country has been unemployment, insecurity, hunger, indigence and national oppression.
>
> Over the years, the Lithuanian people languished under the oppression of that reactionary regime. The Smetona clique kept our toiling and talented people in a vice of lawlessness and misrule . . . Every independent word and free thought were suppressed ruthlessly and at once . . . The interests of the Lithuanian people called for a constant and close unity and friendship with the Soviet Union. However, Smetona and his myrmidons pursued a hostile policy *vis-à-vis* the USSR . . .

It is hardly suprising that, nowadays, the Lithuanians insist that the accession to the USSR in 1940 was illegal.

The Communization of the three republics moved briskly forward. Agriculture was collectivized, industry was nationalized, the churches were persecuted or dissolved, and society was thoroughly purged. In Estonia, for example, about 2000 people were executed and 19,000 deported, and a further 33,000 were carried off by the Soviets during their retreat in 1941. In all, Estonia lost 94,000 people in 1940–41, out of a population of 1.13 million. Furthermore, two areas along the border with the USSR were transferred from Estonia to the Russian Republic.

On 22 June 1941, Hitler invaded the Soviet Union. Lithuania, Latvia and Estonia were occupied by the Germans in July. The fighting was heaviest in Estonia, where large numbers of Soviet troops were cut off. When calm had been restored, the Germans set about preparing for the incorporation of the three republics into the *Reich*. There were about 253,000 Jews in the Baltic countries, including the Vilnius region that had been added to Lithuania by Stalin: the city of Vilnius was then the Jewish capital of Eastern Europe. Of the 150,000 Jews in Lithuania, 100,000 in Latvia and about 1000 in Estonia, 90 per cent were murdered by the Nazis. In addition, by the end of the war, Estonia had lost about 100,000 people, including 70,000 refugees to the West, on top of its 900 murdered Jews and the 94,000 people it had lost in the first Soviet occupation; by 1945, its population had dropped from 1.13 million to no more than 850,000.

Vilnius was liberated – or, rather reconquered – by the Red Army on 13 July 1944, Kaunas on 1 August and Riga on 8 August; the German armies in Tallinn surrendered on 22 September. The NKVD proceeded to restore Soviet control in the three republics in the usual manner: hundreds of thousands of people were deported to the east, 60 per cent of whom would never return. One estimate is that 320,000 people out of a total population of 2 million were deported from Latvia, and as a result, Latvia's population now is 54 per cent Lett, 33 per cent Russian. Stalin also deported about 200,000 Lithuanians and 91,000 Estonians. Finally, during a series of purges of 'bourgeois nationalists' in 1949–53, coinciding with the other purges in Eastern Europe, a few thousand more were executed or deported.

Anti-Soviet guerrilla movements subsisted for ten years after the war in all three Baltic countries, as well as in Poland and the

Ukraine; in Estonia, they were called the 'forest brethren'. The guerrillas tried to defend peasants against forced collectivization, which resumed in 1949, but were never more than an irritant to the Soviet occupation forces. By 1950, the three republics were thoroughly integrated into the Soviet Union.

The revival of the Baltic states

From the beginnings of Mikhail Gobrachev's *glasnost*, nationalist agitation in the three republics turned rapidly into anti-Soviet demonstrations. In the spring of 1988, organizations sprang up in all of them demanding a degree of independence from Moscow that stopped just short of secession. In Lithuania, for example, the *Sajudis* ('Movement') was established on 3 June by rebellious members of the Institute of Philosophy of the Lithuanian Academy of Sciences. These groups wanted their countries to manage their own economies and to have their own representatives at the United Nations (like the Ukraine and Byelorussia), and they openly discussed the possibility of running candidates in elections. The leaderships of the Communist parties in all three countries had to scramble to catch up.

The three nations' flags, suppressed in 1940, reappeared in 1988, with official toleration. The governments made strenuous efforts to patch up relations with the churches, particularly in Lithuania which is strongly Catholic. Vilnius Cathedral, turned into a museum by Stalin, was returned to the Church.

Estonia led the way in 1988, forming the 'Estonian Front', the nearest thing to an opposition party anywhere in the Soviet Union since immediately after the Revolution. The Communist party secretary was dismissed on 16 June and replaced by Vaino Valas, who had shared a room with Mikhail Gorbachev when they had both attended a Komsomol (Young Communst) party school 30 years before. He immediately won the hearts of Estonians by addressing his first Central Committee meeting in Estonian rather than in Russian. This was not, however, enough to retain their affections.

All these signs of revived nationalism were permitted by the government in Moscow. The public demonstrations in all three countries were peaceful and, to begin with, did not involve overt demands for full independence. In each case, people demonstrated on the anniversary on their countries' incorporation into the Soviet Union, in June 1940. Then on 24 February 1988, 20,000–30,000 people demonstrated in Tallinn to commemorate another significant day – the day Estonia had won its independence from Russia in 1920.

In November 1988, Gorbachev presented a series of constitutional amendments to a meeting of the Supreme Soviet (parliament) in Moscow. The reforms had been much discussed in advance, and the Estonian parliament, in a quite unprecedented gesture, had voted unanimously to reject them, especially the provisions that increased the Soviet president's powers and reduced those of the USSR's constituent republics. The Estonian objections were overruled in Moscow, but afterwards, the Estonians once again proclaimed that they could themselves determine which parts of Soviet legislation they would adopt. Then they voted to make Estonian their national language. The Russian minority there – comprising one third of the population – staged strikes in protest, and Gorbachev and the Politburo fulminated, but the independence movement continued to gain momentum. On 23 August 1989 – the 50th anniversary of the Hitler–Stalin Pact – a human chain was formed that reached from Tallinn in Estonia to Vilnius in Lithuania.

Gorbachev had hoped that the three republics would take the lead and succeed in economic reform, thus demonstrating the advantages of *perestroika*, and on 1 January 1990, they were given a great measure of economic independence. Unfortunately for him, the citizens of the three countries, though delighted at the opportunity to recover their economic independence, used the opportunity to put their political demands first. Their governments had then to confront the difficulties of turning political agitation into practical reform.

In the autumn of 1989, Lithuania took over the lead from Estonia. On 7 December its parliament voted to repeal Article VI of its constitution, the clause that provided for the 'leading role' of the Communist party, and Lithuania was thus the first of the Soviet republics to abandon the Communist model. Three days later, local elections gave nationalists an 80 per cent majority in Estonia and 60 per cent in Latvia. The Lithuanian Communist

Party, in a desperate attempt to preserve itself, voted on 20 December to split from the Communist Party of the Soviet Union (CPSU). That act of secession was vehemently denounced by Moscow, which decided to send a delegation headed by Gorbachev himself to persuade the Lithuanian party to change its mind. The conflict escalated rapidly. The *Sajudis* declared that its objective was full independence: the annexation of 1940 had been illegal and therefore Lithuania had no need to consult Moscow about its plans. Besides, the Soviet constitution made provision for any republic that may want to secede.

Gorbachev arrived on 11 January, and toured Lithuania, arguing with party members, intellectuals and crowds in the street. Everywhere he went, he was received courteously, listened to carefully and told firmly that Lithuania would make its own decisions. He promised to prepare a new law to set out the means by which republics might secede from the union and, for the first time, admitted that the leading role of the CPSU might have to be abandoned. He returned to Moscow just in time to confront another explosion in Azerbaijan.

Lithuania held elections on 24 February and 4 March, and the *Sajudis* won a large majority. On Sunday, 11 March, the newly elected Lithuanian Supreme Soviet chose as president the *Sajudis* leader, Vytautas Landsbergis, a musician, and voted unanimously that Lithuania was now independent. The confrontation escalated abruptly. In elections in Estonia and Latvia, substantial majorities voted for independence, but the large Russian minorities in both republics – one third of the population – ensured that there would not be the two-thirds majority needed to change the constitution. Riga, the capital of Latvia, which has a Russian majority, voted against independence. Estonia had tried to avoid that difficulty two weeks earlier, by electing a separate congress and limiting the suffrage to people who were citizens, or descendants of those who were citizens, of Estonia before it was annexed to the Soviet Union. This congress voted for independence, but the Soviet government denied its validity. Then, on 13 April, Gorbachev announced an economic blockade of Lithuania; oil supplies were cut off five days later.

On 30 March 1990, Estonia's Supreme Soviet declared that the annexation of 1940 had been illegal and therefore Soviet laws did not apply to Estonia – but it did not take the final step of declaring the country independent. On 4 May, Latvia's parliament voted for independence, but ruled that there should be a transition period, of undetermined length, before it finally separated from the USSR.

The economic sanctions applied against Lithuania were intolerable, and the Soviet army had already demonstrated its power by sending its tanks rumbling through Vilnius on the day that parliament had voted for independence. In May, Lithuania was forced to seek a compromise. The West, in the persons of President Mitterrand of France and Chancellor Kohl of West Germany, also urged compromise, and when Gorbachev visited Washington in June 1990, he was told that a new trade agreement between the United States and the USSR would not be ratified by Congress unless the blockade of Lithuania were lifted.

Although Gorbachev may have been looking for a face-saving formula, to permit the three Baltic republics to leave the Soviet Union after a transition period of two to five years, it was not at all clear that he would get it. There were large anti-independence demonstrations by Russian residents of the three republics, including many of the military, and in Moscow, the debate on the future of the Baltic republics was inextricably involved in the debate on the future of the Soviet Union itself.

The border questions

There is a substantial Polish minority in Lithuania. Poland ruled Vilnius from 1386 until the Russian annexation in 1795, and in 1920, it retook it and southern Lithuania on the grounds that they were part of Poland. In 1939, Stalin annexed eastern Poland and restored Vilnius to Lithuania. There are still 258,000 Poles living in and around the capital, although the city itself is now chiefly Lithuanian; there had been a Jewish majority before the war, but almost all the Jews were murdered.

In due course, Lithuania also inherited Memel (now Klaipeda) from Germany, but not any other part of East Prussia, which was divided between Poland and Russia. Gorbachev has reminded Lithuanians that even if they win their independence, the Soviet Union may keep Klaipeda, which is one of the main Soviet naval bases on the Baltic and has the largest concentration of Russians.

Doubtless this reminder was part of the psychological war he is waging against Lithuania.

If Lithuania were to leave the Soviet Union, there would also be a small Russian enclave around Kaliningrad (Königsberg) isolated on the Baltic between Poland and Lithuania and one of the most miserable and neglected parts of the Soviet Union. Perhaps the USSR will demand a 'Soviet Corridor'.

The other territorial dispute concerns Estonia, which would like to recover the two districts added to the Russian Republic in 1945. It is not very probable that it will succeed.

Postscript

The division of Europe that began with the invasion of Poland in 1939, ended 50 years later in the revolutions of 1989. It was one of the great turning points of history – but the work was not finished at Christmas with the execution of Nicolae Ceauşescu. Communists still clung to power in Yugoslavia, Albania and the Soviet Union, and a spirit of murderous contention prevailed in Romania. Tyrannies had been overthrown in six countries, but it will be years before any of them, even the most favoured, settle down into the prosperity and stability that prevails in Western Europe.

The changes of 1989 will affect the West almost as much as the East. The most remarkable transformation concerns Germany. At a Nato summit in December 1989, Margaret Thatcher proclaimed that the question of German reunification was 'not on the agenda'. George Bush said much the same thing, neither of them admitting that the decision was not theirs to make. The Germans, led by Helmut Kohl, paid no attention to their allies' doubts. On 1 July 1990, the two Germanies merged their currencies and economies, and a few days earlier, the two parliaments decided to hold national elections in December, consummating their union. They had not consulted Thatcher, or Bush, or Mikhail Gorbachev. Germany thus recovered at last her rightful position in Europe, and the rest of the continent now has to scramble to adjust to the new realities. In political terms, France and Britain – which, after 1945, had both managed to exert influence quite out of proportion to their real weight in the world – will doubtless find the adjustment most difficult. Germany, quite apart from the problems of absorbing the former Democratic Republic, must now also adapt itself to the new role of Europe's uncontested leader.

It is fairly clear that the new Europe that will emerge by the end of the century will be organized around the European Community, which will continue to lurch towards fuller political and economic unity. The Community has decided to postpone the question of admitting new members until 1993, when the last economic barriers between its 12 present members will have been eliminated; most of them hope then to institute a common currency. By that time, presumably, the Warsaw Pact will have withered away completely, and all Soviet troops and military installations in Eastern Europe will have been withdrawn. There will be very large reductions in American forces in Europe, and NATO will play a much smaller role in European affairs. That is the easy part: the challenge for the 1990s is to integrate Eastern Europe with the West as quickly as possible, and with the least pain.

It is no longer very useful to speak of 'Eastern Europe' as though it were still a single bloc. There are great differences between each individual country and a clear division between the northern part of the region and the south. The frontier still runs between the lands once ruled by the Habsburgs and those ruled by the Ottomans, and 45 years of Stalinism did not alter the underlying structures of the Balkans.

East Germany, Poland, Czechoslovakia and Hungary can see where they are going, and how to get there. It will be a painful journey and will require every help that Western Europe can give, but the fact that they have a destination and a road map means that they can be reasonably sure of arriving. After all Spain, Italy and West Germany have travelled the same road, although their journey was from desolation and Fascism to democratic prosperity – while Poland and the rest are leaving behind desolation and Communism.

The future of the Balkans is shrouded in doubt. No one can predict what will become of Romania, Yugoslavia, Albania and Bulgaria: their revolutions are not yet accomplished. The old regime was swept away in Romania, but the old habits remain. Two of Yugoslavia's six republics – the ones that were once part of Austria-Hungary – have abandoned Communism, but the others have not, and the federation's very survival is in doubt. Albania is bringing up the rear: in July 1990, as the *sirocco*, the hot wind from the desert, blew across the Balkans, the first mass demonstrations took place in Tirana.

East Germany has the easiest course ahead of it. It will be absorbed into the Federal Republic, and in a few years, there will be little difference in living standards and political behaviour between Saxony and Bavaria. It will take longer to rebuild the dreary cities and to clean up the environmental disasters of the former Democratic Republic, but Germany is rich and the Germans are industrious and determined.

The environmental damage is as bad in Czehcoslovakia, and the transition to health and prosperity will take longer and be more difficult. Poland is in even worse shape, its industries hopelessly inefficient and still producing goods for the Soviet market – which no longer needs or can afford to buy junk from Poland – in exchange for cheap oil. The conversion of Poland will be very costly and very painful, but it has rich land and an educated population. It is already enjoying the delights of democratic politics as Solidarity's leaders squabble among themselves, and on 1 January 1990, it launched itself boldly upon the waves of economic reform.

Furthermore, Poland, like Czechoslovakia, can at last call on its debtors to redeem themselves. The West, starting with Germany, has had debts outstanding to Czechoslovakia since 1938, and to Poland since 1939. The greatest achievement of post-war diplomacy has been the reconciliation between France and Germany, a task begun in the 1940s and completed, imperceptibly, over the decades since then. It is now time to begin the reconciliation between Germany and Poland, by the same method.

East Germany joined the European Community on 1 July 1990, at the moment of its economic union with the Federal Republic. Poland, Czechoslovakia and Hungary (and Austria, too) have all stated that it is their national ambition to join the Community. Under Article 237 of the Treaty of Rome, 'Any European state may apply to become a member of the Community' – which is not the same as promising them all admittance. They might become associate members first, but it is beyond question that it will be another decade at least before Poland can face full membership. At the best, it might join in the 1990s, and then go through a long transition period.

Whatever the sequence, it will be an immense task to admit

a further four member states – Poland, Czechoslovakia, Austria and Hungary – at the same time as absorbing East Germany, adding another 86 million people in all. Some problems may be less difficult: Austria's neutrality was a barrier to her membership of the Community before the collapse of the Warsaw Pact, and that particular question may now be resolved in the general reordering of European security arrangements. But the institutional problems of integrating four new members, speaking three more languages (or four, counting Slovak), while three of the applicants escape painfully from 45 years of Communist control, are enough to daunt the bravest of Community bureaucrats. Turkey, Cyprus and Malta have also applied to join the EC.

But Community membership is the way forward for the newly liberated states of Eastern Europe. Indeed, there is a certain inevitability about it, already reflected in the public pronouncements of some of the Community's leaders, including Helmut Kohl. The unification of Germany and the prospect that, in five years or so, those 18 million East Germans will be as productive as the rest, means that Poland and Czechoslovakia, and probably Austria and Hungary, too, will be welcomed into the European Community to help ballast the ship. They all need the West – but they are needed, too. It is not that Europe should still distrust Germany: the Federal Republic has proved its democratic credentials over 40 years, and the DDR did so most dramatically in 1989. But the weight of a united Germany in a 12-member Community would be too great, and the closer the union the greater the weight. Economic union means a common currency, and that, in turn, would mean that the Community's currency and economy would be directed by the *Bundesbank*. The addition of Poland, Czechoslovakia, Austria and Hungary would redress the balance.

The future is much less clear for the rest of Eastern Europe. The Baltic countries, when they recover their independence, will look to Scandinavia for assistance. They are small enough and have a well-enough educated labour force to be brought up to European standards fairly rapidly, and to join the European Community in whatever association, even membership, that the Scandinavians finally adopt.

But what about the Balkans? If it might take Poland 15 or 20 years to catch up with the West, how long would it take Romania

– or Albania? Yugoslavia, meanwhile, is still faced with troubles inherited from centuries or even millennia past. Like the rest of Eastern Europe, it must struggle to escape from the economic disasters of Communism, while its major component, Serbia, is prey to an old-fashioned Balkan demagogue, Slobodan Milosevic, who has risen to power on the simple programme of suppressing the Albanians of Kosovo and restoring Serbian hegemony over the whole country. He is a throwback to the 1930s, quite out of place in modern Europe.

But the greatest question facing Europe is not how long it will take for Poland or Czechoslovakia to recover from Communism, or for Yugoslavia to escape from Serbian Fascism or for Romania to recover its soul. Although these are important matters that will occupy the chancelleries for the rest of the century, the disposition of the Soviet empire is far more important.

If the USSR now breaks up, the future of some of its constituent republics is clear enough: the Baltic republics and Moldavia will cast in their lot with Europe, and so, perhaps, will Karelia, which was part of Finland until it was annexed by Stalin in 1944. But what about Byelorussia, which in earlier centuries was united to Poland, or the Ukraine, a country the size and population of France, whose western territories were part of Poland until 1939? And what about Russia?

Mikhail Gorbachev advocates a 'common European house', a structure of undetermined architecture, stretching from Sligo to Sakhalin. It is a concept at least as vague as de Gaulle's 'Europe from the Atlantic to the Urals', and the complete antithesis of the European Community. The Community is based upon a series of excruciatingly precise blueprints, each negotiated in every detail by its members. That is its strength and the reason for its success.

The 12 present members of the Community, and the others that will join, are not going to permit their laboriously constructed edifice to be swallowed in some amorphous federation including all 92 nationalities that comprise the Soviet Union. At best, there may be a series of concentric circles, with the Community at the centre and other nations grouped around it according to their level of economic and political development. This is not to deny that there is such a thing as a common European heritage, or that

Leningrad, Moscow and Kiev are European cities. Perhaps one day, after the Community has been enlarged to include Eastern Europe, the Ukraine and even Russia will enter into an association with it.

In the meantime, Europe's problems are to preserve its own integrity, ensure the further peaceful evolution of Eastern Europe – and help the Soviet Union escape from its frightful past. The revolution that began in Poland and Hungary in 1989 is now sweeping across the vast expanses of the USSR. It is certain to be very difficult and quite likely to be very violent: it is highly unlikely that there will be a 'velvet revolution' in Moscow as there was in Prague. The lesson of 1989 is that the Soviet Communist system of government is inevitably going to collapse, peacefully or violently. The last time the Russian empire disintegrated, in 1917, there ensued civil wars that killed millions of people, and a totalitarian government emerged that was a desperate threat to the peace of the world for 70 years. The possible consequences of a violent dissolution of the USSR are again civil war and a revival of totalitarianism, or a series of totalitarian regimes fighting each other. It should be the West's chief concern, overriding all other considerations, to prevent such an outcome.

All Europe's disasters in the 20th century began in 1914, with the First World War, which sprang from the institutional hostility of the great powers. That cataclysm left Germany and the Soviet Union isolated, resentful and aggressive, and led directly to the Second World War. After 1945, French and German diplomats, using their countries' devastated condition and the Soviet menace, succeeded in breaking down Germany's isolation and its long hostility to France. The work was only half done because Germany was divided and its eastern zone was kept in a state of perpetual enmity towards the West. The unnatural division of Europe was a direct consequence and continuation of the war, and ended dramatically in 1989, just 50 years after Hitler marched into Poland. Now all that remains is to end the isolation of Russia, which began when Lenin and Trotsky ordered the assault on the Winter Palace in October 1917.

The Collapse of Communism a Chronology

1989

Jan 11   *Montenegro, Yugoslavia*: the government and party leadership resign after mass demonstrations engineered by the Serbian leader, Slobodan Milosevic.

Jan 15   *Czechoslavakia*: 5000 demonstrators in Prague's Wenceslas Square commemorate Jan Palach's suicide in 1969. Václav Havel and other dissidents arrested; Havel given nine months' jail sentence on 21 February.

Feb 6   *Poland*: first 'round table' meeting between government and Solidarity in Warsaw.

Feb 11   *Hungary*: government approves creation of independent parties.

Feb 15   *Afghanistan*: last Soviet troops withdraw.

Mar 13   *Romania*: reports published that six retired officials had written a letter of protest to Ceauşescu.

Mar 26   *Soviet Union*: partially free elections bring many dissidents into the new parliament and the defeat of many party notables.

Apr 1   *Angola*: Cuban troops begin withdrawal.

Apr 7   *Poland*: agreement to legalize Solidarity and hold partially free elections.

Apr 17   *China*: first pro-democracy demonstrations at Hu Yaobang's funeral in Peking.

May 2   *Hungary*: border fences dismantled.

May 8   *Hungary*: János Kádár forced to retire as party president.

May 17   *Czechoslovakia*: Havel released from jail.

Jun 4   *China*: Deng Xiao-ping sends tanks into Peking's Tiananmen Square to break up demonstrations.
Poland: elections produce anti-Communist landslide.

Jun 16   *Hungary*: Imre Nagy reburied in Budapest during huge anti-Communist rally attended by prime minister Miklós Németh and other reform Communists.

Jul 6   *France*: in a speech to the Council of Europe in Strasbourg, Gorbachev says, 'Any interference in domestic affairs and any attempt to restrict the sovereignty of states – friends, allies or others – is inadmissible.' He rules out 'the very possibility of the use of force or threat of force – alliance against alliance, inside the alliance, anywhere . . .'.

Aug 21   *Czechoslovakia*: small demonstration (which Havel had advised against) on anniversary of 1968 invasion broken up by police in Prague.

Aug 23   *Baltic republics*: human chain is formed from Tallinn in Estonia to Vilnius in Lithuania to mark 50th anniversary of Hitler–Stalin Pact.

Aug 24   *Poland*: Solidarity leader Tadeusz Mazowiecki is confirmed as prime minister, and goes on to form the first non–Communist government in Eastern Europe since 1948.

Sep   *Ethiopia*: last Cuban troops withdraw.

Sep 10   *Hungary*: border with Austria is opened to East Germans wishing to leave; more than 13,000 leave in the next four days.

Sep 19   *Hungary*: government and opposition agree on free elections in 1990.

Sep 26   *Cambodia*: last Vietnamese troops withdraw.

Sep 30   *Hungary and Czechoslovakia*: by this date, 30,000 more East Germans have gone West through these countries.

Oct 7   *East Germany*: Communist party celebrates the state's 40th anniversary. Police break up anti-regime demonstrations in Berlin, Leipzig and Dresden. Weekly demonstrations continue every Monday in Leipzig.
Hungary: Communist party dissolves and now calls itself the Socialist party.

Oct 9   *East Germany*: police ordered to shoot to break up demonstration of 70,000 people in Leipzig. The order is cancelled at last moment.

Oct 18   *East Germany*: President Erich Honecker resigns and is replaced by Egon Krenz.

Oct 25   *Finland*: Gorbachev in Helsinki, affirms that the USSR has no moral or political right to interfere in the internal affairs of its neighbours. His spokesman says: 'The Brezhnev doctrine is dead.'

Nov 3   *Bulgaria*: police break up demonstration of Eco-Glasnost supporters during international environment conference in Sofia.

Nov 7   *East Germany*: government resigns.

Nov 8   *East Germany*: Politburo resigns.

Nov 9   *East Germany*: new Communist government declares the borders open. East Berliners allowed through Berlin Wall freely for the first time since 1961.

Nov 10   *Bulgaria*: Communist party leader Todor Zhivkov deposed and replaced by reform Communist Petar Mladenov.

Nov 17   *Czechoslovakia*: anti-government demonstration in Prague broken up by police.

Nov 18   *Bulgaria*: first large demonstration in Sofia demanding free elections.

Nov 19   *Czechoslovakia*: tens of thousands demonstrate in Prague against police brutality. Opposition groups form Civic Forum.

Nov 20   *Czechoslovakia*: 200,000 people demonstrate in Prague's Wenceslas Square. Demonstrations continue daily, each larger than the last.

Nov 24   *Czechoslovakia*: Alexander Dubček returns to Prague and addresses the crowd. Miloš Jakeš and the rest of the Communist party Politburo resign, followed by the government.
Romania: Communist party congress opens and reaffirms faith in the correctness of President Ceauşescu's polices.

Nov 26   *Hungary*: referendum rejects government proposal for an immediate presidential election.

Nov 27   *Romania*: Communist party re-elects Ceauşescu to a further five-year term as general secretary.
Czechoslovakia: Civic Forum directs two-hour general strike in support of democracy.

Nov 28   *Czechoslovakia*: Communist party promises to hold free elections and abandon 'leading role' of the party.

Dec   *Mongolia*: Mongolian Democratic Union formed in Ulan Bator and holds first demonstrations to demand democracy.

Dec 1   *East Germany* parliament scraps 'leading role' of the party.

Dec 3   *East Germany* Egon Krenz, party Politburo and Central Committee all resign.

Dec 7   *Czechoslovakia*: government resigns.
Lithuania: parliament votes to repeal 'leading role' of Communist party.

Dec 10   *Czechoslovakia*: new government with non-Communist majority formed. President Gustáv Husák resigns.

Dec 14   *Romania*: first demonstrations against Ceauşescu in Timisoara.

Dec 15   *Soviet Union*: Andrei Sakharov dies in Moscow.

Dec 17   *Romania*: Ceauşescu orders army and police to suppress opposition. Massacre in Timisoara.

Dec 19   *Croatia, Yugoslavia*: state assembly passes law permitting free elections in 1990.

Dec 20   *Lithuania*: Communist party declares itself independent of the Soviet party.

Dec 21   *Romania*: Ceauşescu addresses pro-government rally in Bucharest. He is shouted down by protestors.

Dec 22   *Romania*: Demonstrators storm government buildings in Bucharest. The army changes sides. Ceauşescu escapes by helicopter with his wife; they are arrested later. National Salvation Council proclaimed. There is heavy fighting for the next three days.

Dec 24   *Slovenia, Yugoslavia*: Communist party conference approves free elections in 1990.

Dec 25   *Romania*: National Salvation Council orders Ceauşescus tried and shot.

Dec 28   *Czechoslovakia*: Alexander Dubček elected chairman of Czechoslovak National Assembly.

Dec 29   *Czechoslovakia*: Václav Havel elected president of Czechoslovakia.

1990

Jan 1   *Poland*: introduction of fundamental economic reforms, ending price controls and subsidies; currency becomes partially convertible.
Yugoslavia: currency becomes convertible and is tied to *Deutschmark*.

Jan 13   *Soviet Union*: violent ethnic disturbances break out in Azerbaijan.

Jan 15   *Bulgaria*: repeal of 'leading role' of the Communist party and promise of free elections in June 1990.

Jan 22   *Yugoslavia*: Yugoslav Communist Pary congress votes to abandon 'leading role', and then splits.

Jan 28   *Poland*: Polish Communist Party dissolves itself, and splits.

Jan 29   *East Germany*: Erich Honecker arrested.
         Bulgaria: Todor Zhivkov arrested.

Jan 30   *Soviet Union*: Gorbachev admits inevitability of German reunification.

Feb 1   *Bulgaria*: government resigns. Mladenov replaced as party leader by Alexander Lilov.

Feb 3   *Romania*: National Salvation Council resigns and is replaced by coalition government.

Feb 4   *Soviet Union*: 100,000 people demonstrate against Communist party in Moscow.

Feb 7   *Soviet Union*: Communist party renounces its 'leading role'.

Feb 24   *Lithuania*: Communists defeated in elections.

Feb 25   *Nicaragua*: Sandinistas defeated in elections.

Mar 11   *Lithuania*: parliament declares independence from Soviet Union.

Mar 12   *Mongolia*: Communist party proposes free elections.

Mar 18   *East Germany*: first free election since 1932. Christian Democrats and allies win 48 per cent of the vote.
         Latvia and Estonia: first round of elections give independence parties a majority.
         Soviet Union: second round of local elections bring opposition many gains, including Moscow and Leningrad.

Mar 25   *Hungary*: elections ensure non-Communist government.

Mar 30   *Estonia*: parliament votes that the country's annexation by the USSR was illegal, and therefore Soviet laws invalid in Estonia, but does not vote for outright independence.

Apr 3   *Bulgaria*: Bulgarian Communist party changes its name to Socialist party.

Apr 8   *Slovenia, Yugoslavia*: in elections, Communists win only 20 per cent. Non-Communist government formed after further rounds of voting, on 12 and 22 April.

Apr 12   *East Germany*: new coalition govenrment takes office, with no Communist ministers.

Apr 13   *Soviet Union*: responsibility admitted for Katyn massacre of Polish officers in 1941. Gorbachev announces economic blockade of Lithuania.

Apr 18   *Lithuania*: all oil and other supplies from Soviet Union are cut off.

Apr 22   *Croatia, Yugoslavia*: Communists defeated in elections. Second round on 6 and 7 May confirm the result.

May 4   *Latvia*: parliament votes for indpendence, but with indeterminate transition period.

May 9   *Albania*: government announces loosening of restrictions on foreign travel and religious observance, and economic reforms.

May 18   *East Germany*: treaty signed with West Germany merging their currencies and instituting a market economy in East Germany, to take effect on 1 July.

May 20   *Romania*: first round of presidential and parliamentary elections. Ion Iliescu and National Salvation Council win landslide.

May 27   *Poland*: local elections sweep away Communist authorities throughout the country.

Jun 8–9   *Czechoslovakia*: parliamentary elections. Civic Forum wins.

Jun 10   *Bulgaria*: parliamentary elections held. Socialist party (ex-Communists) wins.

Jun 28   *Albania*: Albanians began to take refuge in foreign embassies in Tirana.

Jul 6   *Bulgaria*: Mladenov resigns.

Jul 22–29 *Mongolia*: Elections. Communists win.

Bibliography

General

Dornberg, John, *Eastern Europe: A Communist Kaleidoscope*, New York, Dial Press, 1980.

Garton Ash, Timothy, *The Uses of Adversity: Essays on the Fate of Central Europe*, New York, Vintage, 1990.

—, *The Magic Lantern*, New York, Random House, 1990.

Gunther, John, *Behind the Curtain*, New York, Harper & Brothers, 1949.

Gwertzman, Bernard & Kaufman, Michael (eds), *The Collapse of Communism, by the Correspondents of* The New York Times, New York, Random House, 1990.

Kertesz, Stephen D. (ed.), *East-Central Europe and the World; Developments in the Post-Stalin Era*, South Bend, Indiana, University of Notre Dame Press, 1962.

Khrushchev, Nikita, *Khrushchev Remembers*, trans. Strobe Talbot, Boston, Little, Brown, 1974.

Roucek, Joseph S., *Balkan Politics: International Relations in No Man's Land*, Stanford, California, Stanford University Press, 1948.

Werth, Alexander, *Russia at War*, New York, E. P. Dutton, 1964.

Wolff, Robert Lee, *The Balkans in Our Time*, Cambridge, Mass., Harvard University Press, 1956.

Albania

Amery, Julian, *Sons of the Eagle*, London, Macmillan, 1948.

Keefe, Eugene (ed.), *Area Handbook for Albania*, Washington, American University, 1971.

Marmullaku, Ramadan, *Albania and the Albanians*, London, Archon Books, 1975.

Page, Bruce et al., *The Philby Conspiracy*, New York, Doubleday & Co, 1968.

Prifti, Peter R., *Socialist Albania since 1945*, Cambridge, Mass., MIT Press, 1978.

Bulgaria

Dellin, L. A. D. (ed.), *Bulgaria*, New York, Frederick A. Praeger, 1957.
Keefe, Eugene K. et al, *Area Handbook for Bulgaria*, Washington, American University, 1973.

Czechoslovakia

Levy, Alan, *So Many Heroes*, Sagaponack, New York, Second Chance Press, 1980.
Littell, Robert (ed.), *The Czech Black Book: An eyewitness, documented account of the invasion of Czechoslovakia*, New York, Frederick A. Praeger, 1969.
Loebl, Eugen, *Stalinism in Prague*, trans. Maurice Michael, New York, Grove Press, 1969.
London, Artur, *L'Aveu: Dans l'engrenage du procès de Prague*, Paris, Gallimard, 1968.
Nyrop, Richard F., *Czechoslovakia, A Country Study*, Washington, American University, 1982.
Windsor, Philip & Roberts, Adam, *Czechoslovakia 1968: Reform, Repression and Resistance*, New York, Colombia University Press, 1969.
Ripka, Hubert, *Czechoslovakia Enslaved: The Story of the Communist Coup d'État*, London, Victor Gollancz, 1950.
Shawcross, William, *Dubček*, New York, Simon & Schuster, 1970.
Sterling, Claire, *The Masaryk Case*, New York, Harper & Row, 1969.

East Germany

Childs, David, *The GDR: Moscow's German Ally*, London, George Allen & Unwin, 1983.
Dornberg, John, *The Other Germany*, New York, Doubleday, 1968.
Keefe, Eugene K. et al., *Area Handbook for East Germany*, Washington, American University, 1972.
Legters, Lyman (ed.), *The German Democratic Republic*, Boulder, Colorado, Westview Press, 1978.
Leonard, Wolfgang, *Child of the Revolution*, Chicago, Henry Regnery, 1959.
Mee, Charles, *Meeting at Potsdam*, New York, M. Evans, 1975.
Steele, Jonathan, *Inside East Germany*, New York, Urizen Books, 1977.
Tusa, Ann & Tusa, John, *The Berlin Blockade*, London, Hodder & Stoughton, 1988.

Wyden, Peter, *Wall: The Story of Divided Berlin*, New York, Simon & Schuster, 1989.

Hungary

Aczél, Támás, *Ten Years After*, London, MacGibbon & Kee, 1966.

Aczél, Támás & Meray, Tibor, *The Revolt of the Mind*, New York, Frederick A. Praeger, 1959.

Barber, Noel, *Seven Days of Freedom: The Hungarian Uprising, 1956*, New York, Stein & Day, 1974.

Gadney, Reg, *Cry Hungary! Uprising 1956*, New York, Athenaeum, 1986.

Hoensch, Jorg K., *A History of Modern Hungary, 1867–1986*, London & New York, Longman, 1988.

Kecskemeti, Paul, *The Unexpected Revolution*, Stanford University Press, California, 1961.

Lasky, Melvin (ed.), *The Hungarian Revolution*, New York, Congress for Cultural Freedom/Frederick A. Praeger, 1957.

Lomax, Bill, *Hungary, 1956*, London, Allison & Busby, 1976.

Nagy, Imre, *On Communism: In Defence of the New Course*, London, Thames & Hudson, 1957.

Pryce-Jones, David, *The Hungarian Revolution*, London, Benn, 1969.

Shawcross, William, *Crime and Compromise*, London, Weidenfeld & Nicolson, 1974.

Vali, Ferenc A., *Rift and Revolt in Hungary*, Cambridge, Mass., Harvard University Press, 1961.

Zinner, Paul, *Revolution in Hungary*, Boulder, Colorado University Press, 1962.

Poland

Ascheron, Neal, *The Struggles for Poland*, New York, Random House, 1987.

—, *The Polish August: The Self-Limiting Revolution*, New York, Viking Press, 1981.

Bethell, Nicholas, *Gomulka: His Poland and His Communism*, London, Pelican, 1972.

Brumberg, Abraham (ed.), *Poland: Genesis of a Revolution*, New York, Vintage Books, 1983.

Davies, Norman, *God's Playground: A History of Poland*, Oxford University Press, 1981.

Garlinsky, Josef, *Poland in the Second World War*, New York, Hippocrene Books, 1985.

Garton Ash, Timothy, *The Polish Revolution: Solidarity*, New York, Charles Scribner's Sons, 1983.
Korbinski, Stefan, *Fighting Warsaw*, New York, Macmillan, 1959.
—, *Warsaw in Chains*, New York, Macmillan, 1959.
Steven, Stewart, *The Poles*, New York, Macmillan, 1982.
Syrop, Konrad, *Spring in October*, New York, Frederick A. Praeger, 1957.
Torańska, Teresa, *'Them' – Stalin's Polish Puppets*, New York, Harper & Row, 1987.
Weschler, Lawrence, *The Passion of Poland, from Solidarity through the State of War*, New York, Pantheon, 1982.

Romania

Floyd, David, *Rumania: Russia's Dissident Ally*, New York, Frederick A. Praeger, 1965.
Fischer-Galati, Stephen, *The Socialist Republic of Rumania*, Baltimore, Johns Hopkins Press, 1969.
Ionescu, Ghita, *Communism in Romania*, Oxford University Press, 1964.
Keefe, Eugene K. et al, *Area Handbook for Rumania*, Washington, American University, 1972.

The USSR (including the Baltic republics

Cohen, Stephen F. & van den Heuvel, Katrina (eds), *Voices of Glasnost: Interviews with Gorbachev's Reformers*, New York, W. W. Norton, 1989.
Doder, Dusko, *Shadows and Whispers: Power Politics inside the Kremlin, from Brezhnev to Gorbachev*, New York, Random House, 1986.
Frankland, Mark, *The Sixth Continent: Mikhail Gorbachev and the Soviet Union*, New York, Harper & Row, 1987.
Manning, Clarence, *The Forgotten Republics*, New York, Philosophical Library, 1952.
Raun, Toivo, *Estonia and the Estonians*, Stanford, California, Hoover Institute, 1987.
Sabaliunas, Leonas, *Lithuania in Crisis*, Bloomington, Indiana University Press, 1972.
Walker, Martin, *The Waking Giant*, New York, Pantheon, 1986.

Yugoslavia

Beloff, Nora, *Tito's Flawed Legacy*, Boulder, Colorado, Westview Press; London, Victor Gollancz, 1985.

Dedijer, Vladimir, *Tito Speaks: His Self-Portrait and Struggle with Stalin*, London, Weidenfeld & Nicolson, 1953.

Djilas, Milovan, *Conversations with Stalin*, trans. Michael B. Petrovich, New York, Harcourt, Brace & World, 1962.

Maclean, Fitzroy, *The Heretic: The Life and Times of Josip Broz-Tito*, New York, Harper & Brothers, 1957.

—, *Eastern Approaches*, London, Jonathan Cape, 1949.

Nyrop, Richard (ed.), *Yugoslavia, A Country Study*, Washington, American University, 1981.

Wilson, Duncan, *Tito's Yugoslavia*, Cambridge University Press, 1979.

Index

Adamec, Ladislav, 105, 107, 108
Adenauer, Konrad, 8, 25, 31
Admiralspalast, 19
Afghanistan, 1, 70, 259
Agrarian Union (Bulgaria), 198, 205
AIDS, 226, 239
Albania, 4, 5, 7, 9, 38, 104, 147, 154, 157, 162, 165, 171–84, 222–3, 254, 257, 263, 264, 265
Albanian Communist Party, 175
Alexander, Prince of Battenberg, 189, 190, 193, 194
Alexander, Prince of Cruza, 210
Alexander II, Tsar, 188
Ali, Mehmet, 172
Alia, President Ramiz, 166, 182–4
Allied Control Commission, 18, 22
America, *see* United States
Anatolia, 21
Andropov, Yuri, 70, 128, 131, 132
Angola, 259
Anheuser-Busch, 113
Anti-Fascist Alliance, 19
Anti-Fascist Council for National Liberation of Yugoslavia (AVNOJ), 154
Antonescu, General Ion, 212–13, 214–16, 217
Apostol, Gheorghe, 230
Artukovitch, Andriya, 152
Ascherson, Neil, 58

Association of Young Democrats (Hungary), 142
Atatürk, Kemal, 172, 190
Attlee, Clement, 8, 17
Aurelian, Emperor, 227
Auschwitz, 152
Austria, 13, 37, 79, 105, 106, 116, 132, 141, 147–8, 211, 229, 254, 256–8
AVO (Hungarian Secret Police), 126, 127, 128–30
Azerbaijan, 165, 250, 262

Balkan League, 158, 160, 191
Balli Kombetar (BK), 175
Baltic Republics, 6, 8, 49, 241–52, 257–8, 260, 268
Banat, 117, 210, 221, 227, 229
Barthou, Louis, 150
'Basic Law', 25, 26
Basil II of Bulgaria, King, 186, 192
Bata, Tomáš, 112
Bavaria, 255
Belgrade, 156, 163, 164, 174
Benelux, 22
Beneš, Eduard, 6, 79, 80, 82
Beria, 7, 27, 28, 31, 86, 91, 122
Berlin, 4, 14–15, 16, 17, 19, 20, 21, 22, 24–5, 29, 30, 32, 44, 189, 226
Berlin Assembly, 25
Berlin Blockade, 23–6, 159, 162
Berlin Wall, 1, 4, 14–15, 33–44, 78, 106, 185, 204

Berling, General Zygmunt, 50
Berman, Jakub, 50, 52, 54
Bessarabia, 117, 188, 210, 211, 213, 214, 215, 228–9, 243, 245
Bevin, Ernest, 18, 21
Bierut, Boleslaw, 50, 51, 52, 54, 201
'Big Three', 18
Bismarck, Otto von, 189, 190
'Black Hand' group, 147, 148, 150
Black Sea, 189
Bodnaras, Emil, 217, 219
Bohemia, 78, 79, 117
Bologna, University of, 106
Bonn, 15, 25
Boris, Tsar, 192, 194, 195, 197
Bosnia-Hercegovina, 145–7, 150, 152, 169, 187, 189, 191
Brandenburg, 16, 30, 33
Brandt, Willy, 25, 35, 40, 57
Brasov, 229–30
Brecht, Bertolt, 30
Breslau, 18, 43, 48
Brezhnev, President Leonid, 2, 39, 62, 93, 95, 96, 98, 99, 102–3, 115, 180, 260
Britain, 16, 20–22, 35, 43, 49, 81–2, 92, 131, 155, 157–8, 175, 179, 187, 189, 194, 216, 218–19
Brno, 106
Broz, Josip, see also under Tito, 153
Brucan, Silviu, 230, 233, 234
Bucharest, 115, 204, 209, 210, 217, 224, 231–2, 234, 237–8
Buchenwald, 19
Budapest, 13, 30, 37, 53, 115, 116, 117–18, 125, 126–7, 130, 134, 137
Budweis, 78, 113
Bujak, Zbigniew, 66
Bukharin, 7, 87
Bukovina, 117, 210, 213, 229, 246
Bulgaria, 1, 4, 7, 37, 53, 147, 150, 160, 185–208, 216, 261, 262, 263, 264, 266

Bulgarian Communist Party, 4, 185, 192, 194, 204, 263
Bulgarian Socialist Party, 4
Bundesbank, 43, 256
Bundesrepublik Deutschland, see West Germany
Burducea, Father, 218
Bush, President George, 13, 102, 253
Bydgoszcz, 63
Byelorussia, 248
Byrne, James, 21

Calfa, Marian, 108, 109, 110
Cambodia, 260
Canossa, 125
Carnogursky, Jan, 109
Carol of Romania, King, 194, 210, 211
Carol II of Romania, King, 212–13, 214, 216
Carter, President James, 116
Castro, General Fidel, 164
Ceauşescu, Elena, 209, 224–5, 226, 239
Ceauşescu, Nicolae, 1, 4–5, 115, 164, 166, 182, 204, 209, 222–34, 236–9, 253, 259, 261, 262
Central Intelligence Agency (CIA), 27, 178–9
Cepika, Alexej, 82
Černík, Oldřich, 99
Cetniks, 153–4, 155, 156
Charles Habsburg IV, King, 117
Charles of Hohenzollern-Sigmaringen, Prince, 210
'Charter 77', 104, 105, 106, 108
Checkpoint Charlie, 34
Chervenkov, Vulko, 201
China, 32, 38, 164, 180–1, 202, 222–3, 224, 259
Christian Democrats (Germany), 19, 20, 42

Churchill, Winston, 8, 20–1, 28, 50, 155–7, 197, 216, 217

Cierna Nad Tisou, 98

Civic Forum, 107–9, 112, 261, 264

Clay, General Lucius, 15, 24

Clementis, Vladimir, 86, 87, 92

Cluj, 222

Cold War, 8–9, 14, 17, 23, 52, 84, 157

Comecon, 93, 138, 164, 222

Cominform, 22, 23, 158, 161, 176

Comintern, 22, 194

Committee for the Defence of Workers' Rights (KOR), 59, 65

Committee of Free Albanians, 178–179

Congress of Berlin, 189, 190

Constantinople, 187, 210

Corfu, 173, 179

Croatia, 79, 147, 149, 151, 152, 168, 262

Csepel Island, 135

Cuba, 259–60

Curzon line, 18, 50

Cyprus, 189

Czechoslovakia, 1, 3, 4, 5, 6, 7, 8, 9, 18, 22, 23, 34, 38, 39, 52, 53, 55, 57, 67, 76, 77–113, 117, 138, 150, 164, 202–3, 223, 255–8, 259, 260, 261, 262, 264, 266

Czechoslovakian Communist Party, 81, 84, 91

Czechoslovakian minorities, 78

Czechoslovakian National Assembly, 82

Dacia, 227

Dahlem, Franz, 28

Dalmatia, 152, 154, 156

Danzig, 18, 43, 48

Davies, Norman, 51

Deak, István, 121

De Gaulle, General, 176, 257

Dekanozov, V. K., 246

de Maizière, Lothar, 42

Democratic Forum, 143

Democratic Party of Poland, 72

Deutsche Demokratische Republik, *see* East Germany

Deutschmark, 23, 35

Dienstbier, Jiří, 108

Dimitriyevitch, Dragutin, 147

Dimitrov, Georgi, 160, 193, 194, 198–200, 205

Dimitrov, Georgi, 198

Disraeli, Benjamin, 188, 189

Djilas, Milovan, 6, 163, 177, 200

Dobrudja, 188, 191, 194, 196, 210, 211, 213, 215

Dominican Republic, 102

Dragoicheva, Tsola, 197

Dresden, 14, 38, 40

Drtina, Prokop, 82, 83, 104

Dubček, Alexander, 93–102, 103, 105, 107, 108, 109, 111, 164, 261, 262

Dubček's Action Programme, 100

Duclos, Jacques, 158

Dulles, General John Foster, 8, 132

Dzhurov, General Dobri, 204

Dzodze, Kotchi, *see* Xoxe, Koci

East Germany, 1, 3, 4, 6, 13–44, 55, 76, 78, 92, 106, 113, 203, 255, 256, 260, 261, 262, 263, 266–7

East Prussia, 18, 43, 81

Eastern Rumelia, 189–90

'Eco-Glasnost', 203

Egypt, 131

Eichmann, Adolf, 116, 118

Eisenhower, President Dwight, 16, 28, 60

Emmanuel III of Albania, King Victor, 174

Erhard, Professor Ludwig, 23, 27, 44

Esterhazy family, 119

Estonia, 241–8, 263

Ethiopia, 260
European Community, 44, 76, 167, 254, 255, 256, 257
European Security Conference, 184

Farkhas, Milhaly, 118, 125
Fascist Iron Guard, 212, 214, 218
Fatherland Front, 197
Fechter, Peter, 34
Ferdinand, Archduke Franz, 147, 150, 159
Ferdinand of Coburg, Prince, 190, 191, 192, 211
Field, Noël, 27
Fierlinger, Zdeněk, 80
Finland, 39, 242, 245, 260
First Balkan war, 191
Fiume, 158
France, 79, 81–2, 117, 131, 258, 260
Free Democrats (East Germany), see Liberals
French Resistance, 45
French Socialist Party, 94

Gaulle, General de, see De Gaulle, General
Gdańsk, 3, 48, 53, 57, 58, 60, 61, 62
Gdynia, 53, 57
Georgescu, Teshari, 217, 218, 220
Gerasimov, Gennadi, 39
Geremek, Bronislaw, 60
German Communist Party (KPD), 16, 19
German Democratic Republic, see East Germany
German Federal Republic, see West Germany
Germany, 14–15, 21, 253
Gero, Ernö, 118, 124, 125, 126–30, 134
Gestapo, 19, 47, 87, 117, 118, 194
Gheorghiu-Dej, Gheorghe, 201, 217, 218, 219, 220, 221–4
Gierek, Edward, 52, 57–9, 60, 64, 65

Gimes, Miklós, 135, 140
Gladstone, William, 187
Goering, Hermann, 194
Gomułka, Władisław, 7, 49, 51, 52–3, 55, 56, 57, 58, 95, 96, 98, 124, 130
Good Soldier Svejk, The, 104
Gorbachev, President Mikhail, 2–3, 4–5, 36, 37, 38, 39, 67, 70, 73, 96, 103, 105, 111, 138, 140, 182, 185, 203, 204–7, 208, 234, 241–2, 248–51, 253, 257, 260
Gottwald, Klement, 80, 81, 82, 83, 86, 91, 96
Gottwaldov, 112
Great Britain, see Britain
Greece, 2, 151, 157, 162, 172–3, 175, 191, 192, 196, 201, 216
Green International, 193
Grósz, Károly, 139, 140, 142
Grotewohl, Otto, 17, 19, 26, 29
Groza, Petru, 218–19
Gysi, George, 191

Habsburg Empire, 145
Hallstein, Walter, 32
Hamid II, Sultan Abdul, 191
Harich, Wolfgang, 31
Hasek, Jaroslav, 104
Havel, Václav, 5, 37, 77, 101, 104, 106, 108, 109–13, 259, 260, 261, 262
Hay, Gyula, 133
Helsinki, 39, 184
Helsinki Final Act, 60, 103–4, 202, 229
Henlein, Konrad, 79
Heydrich, Reinhard, 79
Himmler, Heinrich, 79
Hitler, Adolf, 15, 16, 17, 19, 23, 24, 45, 47, 48, 78, 79, 89, 91, 117, 118, 150–1, 152, 159, 174, 194, 195, 196–211, 212, 214, 225, 228, 242, 243–6, 247

Hitler-Stalin Pact, 212–13, 243–4, 249, 260

Holocaust, 42, 47, 118

Honecker, Erich, 3, 4, 30, 33, 34, 36, 38, 40, 41, 62, 201, 260, 262

Horthy, Admiral Miklós, 117, 118, 122

Hoxha, Enver, 165, 171–2, 174, 175–8, 180–2, 201

Hradčany Castle, 99

Hungarian Communist Party, 36, 131

Hungarian National Independence Front, 119

Hungarian Revolutionary Workers' Peasant Government, 134–5

Hungarian Uprising, 56, 115

Hungarian Writers' Association, 133

Hungary, 3, 6, 7, 8, 13–14, 30, 31, 37–8, 39, 53, 76, 105, 106, 115–43, 150, 211, 214, 216, 222, 227–8, 229, 236, 245, 256–8, 259, 260, 261, 263, 267

Husák, Gustáv, 3, 62, 67, 83, 86, 91, 92, 101, 103, 109, 112, 261

Huta Warszawa steel works, 62

Iliescu, Ion, 233–4, 236–9, 263

Institute of Philosophy of the Lithuanian Academy of Sciences, 248

Internal Macedonian Revolutionary Organization (IMRO), 150, 191, 193–4, 197

International Brigade (Spain), 28, 194

International Court of Justice, 179

International Human Rights Day, 105

International Monetary Fund (IMF), 75, 168

International Red Cross, 50

International Workers' Organization, 60

Ionescu, Ghita, 220

Iran, 231

Iron Curtain, 8, 13, 21, 84, 226

Israel, 89, 131, 138, 200, 202, 220, 223, 229

Istria, 158

Italy, 149, 154, 173, 175

Jakeš, Miloš, 104, 107, 204, 261

Jaruzelski, General Wojciech, 2, 3, 4–5, 8, 52, 58, 62, 64, 65, 66, 67, 68–9, 70, 73, 74

'June Revolt', 27–30

Kádár, János, 3, 95, 100, 118, 121, 126, 128, 131, 133, 134, 135, 136–42, 259

Kaganovitch, 122

Kalinin, Mikhail, 158

Kaliningrad (Königsberg), 18, 252

Kamenev, 7

Kanal, 45

Kania, Stanislaw, 61, 64

Karadjordjevic, King Peter, 147, 149, 155, 157

Karelia, 245

Kastriota, George, 172, 173

Katyn Forest massacre, 47, 50, 76, 263

Kennedy, President John F., 34

Kennen, George, 8, 16

KGB, 47, 87, 100, 159

Khrushchev, President Nikita, 7, 24, 28, 31, 32–3, 34, 54, 55, 56, 98, 122, 123, 124, 125, 130, 132, 136, 137, 159, 164, 180–1, 202, 222, 223

Kissinger, Henry, 224

Kiszczak, General Czeslaw, 71, 73

Klaipeda, *see* Memel

Klaus, Václav, 109

Koestler, Arthur, 87

Kohl, President Helmut, 40, 43, 251, 253, 256
Kolarov, Vasil, 199, 200
Kommandatura, 24
Königsberg, 18, 252
KOR, *see* Committee for the Defence of Workers' Rights
Korea, 1
Korov, Sergei, 7
Kosovo, 145, 146, 165–7, 172, 174, 183, 257
Kostov, Traicho, 7, 89, 196, 197, 199, 200, 204
Kovács, István, 133
KPD, *see* German Communist Party
Kraków, 47, 53
Krenz, Egon, 38, 39, 40, 41, 260, 261
Kriegel, Frantisek, 100
Kukan, Milan, 169
Kun, Béla, 116, 118, 211
Kuron, Jacek, 59

Länder, 20–21, 25, 26, 43, 47
Landsbergis, Vytautas, 250
Latvia, 241–8, 263, 264
League of Nations, 245
Leipzig, 4, 14, 30, 38, 39, 204, 260
Lenin, Vladimir Ilyich, 1, 29, 65, 186, 242, 245, 258
Lenin shipyard, 57, 59, 62, 65, 69, 193
Liberals (German), 19, 20, 42
Lidice massacre, 79
Lilov, Alexander, 205
Lithuania, 241–8, 261, 262, 263
'Little Entente', 79, 117, 150, 212
Lloyd George, David, 211
Lodz, 58
Loebel, Eugen, 85–6, 87, 88, 89
London, 22, 49
London, Arthur, 86, 87, 88, 89, 90
Losonczy, Geza, 135, 140
Lublin Committee, 50
Luca, Vasile, 217, 219, 220

Lucas, László, *see* Luca, Vasile
Lukhanov, Andrei, 204, 205
Lulchev, Kosta, 198
Lupescu, Magda, 211
Lvov, 48, 50
Lwow, *see* Lvov

Macedonia, 145, 148, 152, 169, 173, 187–8, 191, 192, 193, 195–6
Magyars, 116–17, 186
Malenkov, 7, 27, 28, 122, 123, 130
Maleter, Pál, 127, 132, 133, 135, 140
Manascu, Corneliu, 230, 233
Markov, Georgi, 206
Markovic, Ante, 168, 169
Marshall, General George, 21
Marshall Plan, 21, 27, 81, 120
Marx, Karl, 163, 186
Masaryk, Jan, 80, 82, 83, 84
Masaryk, Tomáš, 80, 92, 117
Masur, Kurt, 38
Matyas, 125
Mazowiecki, Tadeusz, 48, 60, 73, 260
Mecklenburg, 16, 41
Memel, 251
Merker, Paul, 27
Michnik, Adam, 59
Mihajlović, Colonel Draza, 153, 155, 156–7, 175, 198
Mikolajczyk, Stanislaw, 51
Mikoyan, Anastas, 7, 128
Mikulic, Branco, 167
Milea, General Vasile, 231
Military Council of National Salvation (Poland), 66, 67
Milosevic, Slobodan, 166, 168, 257, 259
Minc, Hilary, 50, 54
Mindszenty, Cardinal Józef, 122, 130, 134
Mitterrand, President François, 251
Mladenov, Petar, 204–6, 264
Moczar, General Mieczyslaw, 56, 57
Modrow, Hans, 40–41, 42

Moldavia, 210, 229, 235, 257
Molotov, V. N., 7, 49, 122, 160, 177, 213, 215, 243, 245, 246
Mongolia, 261, 263
Monroe Doctrine, 102
Montenegro, 145, 146, 152, 154, 167, 188, 259
Munnich, Ferenc, 128, 131, 133
Mussolini, Benito, 150, 151, 174

Nagorno-Karabakh, 165
Nagy, Imre, 98, 106, 118, 119, 121–5, 126–33, 134, 135, 143, 260
Nasser, Gemal Abdel, 163–4
National Democratic Front (Romania), 219
National Front (Czechoslovakia), 80, 95
National Liberation Movement (Albania), 175
National Salvation Council (Romania), 233–6, 262
NATO (North Atlantic Treaty Organization), 8, 22, 26, 43, 62, 102, 253
Nehru, Jawaharlal, 163–4
Németh, Miklós, 140, 141, 260
'New Forum' (East Germany), 37
Nicaragua, 263
Nicolson, Harold, 211
Nixon, President Richard, 181
NKVD, see Soviet Secret Police
Noli, Fan, 173
North Korea, 224
Nosek, Václav, 80, 82
Novotný, Antonin, 91, 92, 93, 94, 95–7, 104, 111
Nowy-Huta steel plant, 53
Nyers, Reszo, 140

Obrenović, King Alexander, 147, 148
Obrenović, Milos, 146
'October, The', 56

October Revolution, 122
Oder-Neisse Line, 17, 51, 57
Odessa, 214
Olympic Games, 35
Orwell, George, 5, 225
Ostmark, 23, 25, 35, 40
Ostrava, 106
Ottoman Empire, 145, 172, 187, 190, 210

Pacem in Terris, 122
Palach, Jan, 101, 259
Panama, 252
Paris, 26
'Partisans, The', 56–7
Parvulescu, Constantin, 230
Patrascanu, Lucretiu, 7, 89, 217, 218, 219, 223
Patriotic People's Front (Hungary), 136, 138
Patton, Commander George, 80
Pauker, Ana, 197, 217, 219–20, 222, 223
Paul of Yugoslavia, Prince, 194
Pavelic, Ante, 152, 154
Peasants' Party (Poland), 72
Peter, Gábor, 118, 119, 123
Petkov, Nokola, 198
Petrovic, Karadjorje, 146
Philby, Kim, 179
Pieck, Wilhelm, 17, 26, 29
Pilzin, see Plzeň
Plzeň (Pilzen), 78, 80, 92, 113
Poland, 3, 4, 5, 6, 7, 8, 13, 17–18, 31, 35, 36, 39, 40, 42, 43, 44–76, 79, 106, 113, 142, 156, 178, 243, 244, 251, 254, 255, 256–8, 259, 260, 262, 264, 267–8
Polish Home Army, 45, 47, 50
Polish minorities, 48
Polish United Workers' Party, 51, 54, 65
Polish Workers' Party (PPR), 49, 51, 262

Politburo, 27, 100, 105, 108, 123, 131, 132, 160–1, 201, 223, 249, 251, 253

Pope John Paul II, 59, 67

Popieluszko, Father Jerzy, 67

Poszgay, Imre, 140, 142, 143

Potsdam, 16, 17, 18

Potsdam Conference, 51

Potsdamer Platz, 33

Poznań, 54, 123

Prague, 4, 32–8, 77, 80, 81, 83, 84, 90

'Prague Spring', 34, 76, 87, 90, 92, 94–102, 103, 105, 106, 107, 204

Prague University, 108

Princip, Gavril, 147

Provisional Council for National Unity (Romania), 236

Radić, Stejpan, 149

Radio Free Europe, 133

Radom, 59

Rajk, László, 7, 86, 87, 89, 118, 119, 120–21, 123–4, 126, 141

Rákosi, Matyas, 118, 120–22, 123–5, 134, 136, 201

Rakowski, Mieczyslaw, 64, 71, 72

Red Army, 3, 5, 6, 15, 16, 45, 47, 50, 51, 52, 59, 69, 76, 80, 84, 85, 98, 116, 118, 119, 135, 136, 156, 176, 195, 196, 214–15, 217–18, 229, 241, 244–5, 247

Reichstag, 15, 194

Reuter, Walter, 24, 25

Ribbentrop, J. von, 117, 213, 243, 244

Riding, Alan, 230

Ripka, Hubert, 90, 94

Rokossowski, Marshal Konstantin, 51, 55, 56

Romania, 1, 4–5, 6, 7, 32, 77, 79, 103, 113, 116, 135, 147, 150, 178, 189, 191, 195, 201, 203, 206, 209–39, 245, 254, 259, 261, 262, 263, 268

Romanian Communist Party, 217, 222

Romanian Orthodox Church, 220

Romanian Workers' Party, 222

Roosevelt, President Franklin D., 50, 156

Royal Air Force, 15

Russian Revolution, 17

Sachsenhausen, 19

Sadovy, John, 129–30

Salonika, 190

Samuel, Tsar, 186, 187

San Stefano, 189, 192

Sarajevo, 147

Saxony, 16, 255

Schabowski, Günter, 39

Scutari, *see* Shkodër

Secret Intelligence Service (SIS), 179

Securitate (Romanian Secret Police), 4, 115, 226, 230, 232–4

SED, *see* Socialist United Party

Sejna, General Jan, 95

Serbia, 146–7, 148, 149, 153, 166–7, 172, 173, 188, 189, 190, 191, 192

Serov, General Ivan, 133

Shao-chi, Liu, 130

Shehu, Mehmet, 175, 178, 180, 182

Shkodër, 183

Šik, Ota, 93

Silesia, 18, 43, 48, 60, 66, 81

Sima, Horia, 212, 213

Simeon I, King, 186

Simeon II, Tsar, 195, 198

Sinatra, Frank, 39

Skanderbeg, George, *see* Kastriota, George

Slanský, Rudolf, 7, 28, 81, 86, 87, 89, 91, 111, 121

Slovak uprising, 83, 93

Slovakia, 78, 83, 86, 92–3, 95, 106, 111, 116, 117
Slovenia, 117, 145, 149, 152, 168, 263
Smallholders' Party (Hungary), 119, 133
Smid, Martin, 106
Social Democrats (Germany), 42
Socialist Party (Bulgaria), 207
Socialist Party (Hungary), 142–3
Socialist United Party of Germany (SED), 20, 26, 28, 29, 31
Sofia, 189, 190, 191, 194, 206, 207
Solidarity, 2, 35, 37, 59–76, 142, 207, 255, 259, 260
Soviet Communist Party (SPD), 3, 7, 19, 20, 25, 28, 54, 64, 91, 158, 250
Soviet Secret Police (NKVD), 47, 49, 87, 159, 247
Soviet Union, 1, 2, 3, 5, 7, 8, 9, 15, 16, 18, 20, 23, 25, 27, 31–3, 35, 36, 39, 42, 43, 47, 49, 51, 55, 63, 67, 69, 70, 76, 79, 81, 84–5, 87, 89, 93, 94, 100, 103, 105, 108, 111, 112, 117, 118, 128, 129, 130, 132, 135–6, 138, 143, 150, 155, 159, 164, 174, 177, 181–2, 184, 196–8, 207, 208, 211, 214, 215, 217, 218, 221–3, 228–9, 234–5, 241–52, 257–8, 259, 261, 262, 263, 268
SPD, *see* Soviet Communist Party
Spain, 149
Speer, Albert, 225
Stadthaus, 25
Stalin, Joseph, 4, 7, 17, 18, 20, 23, 24, 26, 27, 45, 47, 48–9, 50, 53, 54, 78, 79, 81, 85, 89, 91, 96, 117, 118–23, 125, 153, 155, 158, 159–64, 175–7, 181, 190, 194–5, 198, 199, 200, 211, 215, 216, 217, 220–21, 228, 242, 243–4, 246–7, 251, 257
Stalinallee, 29, 30

Stalingrad, 8, 196
Stambolinski, Alexander, 193
Stasi (East German Secret Police), 42
Stepinac, Archbishop, 152, 156, 163
Stettin, 18, 43, 48
Štrougal, Lubomír, 105
Sudeten Germans, 18
Sudetenland, 78, 79, 81, 113
Suez crisis, 131–2
Sukarno, Achmed, 163
Suslov, Mikhail, 128
Svoboda, Ludvik, 80, 98, 100, 103
Szalasi, Ferenc, 118
Szczecin, 48, 53, 60
Szeklers, 221–2
Szilagyi, Jószef, 135, 140

Tallinn, 247, 249, 260
Tass, 100
Tatarascu, Gheorghiu, 218–19
Technological University for Building Industry, Budapest, 124, 126
Tehran Conference, 50
Těšín, 111
Thälmann, Ernest, 17
Thatcher, Margaret, 40, 253
Third International 22
Third Reich, 19, 23, 47, 79, 118, 247
Thuringia, 16
Tienanmen Square, 38, 141
Tildy, Zoltán, 119, 133
Timisoara, 204, 229, 230–1, 232, 262
Tirana, 171, 180, 255
Tirgu-Mures, 236
Tito, President, 7, 52, 82, 85, 120, 124, 125, 130, 152, 153, 154–68, 174, 175, 180–1, 196, 200, 222
Tokes, László, 230
Tomášek, Cardinal, 107
Torańska, Teresa, 53
Trajan, Emperor, 227
Trans-Carpathian Ruthenia, 117

Transnitria, 214

Transylvania, 117, 210, 211, 214, 215, 221, 222, 227, 228, 229, 235, 236

Treaty of Brussels, 22

Treaty of Bucharest, 191

Treaty of London, 191

Treaty of Peace, 124

Treaty of Rome, 255

Treaty of Trianon, 116

Treaty of Versailles, 211

Trieste, 158

Triple Entente, 192

Trotsky, Leon, 7, 87, 258

Truman, President Harry S., 8, 16, 17, 18, 21, 22

Truman Doctrine, 21, 102

Tse-tung, Chairman Mao, 32, 130, 159, 181

Tudjman, Franjo, 169

Turkey, 21, 172, 186–7, 188, 206, 228

Ukraine, 178, 229, 248

Ulbricht, Walter, 17, 19, 26, 28, 31–3, 34–5

Union of Democratic Forces, 207

Union of Polish Patriots (ZPP), 50

United Nations, 35, 83, 131, 132, 184, 248

United Nations Declaration on Human Rights, 203

United States, 21, 25, 32, 43, 81, 89, 120, 132, 157, 162, 184, 200, 218–19, 251

Urbanek, Karel, 108

Urbsys, Jonas, 246

US Air Force, 15, 157

US Army, 21

USSR, see Soviet Union

Ustachis, 150, 152, 154, 156, 193

Vaculík, Ludvik, 97

Valas, Vaino, 248

Vali, Ferenc, 125

Vienna, 37

Vietnam, 1

Vilnius, 48, 50, 243, 244, 247, 248, 249, 251, 260

Vistula, 45

Vlad the Impaler (Vladul Tepes Culad), 210

Vojvodina, 145, 147, 166–7

Volkskammer, 40

Vyshinsky, Andrei, 198, 218, 246

Wajda, Andrej, 45

Walentynowicz, Anna, 59

Wałęsa, Lech, 3, 37, 59, 62, 63, 65, 67, 69, 70–1, 72, 75

Wallachie, 210

Wandlitz, 41

Wannsee Conference, 79

Warsaw, 3, 37–8, 45, 62, 67

Warsaw Pact, 4, 5, 43, 55, 62, 65, 74, 95, 96, 97, 98, 108, 130, 131, 138, 143, 164, 180, 223, 254, 256

Warsaw Uprising, 48

Washington DC, 13, 26

Wehrmacht, 15, 49, 116, 153, 196, 245

Weimar Republic, 78, 150

Wenceslas Square, 101, 106–7

West Germany, 1, 13, 31, 41–3, 48, 242, 253, 254, 256

Western European Union, 22

Wojtyła, Karol, 59

World Bank, 35

World War I, 148, 173, 189, 192, 210, 241, 258

World War II, 5, 6, 47, 48, 79, 116, 117, 165, 195, 199, 211, 228, 258

Wrocław, 48

Wyszynski, Cardinal, 54

Xiao-Ping, Deng, 141, 181, 259

Xoxe, Koci, 7, 89, 176–8

Yagoda, 87

Yalta, 16, 17, 18, 50, 156–7, 197, 218

Yaobang, Hu, 259

Yugoslav Communist Party, 161, 262

Yugoslavia, 4, 5, 6, 9, 23, 32, 79, 116, 125, 132, 145–69, 175, 176, 192–3, 216, 254, 257, 269

Yugov, Anton, 201, 205

Zevno, 193

Zhdanov, Andrei, 246

Zhelev, Professor Zhelio, 207

Zhivkov, Todor, 4, 185, 201–2, 203–5, 262

Zhivkovitch, Peter, 148, 149

Zielinski, Adam, 72

Zinoviev, 7, 87

Zionism, 87–9

Zlin, 112–13

Zog, King (Zogu, Ahmet Bey), 173–5, 178–9, 194

Zorin, Valerian, 82